The tiruvAcagam

of the Tamil Poet, Saint and Sage

MAnikka-vACagar

by

Rev.G.U.Pope

Oxford, Clarendon Press, 1900

(Part I - Hymns 1 -10)

HYMN 1 (civapurANam)
Civan's way of Old (or)
Civan's Course from Everlasting

This has always been considered the first of MAnikka-vACagar's poems, and it has all the characteristics of a preface, as enumerated in the NannUl; but its very technical completeness makes its genuineness doubtful; and it rather apperars to have been added by the Tillai assembly when the lyrics of the Saint were first collected. In the VAthavUrar purANam(V II) it is said that after the divine Master had returned to Kailacam, the sage with the 999 devotees remained under the Kurunthu tree at Perunn-turrai, where the God had first appeared to him; erected a shrine there, and spent this time in adoration and praise, until his fellow-worshippers passed through the fire to Civan, leaving him alone. To this, the first period of his religious history, the following three poems belong; and also according to tradition, lyrics 19, 20, 23-29, 32-34, 36, 38, 39, 41-48, and perhaps a few others.
Here all the Tamil lines are of four feet, except the last, which has three only. The connection is VeNTaLai. The metre is veng-kalipA.

SALUTATIONS
Hail, the five letters! Hail, foot of the Lord !
Hail, foot of Him Who not for an instant quits my heart !
Hail, foot of the Guru-pearl that rules in GOgari !

Hail, foot of Him Who becomes, abides, draws near as the Agamam !
Hail, foot of Him, the One, the Not-One, and the King ! (5)

Victory to the foot of the King, who soothed my soul's unrest and made me His !
Victory to the jewelled foot of Pinnagan, who severs continuity of birth !
Victory to the flower-foot of Him Who is far from those without !
Victory to the anklets of the King, rejoicing 'mid those that fold adoring hands !
Victory to the anklets of the glorious One, who uplifts those that bow the head ! (10)

Praise to the foot of ICan ! Praise to my Father's foot !
Praise to the foot of the Teacher ! Praise to Civan's roseate foot !
Praise to the foot of the Stainless, who in love stood near !
Praise to the foot of the King, who cuts off delusive birth !
Praise to the foot of glorious Perun-turrai's God ! (15)
Praise to the Mount, in grace affording pleasures that cloy not !

INTRODUCTION
Because He, Civan, within my thought abides,
By His grace alone, bowing before His feet,
With joyous thought, Civan's 'Ways of Old' I'll tell,
That thus my former 'deeds' may wholly pass. (20)

I came, attained the grace the 'Brow-eyed' showed,
Adored the beauteous foot by thought unreached.

O Thou, Who fill'st the heaven, Who fill'st the earth, art
manifested light,
Transcending thought, Thou boundless One ! Thy glory
great
I, man of evil 'deeds' know not the way to praise ! (25)

HIS VARIOUS EMBODIMENTS

Grass was I, shrub was I, worm, tree,
Full many a kind of beast, bird, snake,
Stone, man, and demon. 'Midst Thy hosts I served.
The form of mighty Asuras, ascetics, gods I bore.
Within these immobile and mobile forms of life, (30)
In every species born, weary I've grown, great Lord !

HE FOUND THE MASTER

Truly, seeing Thy golden feet this day, I've gained release.
O Truth! as the OngAram dwelling in my soul,
That I may 'scape. O spotless one ! O Master of the bull !
Lord of the VEdas! Rising, sinking, spreading, subtile One !
(35)
Thou art the heat ! and Thou the cold ! the Master Thou, O
spotless One !
Thou cam'st in grace, that all things false might flee,
True Wisdom, gleaming bright in splendour true,
To me, void of all wisdom, blissful Lord !
O Wisdom fair, causing unwisdom' self to flee far off ! (40)

CIVAN'S FIVE OPERATIONS

Thou know'st no increase, measure, end ! All worlds
Thou dost create, protect, destroy, enrich with grace,
Release. Thou causest me to enter 'mid Thy servant band.
More subtile Thou than fragrance. Thou'art afar, art near.

Thou art the Mystic word, transcending word and thought.
(45)
As when are mingled milk, sweet juice of cane and butter,
Thou dost distil, like honey, in the thought of glorious
devotees,
And cuttest off the continuity of births - our mighty One !

HUMAN EMBODIMENT AND ENLIGHTENMENT BY GRACE

Thou hast the colours five ! While heavenly ones extolled
Thou didst lie hid, our mighty Lord ! In the strong grasp of
deeds, (50)
I lay, hidden amid illusion's shrouding gloom.
Thou binding with rare cords of virtue and of sin,
Didst clothe with outer skin, enveloping with worms and
filth, -
Within my nine-gated dwelling foul bewildered,
By the five senses sore deceived, - (55)
To me, mean as I was, with no good thing, Thou didst grant
grace,
That I, with mind erewhile embruted, - pure one ! - should
Become commingling love, in soul-subduing rapture melt !
Thou cam'st in grace on this same earth, didst show Thy
mighty feet
To me who lay mere slave, - meaner than any dog, - (60)
Essential grace more precious than a mother's love !

EPITHETS OF PRAISE

Spotless splendour ! Brightness of full-blown flower !
O Teacher ! Honied ambrosia ! Lord of Civa-town !
O venerated One, Guardian, Looser of PAcam's tie,
Working in grace of love, that in my mind delultion may
die out ! (65)

Great river of exceeding tenderness, with ceaseless flow !
Ambrosia that satiates not ! Infinite, almighty Lord !
Light unseen that lurks within the souls that sought Thee
not !
Thou Who abidest in my soul, till melting waters flow !
Thou Who art without pleasure or pain, Who yet hast both
! (70)
Loving to loving ones ! Effulgent One, Who all things art,
And their negation too ! Great Master, whom no darkness
gathers round !
First One, Thou'rt End and Midst, and art devoid of these !
Father, Lord, Who drew'st, and mad'st me Thine !
Eye of the minds that see by keenest glance of wisdom
true, (75)
Hard to be eyed ! Subtle understanding, none can
scrutinize !
Holy ! Who comest not, nor goest, nor mingling liv'st !
Guardian who guardest us ! Great Light whom none can
see !
Flood of delight ! Father ! Light of all passing splendours
That appear ! Unutterably subtle Intellect ! (80)
Of all that in this world diverse pronounced as truth
Is known, Thou art the knowledge sure ! Full certitude !
Precious ambrosia, fountain welling up within ! My Owner
Thou !

PASSIONATE INVOCATION
I can't endure, our Guru, in this changing straitened frame
to 'bide.
Aran! All Thy saints made true invoke Thee, (85)
Worshipping abide, and praising Thee, from falsehood
freed,

6

Hither return no more ! That deeds and birth cling not,
To sever bonds of this deceitful sensuous frame the might
is Thine !
Lord who dost dance, trampling dense darkness down !
Dancer in Thillai ! Dweller in the Southern PAndi land !
(90)
Thou Who dost cut off evil birth ! - Adoring ever, Thee they
name,
Whom words declare not; then 'NEATH THY SACRED
FEET
THEY LEARN THE MEANING OF THEIR SONG. The blessed
ones
In Civan's town who dwell, - full many a one, - beneath
The feet of Civan, lowly bending utter praise. (95)

HYMN II . kIrttit tiru akaval
CIVAN'S FAME
THE SACRED SONG OF CIVAN'S RENOWNED ACTS
(composed in Tillai, tiru vAtavUrar purANam, v. 62)
The sacred foot that danced in Tillai's city old
Is His, Who in all varied lives has energized;
Revealed in beauty of innumerous, varied qualities;
In earth, in sky, and in celestial worlds.
All ordered lore hath He revealed, and He made void. (5)
My darkness hath He driven for aye far off.
Within His servants' inmost soul that love o'erflows
He dwells, - His glory and His choice.
On great MahEndra's biding hill
In grace He caused the uttered Agamas appear. (10)
He came with the good goddess,
Pleasant and gracious, mingling with men at KallAdam.
With her whose words are milk in the 'fivefold couch,'

7

He caused sweet grace, that unfailing accumulates, to grow.

In guise of a woodman, of her whose lips are crimson, (15)

He sank in the lovely expanse of the swelling breast.

Becoming a fisherman He caught the shark.

And he received the Agamas, a rich spoil.

Moreover, on MahEndra seated, the self-same Agamas

From His five mouths He graciously spake forth. (20)

In our abode a BrAhman He became,

And as a deathless Guru dwelt in grace.

Assuming diverse forms, and diverse habitudes,

As hundreds of hundreds of thousands of natures,

I Can, Lord of the bull, that the world might be saved, - (25)

He and the Lady, His partner, - came in grace.

Bringing horses, in the Western land,

Right royally He rode in state.

In fair PuttUr, town of the dart, upon the bull He rode,

Made manifest His state and glorious pomp. (30)

In a mirror, at PuttUr of the santhal-wood,

Gave increase to the woodman armed with bow.

His form all flame, that held the 'gram-bag',

In magic beauty exquisite, of old he showed.

He whose extent to Hari and to BrahmA was not known, (35)

In goodness jackals into horse made,

To make him His, He of the sacred foot,

The chargers to the PAndiyan sold,

Nor deigned to take the heaped-up gold.

Our King made me His slave, and in the path of grace to keep, (40)

Made manifest the ancient brightening ray.

Becoming a BrAhman, graciously making me His own,
He showed the magic illusion.
Coming to Madura, the city great and fair,
He became a horse's groom. (45)
And therein too, for the female devotee
He condescended to carry earth.
In Uttara-KOca-Mangai abiding
He showed His special form.
In PUvanam he vouchsafed to appear in beauty, (50)
And showed His ancient spotless form.
In VAthavUr he came sweetly gracious
And caused the sound of His tinkling anklets to be heard.
In Perun-turrai's blissful home, a Blessed One He dwelt,
And guileful, in undimmed lustre hid Himself. (55)
In PUvalam, beauteous, sweet and gracious,
He sin destroyed.
A water-booth he placed, to gain the victory,
And graciously became an attendant who serves water.
He came a guest to VenkAdu. (60)
Beneath the Kurunthu tree He sat that day.
In royal Mangai, in fair beauty throned,
The eight great mystic powers in grace He gave.
Becoming a hunter, and assuming the form He desired,
In the forest with guile He lay hid. (65)
Exhibiting a body, assumed at pleasure,
He bore the fitting form.
In Jackal-town well pleased in grace
He became an earthly babe.
In PANTUr He came to dwell. (70)
In the resplendent island, in the south of DEvUr,
He assumed kingly state.
In sacred ArUr, famed for its honey-dripping groves,

He bestowed the gift of wisdom.
In Idai-maruthu, by hosts attended,
He planted His pure foot. (75)
Assuming the nature of Ekambam,
He became partner with his never-sundered queen.
In glory He dwelt in sacred VAnjiyam,
And delighted in the society of her of perfumed locks. (80)
He became an attendant bearing a mighty bow,
And assumed many various appearances,
He dwelt in a spacious home in KadambUr;
And showed Himself in beauty in the hill IngOy.
He became a Caivan in AiyAru. (85)
He abode with desire in Turutti.
In the 'town of the sacred palm' He dwelt desired.
In Karumalam He manifested His presence.
In the 'Vulture's Hill' He dwelt without a flaw.
In Purrambayam He taught virtues manifold. (90)
In KutRAlam He was for a sign.
Concealing His endless greatness in form of fire,
In beauteous disguise the only primal One assumed a
form,
In magic splendour came in grace,
Took each one's nature into Himself,- (95)
Being the infinite Lord of grace, our king,-
Became a Sage as moonlight bright.
Thro' upper air descending to the beauteous LAND
He came in fairest form and filled with grace,-
Lord of the HILL MahEnthiram, mountain of mystic lore,
(100)
The King of grace, immeasurably great !

If one could tell the way He made me His:

He showed His sacred form of power and grace;
He exhibited His BANNER of sacred ashes;
The RIVER of rapture that straightway (105)
All human vileness sweeps away, in grace He gave:
The Partner of the DAME, in mercy great !
While the great NATHA-DRUM spake loud
He made me His, so that impurity touches not.
He bears the mystic SPEAR, (110)
The splendour He whose flame pure light emits,
Who cuts away the primal threefold bond;
A loving one, the lotus GARLAND blue
In fragrant loveliness He wore;
Hari and BrahmA knew not Him to mete; (115)
On prancing charger forth He rode.
He shows in grace the way knows no return;
The old dominion of the PAndi LAND is His;

He bears to bliss supern His pious saints
Uttara-KOca-Mangai is His TOWN; (120)
To the primeval Beings He gives grace,
The GOD OF GODS His sacred NAME;
His VEHICLE is gift of joy dispels the dark;
His the MOUNT of grace that greatness gives,
Fitted to each one's lofty nature, each one's power; (125)
Meetly in love He makes them His;-
Me, cur, in Tillai filled with good,
He bade draw nigh th'all-glorious company;
Yet, Ah ! He left me here.
That day His servants who gained grace to go with Him,
(130)
Mingled in perfect union with Himself,
While those that gained it not leaped on the fire !

Then did bewilderment come over them,
On earth they rolled, they fell, they wailed,
They rushed with eager foot to reach the sea; (135)
'Our Lord, Our Lord', they wept and called.

While those who gained His foot pressed near,
And cried, 'Celestial Dancer, who to Patanjali gave grace,'
And yearned to gain satiety of bliss,
He dances 'mid the company of beauteous 'Tiger-town',
(140)
That golden beauty like HimAlaya wears,
There to Umai, whose roseate mouth is filled with
sweetness,
And to KAli grants the beauteous smile of His blest
countenance.
Thus the King with His assembled saints
Joyous hath entered 'Tiger-town,' with garners filled,
(145)
High Lord of Kailai that resounds with rapturous song.

HYMN III - thiruvanndappahudi

THE NATURE AND DEVELOPMENT OF THE UNIVERSE

This poem has an introduction of twenty eight lines, after
which the praises of Civan are intermingled with
somewhat intricate but ingenious allegories. The whole
partakes of the nature of a rhapsody, - not without some
sublimity, - and can be fully appreciated by those only who
have studied the whole Caiva system as shown in Notes I-
XVII. It is an imitation, it would seem of the Sanskrit
Catarudriya or Hyme to Rudra. Yet, Civan - the Auspicious
- is imagined by the Tamil Caivaites quite otherwise than
by the northern and more ancient authorities Civan in the

south is the Guru, the friend, ulmost the familiar
companion, of His votaries, and is addressed with a
mixture of awe and of simple affection that has a peculiar
effect . Through all MAnikkaVacagar poems this personal
relation of the God as manifested Guru to His devotees or
disciples is, of course most prominent. I am not aware of
anything quite like this in the mythology of the north
though among the worshippers of Vishnu in His various
incarnations something analogous may exist. Here lines 1-
12 are very intricate, and emphasize two thoughts (1) that
the Supreme in His greatness embraces all, and pervades
the minutest things in His universe; and (2) that He is the
unique Being, whose wondrous and admirable sublimity is
not to be fully comprehended by any finite beings, gods or
men. The two epithets the the Great One (line 6), and the
Beautiful one. (line 12).

The idea of lines 13-16 is peculiar to the Caiva system,
which teaches that there are three great processes carried
on by Civan, the Supreme, in the Universe. In the beginning
of each aeon He evolves the phenomenal universe, and
through countless ages sustains it as the theatre of births
and deaths - of the whole drama of metampsychosis; and
at the end of each aeon He involves the phenomenal
universe in its primal elements. These three processes of
evolution,conservation and involution, are commonly
assigned to three deities, of whom BrahmA is the Creator,
Vishnu the Preserver, and Civan the Destroyer. This
however was seen to give to Civan an office apparently
inferior, and certainly less gracious, than that which
belongs to the other Gods. The South-Indian Caiva system
boldly faces this difficulty. According to it there is really
but one God. He is called, among many other names, Civan

'the Blessed One'. Vishnu and BrahmA and the other so-called gods are but dependent 'souls' like the rest, and at the beginning of each aeon their place and office for that aeon are assigned them by the Supreme as the result of merits accumulated. The BrahmA of the present aeon is the Demiurge or fashioner of The evolved Universe: he puts it into shape, and is the mere agent of Civan. This system invites us to contemplate the universe at the beginning of each aeon awaiting the action of the Supreme. Existence is eternal; it is subject to what are called deluges, or overhelming catastrophes, in which all the heavens, and all the regions of the abyss, all worlds, and all beings are restored to their rudimental condition, after which, by the will and operation of Civan they resume their normal manifestations. What exists at the beginning of an aeon

First, we have the Lord, Pathi, Sivan, PerumAn. He is the First Cause of all things; the only God. Inseparable from Himself, dwelling in Him,is His personified energy or Sakti --- his bride said to be the originator, source, fountain, beginning of all emotion, action, wisdom, and grace. Secondly, we have Souls, lives, atomic existences,the flocks, pacu. These have now no embodiment , no powers, energies, or faculties,abiding like birds sleeping in the night on the branchces of some mighty tree, hardly to be distinguished from the tree itself, save that they live. These are definite in number, and are eternal; no addition can ever be made to the number of souls that are alive in the universe, none of them can ever die. Since, as we shall see, these may gain absolute identification with Civan-PerumAn and thus be embodied no more, the number of embodied souls diminishes; but no soul ceases to exist even after obtaining release, and being taken into God. It may be, according to this system, that the time shall arrive when all embodied lives have obtained release, and then the worlds will for ever cease and Civan be all in all. Each of these souls has its load of deeds which are stored up, and are a' parte ante, eternal; the result of which, in pleasure or in pain, each soul in some embodied form must experience. As the Caiva system says, The fruit of deeds must be eaten '

These souls, at the beginning of each aeon, crouch waiting for their embodiments. There are now no evolved worldsno heaven, no hell, no gods and demons, men. All these have been, and shall be,but now are not. That SOULS may be furnished with embodiments, and with worlds in which they may experience their fate, we have thirdly, the Bond, pAcam the eternal material cause of the creation. This is threefold, pure maya, impure maya and prakrithi, the of offspring of the latter, which is undefined. These three categories PATHI, PACU and PACAM - which we call roughly 'The God, SOUL AND MATTER' Are the subjects expounded in the Caiva Siddhantha Philosophy.

Civan's palpable and subtle existence

The developement of the sphere of the elemental universe,
Its immeasurable nature, and abundant phenomena,
If one would tell their beauty in all its particulars,
As when, more than a hundred millions in number spread abroad,
The thronging atoms are seen in the ray that enters the house, (5)

So is He the GREAT ONE, Who exists in the minutest
elements.
If you would know Him, BrahmA and the rest with MAl,
His greatness, source, glory, and end,
Conjoined with His eternity, His extent, His abiding
essence,
His subtile ant palpable manifestations, (10)
They sought to understand. As the rush of a mighty
whirlwind
The Beauteous One drave them far in whirling course !

The operations of the Supreme

He is the Ancient One, Who creates the Creator of all;
He is the God, Who preserves the Preserver of things
created;
He is the God, Who destroys the Destroyer; (15)
But, thinking without thought, regards the things
destroyed.
To the six sacred sects with their six diverse kinds of men
He is the attainment of deliverance; and Source of being to
the heavenly ones
He is the Possessor of all, Who resembles an insect.
Day by day He to the sun its lustre gave. (20)
In the sacred moon He placed its coolness;
Kindled in the mighty fire its heat;
In the pure ether placed pervasive power;
Endued the ambiant wind with energy;
To the streams that gleam in the shade their savour sweet,
(25)
And to the expanded earth with its strength He gave;
For ever and aye, me and millions other than me,

All in their several cells hath He enclosed.

Forty epithets
See Him the First! See Him the Whole !
See Him Himself, Being without compare ! (30)
See Him adorned with the wild boar's ancient tusk !
See Him Whose girdle is the forest tiger's skin !
See Him with ash besmeared ! Whene'er I think and think,
See, I cannot bear the thought ! I perish overwhelmed !
See, in the sweet voiced lute He is the melody ! (35)
See, each thing, as its essence is, He knows !
See Him, the Infinite ! See Him, the Ancient One !
See Him, the Great One Whom BrahmA and MAl saw not !
See Him, the Wonderful! See, the Manifold !
See Him, the Ancient One, transcending words ! (40)
See, He dwells afar where human thought goes not !
See, He is taken in the net of piety !
See Him that One, Whose title is 'the only One' !
See, He extends throughout the wide extended earth !
See Him, more subtile than an atom small ! (45)
See Him, the King incomparably great !
See Him, the Precious One, rarest of all that's rare!
See, mingling with all beings, each one He cherishes !
See Him, the Subtile One, Whom science fails to see !
See Him, above, below, He spreads ! (50)
See the beginning and the ending He transcends !
See, the 'bond' and 'loosing' He ordains !
See, He is That that stands, and That that goes !
See, He discerns the aeon and its end !
See Him, the Lord Whom all may gain ! (55)
See, Civan Whom the gods know not !

See Him. the Male, the Female, and 'neither one'!
See, even I have seen Him with my eyes !
See, the ambrosial Fount, yielding abounding grace!

Lo, I have seen His mercy s might ! (60)
See, His roseate Foot this earth hath trod !
See Him, even I have known, the Blessed One !
See, in grace He made me His !
See, her His Spouse whose eyes are dark-blue lotus
flowers !
See, Her and Him together stand ! (65)

The Sea and the Cloud

Lines 66-95 are well nigh untranslateable, for they contain
a subtle and intricate allegory, by means of which the
grace of the manifested Civan, who is praised under the
title of the 'Cloud' is set forth. The idea is that the Infinite
sea of rapturous supreme felicity is Civan, but - as the
Cloud in the monsoon season sucks up water from the sea,
and rises in black masses that cover the sky, while all the
phenomena of the wonderful outburst of the beneficient,
but also fearful, monsoon are exhibited - so does the
Supreme manifest Himself as the Guru, the Object of Love,
and Give of grace to His worshippers. In the monsoon
season, lightnings flash from one end of the sky to the
other, crested torrents sweep down over the hills, bearing
with them uprooted plants and trees, and not unseldom
huge snakes that have been disturbed from their rocky
mountain hiding places. The various kinds of 'Gloriosa'
spread forth their beautiful flowers like supplicating

hands, while every valley and hollow is filled with water. Meanwhile, as the heat is most intense just before the burst of the monsoon, the poet pictures a troop of thirsty antelopes, deluded by the mirage which seems to offer them refreshing streams and shade: disappointed they are left to die of thirst in the wilderness. Meanwhile the pain of the fierce heat has ceased. Down the gorges of the hill the torrent rushes, and is received into tanks prepared for it by the expectant husbandmen. These lakes are fragrant with beautiful flowers, and on their banks the maidens have kindled fires with aromatic woods, at which they dry their hair and garments after the refreshing bath. The cultivators may now sow their seed and expect a rich harvest. All this is the work of the black clouds which drew water from the sea to fertilise the earth. In these lines every particular of the description has its mystical meaning, which hardly needs illustration. The student will compare VII, 61-64.

The ancient sea of bliss supreme is THAT indeed !
Appearing like a black vast CLOUD,
Arising in the hill of Petun-turrai blest,
Whilst sacred lightnings flash frorn every point -,
While serpent bright of sensual bondage dies -, (70)
While the sore sorrow of the fervent heat hides itsellf;
While the all-beauteous IIibiscus shines forth,
Swelling in its wrath like our mortal pain,
It sounds forth in mighty grace as a drum.
While the kAnthal stretches out supplicating hands, (75)
And the tender drops of sweet unfailing grace distil,
While the gleaming torrent swells on every side,

And rises to the highest banks of every lake -;
The 'demon-car' of the six sects
Excites the thirst of the large-eyed antelope throng. (80)
And they with eager desire crowd to drink;
And faint with unquenched thirst haste hither and
thither:-
Meanwhile, the heavenly mighty stream
Rises and rushes, crowned with hubbles of delight,
Eddies around, dashes against the bank of our
'embodiment, (85)
And twofold deeds of ours growing from age to age, -
Those mighty trees, roots up and bears away.
It rushes through the cleft of the high hills,
Is imprisoned in the encircling lake,
Where grow the expanded fragrant flowers, (90)
In tank, where rises smoke of the agil, where beetles hum;
And as it swells with ever-rising joy,
The ploughmen-devotees in the field of worship
Sow in rich abundance seed of love
Hail, CLOUD-LIKE god, hard in this universe to reach ! (95)

Ascriptions of Praise

God Who wear'st black snake for girdle, hail !
First One, giving grace to the devout ascetics, hail !
Warrior Who dost remove our fear, all hail !
Thou Who dost ever draw us to Thee, make us Thine, all
hail !
Thou Who dost wipe away sorrows that gather around, all
hail ! (100)
Thou Who giv'st ambrosia rare to those that gain access to
Thee, all hail !

Thou Who in thick darkness dancing dost bend down, all
hail!
Lover of Her with shoulders like the swelling bamboo, hail
!
Thou Who art hostile to the hostile one, our King, all hail !
Thou Who to thy lovers art treasure in distress, all hail !
(105)

Praises

Praise to Thee, our Own, waving the envenomed snake !
Praise to Thee, Great One, Who fill'st our souls with pious
rage !
Praise to Thee, mighty in Thine ash-smeared form !
In every part what moves, Thou mov'st it; what lies still,
Thou lay'st to rest
What stands, Thou dost establish. (110)
Thou Ancient One, transcending speech,
Not grasped by apprehension of the soul !
Not by the eye perceived, nor by sense-organs all.
Thou didst arrange in order, manifest the ether and all
elemcnts.
Like fragrance of the flower uprising everywhere, (115)
Thy greatness without cease all things pervades,
This day to me in condescending grace Thou cam'st
Making this body of destruction fall away, O Being glorious
!
To-day to me in condescending grace Thou cam'st; I praise
Thee ! (120)
Thou Who did'st fashion this decaying frame; I praise Thee
!

As fountain springing in my soul Thou mak'st me glad, I
praise Thee !
Whlle pleasure beyond bound like flower expands
I know not how to bear this body vile !

His hidings of Himself

Bright gems flash'd emerald splendour forth,-
The lightning's play mingling with gleam of gold,- (125)
BrahmA went up to seek Thee; Thou didst hide Thyself !
From them who toiled with mystic scrolls didst hide
Thyself!
From those who in their homes practised virtue, Thou
didst hide Thyself
From those who, in union with Thee, fixed their
contemplative soul
Wlth painfiul effort; Thou didst hide Thyself ! (130)
From those who boasted to see Thee by some rare device,
By that same device, there, -didst Thou hide Thyself!
Benign, regarding all, receiving with abundant grace
As male appearing Thou dost change to neutral form,
And in a bright-browed female form dost hide Thyself ! Far
off (135)
Bidding the senses five depart, passing over every
trackless hill
With frames scarce living, spurning all delights,
Ascetic saints in contemplation dwell;-in their souls Thou
fitly hid'st Thyself!

Seeming one thing, then not, eluding knowledge, Thou
dost hide Thyself !

When e'en of old I strove to find Thee, when to-day I
strive, (140)
Thou hid'st Thyself, Deceiver ! But we've found Thee now !

Worship

Haste, haste ye, garlands of fresh flowers
Around His feet to bind !
Assemble, go around, follow hard on, leave ye no gap.
Lay hold of Him, although He hide Himself, avoid your
grasp ! (145)
The Incomparable told out His nature as it is,
That those like me might hear.
He called, in grace He made me His,
He as a BrAhman showed His glory forth,
Then, while undying love dissolved my frame, I cried;
(150)
I raised enraptured voice above the billowy sea's loud
waves;
In utter wilderment I fell, I rolled, I cried aloud,
Madman distraught, and as a maniac raved;
While those who saw were wildered, who heard it
wonder'd sore.
More than the frenzy wild of raging elephant (155)
Bore me away beyond endurance far. 'Twas then through
all my limbs
Λ honied sweetness He infused, and made me blest.
The ancient city of His foes with fire lit by His beauteous
smile
He caused to fall. Ev'n so that day
With mighty fire of grace our humble dwellings (160)
He destroyed that none were left.

To me as the ripe Nelli fruit in palm He was.

Rapture

What to say I know not, Hail !-to Thee complain.
I mere cur cannot endure ! What He hath done to me
I understand not ! Ah I'm dead ! To me Thy slave (165)
What Thou in grace hast given I know not, tasting am not
satiate,
Though I've imbibed I comprehend it not !
Like flowing billows swell from out the sea of milk
Within my soul He made deep waters rise,
Ambrosia surpassing speech filled every pore. (170)
This is His gracious work !
In every body in this currish state
He filled me full with honied sweetness;
Ambrosial drops most marvellous
He caused throughout my being to distil. (175)
With tender soul, as though He'd make me as Himself,
He formed for me a frame where grace might flow.
And as an elephant explores fields of sweet cane, at last
He sought, and found, and made even me to live. In me
Mercy's pure honey while He mixed, (180)
He gave in grace supernal food: -
Ev'n He Whose nature nor BrahmA knows nor MAl !
Hymn 4 poRRith thiru agaval
THE SACRED AGAVAL OF PRAISE.

THE CREATION OF THE WORLD.
HE CAUSED THE PHENOMENAL UNIVERSE TO APPEAR.
(This seems to the translator to read more like a work of
UmApathi, than of our sage!)

Lines 1-10 The Feet of Civan

While the Four-faced and other heavenly dwellers rose,
Adoring, sacred MAl, whose head with rays is crowned,
With His two feet measured the threefold world,-
While saints from the four quarters praised with all their
sentient powers,
Eager that day Thy foot and crown to know, (5)
He then became a fierce strong boar, and rushing on
Dug down through sevenfold regions, wearied cried at
last:
Eternal Source of all, to Thee be triumphs manifold !'
Yet though He worship paid, Thy pair of Feet-flowers saw
he not;
Yet Thou to me Thy worshipper art easy of access ! (10)

Lines 11 - 35 Human embodiment

On earth girt by the watery seas, from elephant to ant,
Through many matrices I passed,
Obtained a human form within my mother's womb.
..
Thus was I born into the sad sea of th' afflictive life. (25)
Then during each year as it met me
I gained and hoarded gains. How varied was my life!.
Morning's routine, hunger in noontide hour, and night
For sleep. In journeys oft I lived.
Jet black locks, and crimson lips, and radiant smiles were
hers; (30)
Into love's sea I plunged.
.. (31-35)

In the wide marts where foolish worldlings toil
I lived, still slave to fierce desires.
I lived by sea of learning multiform;
I lived in sorrow men call wealth;
I lived 'mid ancient stings of poverty, (40)
And thus in varied forms and fortunes spent my days.

Lines 42-51 The idea of God comes into his life

Then wondrous thought of the Divine, so-called, arose.
Soon as I knew that BEING, free from hate, unique,
Delusive powers in ever-changing millions
Began beguiling varied play. (45)

Relations, neighbours, came around,
With fluent tongue they urged their 'atheism'
Friends around (such herds of cattle old !)-
Seiz'd me, call'd, hurried to and fro;
The BrAhman said 'the way of penance is supreme'; (50)
And others showed the law of trusting love !
Sectarian disputants complacently
Discordant tenets shouted loud and fought.
Then haughty VedAnt creed unreal came,
Whirled, dashed, and roared like furious hurricane. (55)
LOkAyathan a glistening mighty snake
Brought cruel poisoned heresies.
Whilst these delusions, endless, girt me round,

Lines 59 - 86 His conversion

Lest I should go astray, He laid His hand on me !
As wax before the unwearied fire (60)

With melting soul I worshipt, wept, and bent myself,
Danced, cried aloud, and sang, and prayed.
They say: 'The tooth of elephant and woman's grasp relax not,'
So I with love, real, interrnitting never,
Was pierced, as wedge driven into soft young tree. (65)
All tears, I like the refluent sea was tossed;
Soul was subdued, and body quivered with delight.
While the world called me demon, mocking me,
False shame I threw aside; the folk's abusive word
I took as ornament; nor did I swerve. (70)
My mind was rapt;-a fool, but in my folly wise,-
The goal I sought to reach infinity ! All wondering desire,
As cow yearns for its calf, I moaning, hurried to and fro.

Not ev'n in dreams thought I of other gods.
The One most precious Infinite to earth came down; (75)
Nor did I greatness of the Sage superne contemn,
Who came in grace. Thus from the pair of sacred feet
Like shadow from its substance parting not,
Before, behind, at every point, to it I clung.
My inmost self in strong desire dissolved, I yearned; (80)
Love's river overflowed its banks;
My senses all in Him were centredl; 'Lord !' I cried.
With stammering speech, and quivering frame
I clasped adoring hands; my heart expanding like a flower.
Eyes gleamed with joy and tears distilled. (85)
His love that fails not day by day still burgeons forth !

To the end : Praises

Like mother, Thou hast brought me up, I praise !

God, strong to cancel deeds of ours,
Who didst become in truth a Sage, I praise !
King of golden Madura ! (90)
Guru Pearl, in KUdal shining bright !
Dancing in southern Tillai's court,
This day to me precious ambrosia Thou !
Source of the fourfold mystic Scroll that ne'er grows old !
Civan, whose conquering banner is the Bull ! (95)
Thy varied form gleams as the lightning;-Thee I praise !
In me the stony heart Thou softenest.
Guard me, Thou guarded hill of gold !
Ah, give Thy grace to me !
Thou dost create, Thou tost preserve, Thou dost destroy !
(100)
Father, who dost remove all griefs, I praise !
Ruler, I praise ! My King, I praise !
Mount of shining crystal,-praise !
Monarch, to Thee be praise ! Ambrosia,-praise !
Unfailing refuge are Thy fragrant-feet ! (105)
Thee VEdic Sage, I praise ! Spotless One,- praise !
Thee First, I praise ! Wisdom, I praise !
Thou Goal I seek,praise ! Sweet fruition, Thee I praise !

Our Lord, on Whose bright crest the river flows,
Our Master, praise! Understanding,praise ! (110)
Thou hast beheld the servitude of lowliest me,
O Teacher,-praise ! Minute as atom,-praise !
O Caivan, -praise ! Our Chief, I praise !
Our Sign, I praise ! Virtue, I praise !
ThouWay, I praise ! O Thought, I praise! (115)
Balm, hardly by celestials gained, I praise !
King, easy of access to others, praise !

Monarch in grace, Who savest lest we sink
In hell's hated one-and-twenty rounds, I praise !
Companion,-praise ! My Helper,-praise! (120)
0 Bliss of life, I praise ! My Treasure,praisc !
0 free from bonds,praisc ! First One,praise !
Father,praise ! Haran,praise !
Thou One, transcending word and understanding,praise !
Yield of the world girt by the extended sea, praise! (125)
Beauty rare, yet easy of access, I praise !

Eye like an azure cloud, I praise !
Abiding Mount of sacred grace, I praise !
Me, too, Thou mad'st a man,Thy twin feet
Thou placed'st on my head, O Warrior,praise ! (130)
Thou dost wipe off all sorrow from adoring hand, praise !
Sea of imperishable rapture, praise ,
Thou dost transcend all forms that pass and come
renewed, praise !
First One surpassing all, praise !
Bridegroom of Her with fawnlike eyes, praise ! (135)
Mother of the Immortals in the heavenly land,praise!
Fivefold Thou dost in earth extend,-praise !
Fourfold Thou dost exist in the water,-praise !
Threefold in fire Thou shinest,-praise !
Twofold in the air Thou art all glorious, -praise ! (140)
One in the ether Thou hast sprung forth,praise !
Ambrosia of the troubled mind,praise !
Hard to be approached by gods e'en in a dream,praise !
In waking hour to me a cur Thou gavest grace,praise !

Father, Who dwell'st in Idai-maruthu,praise ! (145)
Thou bearest Gangai on Thy crest, praise !

King in ArUr abiding,praise !
Lord of glorious Tiru-aiyAru,praise !
Our Prince of AnnAmalai,praise !
Sea of ambrosia, filling all the place,- praise ! (150)
Our Father dwelling in Ekambam, praise !
Thou Who in form art half a woman,-praise !
Who dwell'st supreme in Perun-turrai,-praise!
Civan Who dwell'st in Sira-palli,-praise !
None other refuge here I know, -praise ! (155)
Our Dancer in KutRAlam,-praise !
Our King dwelling in GOkazi, praise !
Our Father of IngOy's Mount, praise !
Beauteous One of seemly Paranam, praise !
Idangan Who dwell'st in KadambUr, praise ! (160)
Father, gracious to those that come to Thee, praise !
Beneath the Itti tree to six,

King, Thou wert gracious, and to th' elephant,-praise !
Civan, Lord of the southern land,praise !
King of our country folk,-praise ! (165)
Thou wert gracious to the litter of the boar,-praise !
Lord of glorious Kailai's Mountpraise !
Father, Who grants us grace,-praise !
King, Who our darkness dissipates,-praise !
I Thy slave languish all alone,-praise ! (170)
In grace remove my guile,-praise !
In grace say to me ' Fear not,-Ôpraise!
Poison became ambrosis by Thy love,-praise !
Father,-praise ! Guru,-praise !
Eternal,-praise ! Pure One,-praise! (175)
Brother,-praise ! Existent One,-praise!
O Great One,-praise ! O Lord,-praise !

30

bhakta
(T-patta)

O Rare One,-praise ! O Pure One,-praise !
Glorious Path of Vedic sages,-praise !
I make my plaint,nor can endure, O First One,-praise !
(180)

Kinsman,-praise ! Life,-praise !
Glory,-praise ! Bliss,-praise !
O Cloud,-praise ! O Bridegroom, praise !
Spouse of Her whose feet are soft,-praise !
I, a cur, Thy slave am perplexed,-praise ! (185)
Our Master Thou, all dazzling bright,-praise !
Eye apprehending forms diverse,-praise !
King, dwelling in the circling, sacred town, I praise !
Lord of the mountain land,-praise !
Thou in Whose locks is the crescent moon,-praise ! (190)
Blessed Lord of the sacred Eagle-mount,-praise !
Aran of hilly PUvanam,-praise !
Formless, in form revealed Thou art,-praise !
Mountain of mercy ever nigh,-praise !
Light transcending utmost bound,-praise ! (195)
Clearness, hard to understand,-praise !
Ray of the flawless Gem, praise !
Loving to those Thou mak'et Thine own,-praise!

Ambrosial grace that satiates not,-praise !
Our Lord, the bearer of a thousand names,-praise ! (200)
Thou Whosc garland is the TAli-arrugu,-praise !
Dancer in light expanding far,-praise !
O Beauteous with the santhal wood perfume,-praise !
Bliss, hard for thought to reach,-praise !
On Mandira's mighty mount Thou dwell'st,-praise ! (205)
Thou Who dost undertake to save us,-praise !

Thou Who in grace didst give the tiger's dug to th'
antelope,-praise !
Thou Who didst walk upon the billowy sea,-praise!
I hou didst give grace that day to the black bird,-praise !
Thou didst appear by sense discerned,-praise ! (210)
Fiery One on earth displayed,-praise !
Thou art the First, the Midst, the Last,-praise !
Hell, Paradise, or-pendant Earth not entering,
The heavenly goal Thou gav'st unto the PAndiyan,-praise !
Thou that fillest all, to Thee be praise ! (215)
King of Civa-puram rich with clustering flowers, to Thee
be praise !

God, garlanded with purple lotus flower, to Thee be praise
!
Thou dost cut off bewilderment of those that worship
Thee,-praise !
Praise ! Take in grace this wreath of babbling words
From me, mere cur, that know not to distinguish false from
true ! (220)
Ancient of days Burner of many towns,-praise !
Infinite Lord of splendours infinite,-praise !
Praise ! Praise ! Bhuyanga-PerumAn !
Praise ! Praise ! Ancient-cause of all !
Praise! Praise ! Triumphant praise ! (225)
HYMN V - thirucathakam
THE SACRED CENTO.
RELIGIOUS ENTHUSIASM.

Introduction to the Sacred Cento

This remarkable poem contains a hundred especially flowing and harmonious verses of varying metres. These are divided into ten decades, and the whole are connected by the law which requires that the last word of each verse shall begin the following verse. The whole ten lyrics with their hundred verses are thus linked together. This arrangement, which is very common in Tamil, is called AnthAthi, which I venture to translate 'anaphoretic verse'. This cento is intended to exhibit the progress of the soul through the successful stages of religious experience till it loses itself in the rapture of complete union with the Supreme. The general titile given by one editor is equivalent to 'The Varying Phases of Religious Enthusiasm' at least this is the nearest expression for it that I can find in English. The poem is supposed to have been composed in Tiru-peran-turai immediately after the departure of the Saints, for some time MAnikka-VAcagar's companions, who passed through fire and went home to Civan. From the border of the tank, where the divine conflagration had arisen, into he midst of which his companions had thrown themselves, he returned to the Kondral tree, where he spent a long period in solitary meditation, of which these poems are the sum. He surveys his past experiences, contemplates the work assigned him and while he begins the series of sacred poems by which he was to establish the Caiva system n the hearts of his fellow-countrymen, he never ceases to complain in most touching language, that he is not permitted at once to follow his Master and brethren into the rest and glory of Paradise. This is indeed the burthen of much of his poetry. The titles of the ten decades, into which the poem is divided, indicate in some measure the course of his thoughts and the character of his mental conflicts. There is a most pathetic alternation of rapturous and realising devotion with coldness and apathy, and even, it seems of temporary abandonment to gross sensuality. It is to be doubted whether the whole of these verses are of one period, and I should prefer to think that they really embody his meditations and solloquies up to the period of his final settlement in Cithambaram.

DECAD 1.

THE COGNITION OF THE TRUE.

1. Humble access to the New Master
My frame before Thy fragrant foot is quivering like al1 opening bud;-
My hands above my head I raise; while tears pour down, my melting soul,
The false renouncing,, praises Thee; with songs of triumph praises Thee,-
Nor suffer I adoring hand to rest;-O Master, look on me !
(4)

II. Self-surrender. He accepts the ascetic life.
I ask not bliss of Indra, MAl, or Ayan;-though my house and home
Be ruin'd, friendship form I none save with Thine own; though hell's abys
I enter, I unmurmuring go, if grace divine appoint my lot;-
O King I no other god save Thee I ponder, our Transcendent Good ! (8)

III. He is despised as a mad enthusiast.
Transcendent Good ! Owner and Sire ! Thy servant melting
thinks on Thee.
In raptures meet I utter forth my fever'd soul's ecstatic
joys,
Still wandering from town to town; while men cry out, 'A
madman this;'
And each one speaks, with mind distraught, discordant
words. O, when come death ? (12)

IV. None to be worshipped but Civan
Erewhile was Dakshan's offering death. They ate the flesh,
and poison feared
' Our Father,' cried our friends and worshipt Him with
suppliant voice.
And yet 'Three are the gods that rule in heaven and earth,'
they vainly deem.
What sin is this your haughty minds breathe out, ye
errirng penitents ? (16)

V. I plead no merit- am no real devotee.
No penance have I done, nor bowed, with hand unstinting
scatt'ring flowers;
Born all in vain,-to ' cruel deeds ' a thrall,-the bliss of
Civan's heav'n,
Amongst Thy loving ones, I've fail'd to gain; see, and in
gracc bestow
On me, Thy slave, consummate life beneath Thy feet,
Supernal Lord ! (20)

VI. Grace unfailing to the faithful

They roam'd and cull'd choice varied flowers to lay in
worship at Thy feet,
They deemed that all they sought they should obtain; and
from these loving
hearts
In mystic guile Thou hidest still, abiding not ! In grace
bestow,
Love to Thy glorious foot, that I may ceaseless praise with
perfect song ! (24)

VII. Civan was an ascetic,as am I now.
Erewhile the Maker's-maker bowed, brought blooming
flowers, and everywhere
Sought for Th' All-seeing One, nor found. Our mighty One,
Who dwells beyond,
Here in the wilds with demons danced, a homeless,
friendless one; and there
In tiger-skin arrayed Himself, as madman wand'ring to
and fro ! (28)

VIII. Save Thy servants in the day of doom!
> The wand'ring wind, the fire, the flood, the earth, the
heaven,-a time shall be
When these adown the gulf shall go ! After that hour
unknown has come
The deeds-mighty the soul to bind-Thy slave in wand'ring
days has done
Let the time come for these to pass ! Guard us from these,
our Guardian then ! (32)

IX. Bhavan's our Lord.

Bhavan's our Lord, Whose garland is the cool vast moon,
of heavenly one
The Prince. Civan's our Lord,Who made me His, my
meanness though He saw
Our Lord Supreme is He, and I, His lowly servant, thus
declare !
That earth may know, sound out that Bhuvan is our Lord !
(36)

X. 'Tis wondrous grace that sought me out.

Unmeet was I to enter 'mongst Thy loving ones, my
flawless Gem !
Ambrosia rare ! The way Thou took'st me for Thine own
and mad'st me meet
The very meanest lifting high, Thou didst the heav'nly
ones bring low !
What Thou our Lord to me hast done is as a play men
laugh to see ! (40)

DECAD II

THE IMPARTATION OF DIVINE KNOWLEDGE.

XI. A prayer for perfect love-

'Midmost of Thy devoted ones, like them in mystic dance
to move;
Within Thy home above to gain wish'd entrance, lo, I eager
haste !

O golden-glorious Hill of gems ! Give grace, that ceaseless
love to Thee.
Our Master, in my heart of hearts, melting my very soul,
may 'bide. (44)

XII. Longing for grace alone.

I dread not any birth. To death what should I owe ! Nor do
I crave
Even heaven itself to gain. No power to rule this earth do I
esteem.
O Civan, crowned with cassia-flowers that sweets distil;
our PerumAn !
Our only Lord! I fainting cry: ' When comes the day I find
Thy grace ?' (48)

XIII. Without Thy presence I pine

I ever pine Thy flow'ry feet to see, -Thy slave, dog though I
am !
I sit, no fitting flowers present, my tongue no rising
raptures speaks.
Thou Who the well-strung golden bow didst bend !
Ambrosia of Thy grace
If Thou give not, I PINE,-a wretch forlorn,-what other can I
be? (52)

XIV. Deadness of soul.

My inmost self PINES not, as were befitting, for Thy sacred
Foot;

Nor melts in love; I bring no wreath; speak out no worthy
word of praise
Within the shrine of Him, the King of gods, perform no
service due;
Nor move in dance. To death I haste ! Thou Whom true
wisdom bringeth nigh! (56)

XV. God all in all

Thou art the Heaven; Thou art the Earth; Thou art the
Wind;Thou art the Light!
The Body Thou; the Soul art Thou; Existence, Non-
existence Thou;
Thou art the King; these puppets all Thou dost make move,
dwelling within
That each one says: ' Myself and mine. 'What shall I say?
How render PRAISE (60)

XVI. My praise is pure. Free me from embodiments.

The heavenly ones adore Thee still heaven's bliss to share
! Their minds to Thee
They lowly humble that, on high exalted, men may
worship them;
Thou round whose flower-wreath hum the honey-bees !
Thy slave, I praise
Thee, even I, that Thou may'st save from idle round of
earthly birth ! (64)

XVII. The bliss of Civan's heaven of presence.

The heavenly dwellers chaunt Thy praise; the fourfold
VEdas utter song;
She of the shining locks that shed perfume is sharer of Thy
seat;
There in true love Thy servants all commingling dwell;
there, more and more,
Thy feet with sounding anklets girt do they behold, Thou
hard to know !(68)

XVIII. This abandonment is unendurable.

Thou Whom 'tis hard to know, in sky and in the golden
court revealed,-
Our mighty One ! beneath the jewelled feet where I was
made Thine own,
No more I scatter fragrant flowers, nor wondering weep,
nor melt in love.
'Tis past my power to bear ! How can it be ? I die, insooth, I
die ! (72)

XIX. He is above; we earthly still.

With flow'ry arrows in the spring-time comes the god of
soft desire,
And witching smile of maidens fair, with rosy mouths and
flower-wreathed locks !
Poor soul, that pants and melts through these, Who made
thee His, and thrilled thy frame,
To-day hath gone and dwells in heaven; yet see, thou still
art lingering here ! (76)

XX. O soul be wise!

O soul, that livest here in joy ! Of life's true joys bereft, in
mire
Thou sink'st of 'mighty deeds '! Him Who guards men from
sinking praisest not !
Thou art devising ruin to thyself,I tell thee so full oft;
Thou'rt sinkcing even now beneath the FLOOD of the
distressful sea! (80)

DECAD III.
DYING TO SENSE AND SELF.

This decad describes the mystic experience known by
Caiva Siddhantha, as NAna-Carithai, in which the devotee,
though able to discern God in and above and beyond all
things, continues to perform outward rites (Carithai) and
to avail himself ofall means of grace. See Civa-PragACam
II.48. Since Civan so deigns to manifest, and yet vell, His
presence, the devotee is assiduous n performance of all
prescribed acts of worship, while his soul transcends the
visible, and by NAnam (in this connection = divine faith)
sees God.

XXI. I have relapsed into apathy.

Through Thine expanding locks the FLOOD pours down;
the Bull is Thinc, Lord of the heavenly ones ! -
They sang, and stood, with panting, melting souls,
like torrent, plunging in th' abyss ! and I,
With yearning soul I heard ! Thou mad'st me Thine ! Yet
now
from head to foot, I melt not;from my eyes

The rushing waters pour not down;my heart
is stone;both eyes are wood to SINFUL me ! (84)

XXII. Deadness has come over me.

Thou ent'ring stood'st by me fast bound IN SIN;
as one who says, ' I'm sin's destroyer, come !'
Thyself announcing thus, Thou mad'st me Thine,-
becam'st my mighty Lord. Like iron statue, I
Now sing no praise, nor dance, nor weep, nor wail,
nor faint with bliss. Behold, O Primal One,
To Thee I make my plaint; nor know how this
with me shall end, Thou Who art First and Last !(88)

XXIII. Very vile, but Thine, save me!

Thou'rt Ayan, Thou the fourfold VEdas' Lord;
I know Thee,-I, lowest of men that live;
I know,-and see myself a very cur;-
yet Lord, I'll say I am Thy loving one !
Though such I was, Thou took'st me for Thine own
Thy saints are here no longer, only I,
Vile wretch ! and is it thus Thy greatness shines ?
Our PerumAn, what shall I say to Thee ? (92)

XXIV. Thy votary, though full of sin.

And if I spake, ' Thou'rt ICan, Father, Sire
great PerumAn ;' thus have I ever said;
If I besmear'd, 'twas sacred ash alone
I smear'd, still praising Thee, our PerumAn;
Who erst made those Thine own who'd passed by love

o'er birth and death. In torrent plunged of lust
And guile, behold me, spotless Hill of gems !
Father ! 'Twas such an one Thou mad'st Thine own ! (96)

XXV. The mystery of His being.

Thy colour is not red,-nor white Thy form;-
Thou'rt Many, One; Atom, than Atom far
Subtler; the heavenly host in 'wildered thought
know not the way, Father, to reach Thy feet.
Thou showd'st Thy form, Thy beauty didst display
didst show Thy now'ry feet ! Me wandering, Thine
Thou mad'st, safeguarding me from future ' birth ' !
Our PerumAn, what shall I say, what THINK ? (100)

XXVI. Wonders of grace.

Thou mad'st my THOUGHT Thy THOUGHT ! Of me, mere cur,
Thou mad'st the eye rest on Thy foot's blest flower,
Thou mad'st me bow before that flower alone ! My mouth
Thou mad'st to speak abroad Thy gem-like word !
My senses five to fill Thou cam'st, and mad'st me Thine.
Ambrosial Sea of magic might ! O Mount ! Thyself
Thou gav'st, Thy form like wild of roseate lotus flowers,
to LONELY helpless me. Thou Only-Light ! (104)

XXVII. The voyage

I, LONELY, tost by billows broad of anguish sore,
on the great ' sea of birth,' with none to aid;
Disturbed by winds of mouths roseate like ripened fruit,

lay caught in jaws of the sea monster lust !
' Henceforth,what way to 'scape ? ' I frequent cried ! then thought,
and seiz'd the raft of Thy Five Letters ! So to me,
O Primal One, Thou showd'st a boundless fertile shore,
and mad'st the rash insensate one Thine own ! (108)

XXVIII. What He did for me.

Him none by hearing know; He knoweth no decay;
He hath no kin; naught asking, heareth all !
While people of the land beheld, here on this earth
to me, a cur, He gave a royal seat;
To me, a dog, all things not shown before, He showed;
all things not heard before, He caused to hear;
And guarding me from future ' birth,' He made me His.
Such is the wondrous work our Lord hath wrought for me ! 112

XXIX. His appearing.

The WONDER this ! Say, is there aught like this ?
He made me servant of His loving saints;
Dispell'd my fear, ambrosia pouring forth, He came,
and while my soul dissolv'd, in love made me His own;
The Sire, Male, Female, Neither, Ether pure, was He;
as wondrous Fire; as End of all; beyond all far;
His body like a flower of golden hue;
our Civa-PerumAn, our Lord, OF GODS THE KING ! (116)

XXX. Triumph

The GOD OF GODS, to king of gods unknown;
King of the ' Three '; what teeming worlds create,
Preserve, destroy; the First; Essence divine;
the Sire of sires; Fa,ther, whose half the Mother is;
The King of all ! He came, and made me, too, His own.
Henceforth I'm no one's vassal; none I fear !
We've reached the goal; with servants of His saints
in sea of bliss we evermore shall bathe ! (120)

DECAD IV

THE SOUL'S PURIFICATION.

XXXI. The sluggish soul.

Thou dancest not; thou hast no love for the DANCER'S
foot;
with melting thrill
Thou singest not; thou throbbest not; thou bowest not
down;
the flower of His foot
Thou wearest not; thou crownest it not with flowers;
there's none like Thee,
DEAD HEART !
Thou seekest Him not through every street; thou wailest
not; nothing know
I thou dost ! (124)

XXXII. The ungrateful, treacherous heart.

My Sire came, entered, made His own me who knew
naught; in mercy taught

me all;
Caused me to know the higher path; He loos'd my every
bond !
Despite the gain of changeless, sweetest gifts of
grace,thou'rt changed,
DEAD HEART !
RUINED by thee, to all that's false subjected, thus I
RUINED lie ! 128

XXXIII. Heart unworthy of trust; insensible to complaint

My foolish senseless HEART, that changing, RUIN bringst
to me,
Henceforth I trust thee nevermore;-assuredly on Civan's
mighty arm
The ashes thickly smeared thou saw'st, yet melted'st not;
this, body's bonds
Thou rendest not,-nor can I bid restore the ruin thou hast
wrought. (132)

XXXIV. The utter folly of the fickle mind.

Perish, O restless mind ! before the Master Absolute,
A dog I lay; Thou didst enjoy His fragrant flowery Foot;
But now thou'rt severed like a young and tender shoot; all
former bliss
Hast lost ! Truly I deem Thy wisdom and Thy greatness
measureless ! (136)

XXXV. Insensible to infinite mercy.

When He to heavenly ones inscrutable, of acce~s easy to
His saints,
Our hidden sin destroyed, and made me His, thou knew'st
the melting joy !
Yet, HEART thou hast not, hating all thy hidden sin,
prepar'd an ample field for Him,
Nor bow'd before the Master's healing Feet, the heavenly
goal to gain ! (140)

XXXVI. What remedy?

If 'tis not given to pass the golden gate,-where all may
entrance find,
And whence none e'er departs;-nor yet to melt in love
before the foot
Of Him, my Sire, my Lord;-if there to me abound no more
Ambrosia, every honied sweet;-a sinful man, what can I do
for this ? (144)

XXXVII. A sinner - I quit thee not.

What other sinners are there like to me, cur at the Master's
Foot?
Yet not a whit from me to sever is Thy sacred will; and
thus,
O Primal One, Thy Foot's fair flower if I should quit, arld
yet live on,
My soul is iron, stone my mind; my ear to what shall it
compare ! (148)

XXXVIII. Life, a long exile.

The others all have reached the goal, yet I, who know not
anything,
Haste not to Thee who art all sweetness, Civan, King of
Civa-world;
Thou Spouse of her whose eye is like the tender fawn; long
time
I still abide, cherish this flesh, and so my death-in-life
drags on ! (152)
XXXIX. How do I bear life?

O bliss that ceases not ! O bliss beyond compare ! His
bright flower-foot
He gave; to me of kind more base than dogs, He showed
the perfect way
My Chief, who gave me grace sweeter than mother's love, I
see not now !
Yet in the fire I fall not, wander not o'er hills, nor plunge
me in the sea ! (156)
XL. Still the senses' slave.

'When Cupid's dart in springtide wounds, moonlight will
scorch ;' of this I took!
No heed; like milk 'neath churning stick I'm stirred by
wiles of those of
fawn like eyes.
To Civan's city go I not, where grace as honey to the soul is
given;
To cherish soul within the body, still I eat, and garments
still put on! (160)
DECAD V

THE RENDERING A FIT RETURN

XLI. I did not clearly apprehend Thine appearing.

Like elephant two-handed I saw not
My mind's true germ; I saw but sore distress.
Thou bad'st me, 'come'; yet, 'mid the heavenly ones
'Twas I alone passed not, the senses' slave. (164)

XLII. It must have been illusion. Is HE man?

To all who apprehend that one bright Essence truly is,
As female, male, or lifeless thing Thou art not known;-
To me Thy servant, coming as Thou art, Thou didst appear
!
I saw Thee, yet I saw Thee not ! What visual juggle this
!(168)

XLIII. When shall I really see Thee as Thou art?

Thou Form unique, to even heavenly ones
Unknown ! Thou Mystic Dancer, Who didst make me Thine
!
Me Thine ! On earth, in heaven, or when all these
Have passed away,-WHEN shall I see Thy face? (172)

XLIV. I am of earth, earthy.

Thou Infinite, by men yet seen ! Beyond eye's ken
Thou Essence gleaming bright ! Here, like a fledgling, I
Would gladly leave this faulty frame; yet know I not
Dweller in this sense-world-how I may Thee put on.
(176)

49

XLV. Deadness of soul.

I call not on Thee filled with mighty love,
Nor render praise, nor fall in ecstasy
'Tis with me as when death confronted Thee,
Bowing before those lotus flowers Thy feet. (180)

XLVI. Call me, take me once more.

Call, take me 'midst Thy loving ones, Thou crowned
With cassias, home of sweets and humming bees !-
In 'midst, beneath, above, in all contained,
Thou art, my Sire, ' like oil within the seed ! '(184)

XLVII. The Self-sufficing sought out me.

Fathcr and Mother, Lord ! To all besides.
Sire, Mother, Lord: to Him all these are not !
Erewhile within my inmost soul He entered,
Whom none by thought can know, the Ever-blissful One !
188

XLVIII. I had but a glimpse of His glory.

To Thee, nor wealth, nor want ! From heavenly ones to
worms,
And grass, (no limit), all Thou fillest, -Being rare !
I saw Thy Foot-gem limitless, yet swerved from Thee.
This is the grief I stony-hearted have endured ! (192)

XLIX. An appeal.

My bonds Thou loosed'st, mad'st me Thine ! And all
The loving saints who ashes gave beheld.
Thou didst exalt, within the temple court,
Ev'n me Thou didst exalt, who knew not anything.(196)

L. I was not chosen for my wisdom or might.

Thou Only-Wise ! Ambrosia ! me, a servile cur,
When Thou didst take and make Thine own, was I then
wise ?
Thou saw'st my ignorance that day Thou mad'st me Thine
!
Ah, Lord of grace, was I then wise ? was I then strong
?(200)

DECAD VI.

OVERFLOWINGS OF JOY.

LI. No possible return for such mercies.

O Master, O my Mighty One, my Father, PerumAn, my
births'
Destroyer, Thou Who mad'st me Thine,-an evil wholly
worthless dog,
And throughly base; I cannot think, Thou see'st,-of any
meet return to Thee,
O Shining One, Lord of the Porch,-nor know I aught that I
can do. (204)

LII. I am still the senses' slave

Mean cur, that knew not what to do, I gave myself to gain
those things
That false ones gain, who ne'er have seen Thy flowery Feet
of ruddy gold.
I saw and heard that Thy true saints set free from lies, had
gained Thy fragrant Foot;
Yet I,-false one,-O Warrior strong ! still eat, am clothed,
and here abide. (208)
LIII. I only left !

Thou Warrior strong from out Thy golden city cam'st,
mad'st darkness flee;
With Her the beauteous Queen didst deign to come. The
glorious devotees
Who grace had gained, approached Thy Feet. I saw, yet like
a sightless hog
That roams the village street, shall I still roam a wretch
doomed to live on ? (212)
LIV. My love is weak

Full many a saint through deathless time wrought
penance,members mortified
With frustrate hope to see Thee here ! Yet Thou didst
sinful me Thy servant make.
O Gem ! This frame with foulness filled wears not away. To
see Thy face,
The strong desire and love 'bide not in me; my Prince, how
may I rise ?(216)

LV. Still I live this loathed life.

Thy bride is Umai with the fawn-like eyes ! Thou cam'st and mad'st me Thine
Ambrosia Thou, essential sweetness shed ! O Civan, southern Tillai's King
Thy saints assembled 'neath Thy sacred sign have gone to gather round Thy feet
This loathsome body still I guard, still here I dwell, O MASTER MINE !(220)

LVI . Thy will ordains my exile.

O MASTER MINE ! They think on Thee, Thy loving ones, with rapture filled
They're Thine, Thy Foot I saw them join. Yet here more mean than village cur
I dwell; my heart no rapture feels; my mind is stone, nor melts within.
This body vile I still must guard and here abide,-such is THY WILL ! (224)

LVII. My old life of earthly love.

The way THY WILL ordains befits me well ! Faithless I strayed, I left
Thy saints. A reprobate was I I How did I watch the one belov'd,
The quiverings of the lip, the folds of circling robe, the timid bashfull looks
To read love's symptoms there ! My mind thus ruin to myself wrought out. (228)

LVIII. Was my vocation a mockery then?

Thou honied Sweetness, purest Joy, Souls' Light, Master
Who fill'st with bliss
The frame of those that trust in Thee, Giver of endless gifts
! Of worth.
I void am yet Thy slave; Thou me hast made Thine own; if
this be so
Thy servant's state would show, I plead, Thy gift of grace
was but Thy sport. (232)
LIX. What other refuge have I ?

Thy nature others know not ! Lord ! Me evil cur, lowest of
all,
Hast Thou not made Thine own ? And wilt Thou let me go
cast out from Thee?
Then who will deign to look on me ? What shall I do, O
PerumAn ?
Father, whose sacred form is gleam of gold, where shall I
refuge find? (236)

LX. I have sure hope; yet how unworthy!

I shall enter beneath Thy Foot which is mine ! 'mid saints
that adore I standing
Shall laugh, glad as I gaze on the well-known form!
shameless dog tho' I am !
No melting love is here! To see Thee - to be made Thine
own, - can I
Be meet ? This abject state, Father ! behold, 'tis past my
power to BEAR !(240)

DECAD VII.

THE OVERWHELMING SENSE OF THE DIVINE COMPASSION.

LXI. Praises

I BEAR no more these joys of sense; Hail I CangarA !
Hail ! heaven's ancient Lord. Hail ! our Vidalai !
Hail ! Matchless One ! Hail ! King of heavenly hosts !
Hail ! Tillai's Dancer ! All hail ! our Spotless One ! (244)

LXII. Ectasy.

All hail ! Na ma-ci va ya ! Buyangan ! My senses fail !
All hail ! Na ma ci-va-ya ! Other refuge is there none !
All hail ! Na-ma-ci-va-ya ! Send me not forth from Thee !
All hail! Na-ma-ci-va-ya! Triumph, triumph, Hail! (248)

LXIII. All in all !

Hail ! Loving One, Who deign'st to make false ones like me
Thine own !
Hail ! to Thy Foot ! Hail ! O Lord ! Hail, hail !
Hail ! Sweetness new of mercy's flood ! Earth, water, fire,
Wind, ether, the two lights of heaven,are Thee, O GOD !
(252)

LXIV. Come quickly !

Hail, O my GOD ! In grace behold me; Hail !
Hail ! I pray Thee melt my soul within me, make me Thine !

Hail ! This body strip from off me; quickly give the
heavenly realms !
Hail ! CangarA, Who in Thy braided lock hast GangA placed
! (256)

LXV. Praise.

Hail ! O CangarA, other refuge have I none !
Hail ! Partner of the Queen of glorious form, of ruddy lips,
And gleaming smile, and black bright eye ! Hail ! Rider on
the mighty Bull
Here these earthly joys I bear not, Embiran,I all renounce !
(260)

LXVI. Prostration.

I have myself renounced, even I; Hail, hail, Embiran !
I have not done Thee wrong ! Hail ! Foot to which I service
owe !
Hail ! Faults to forgive is duty of the great !
O cause this earthly life to cease ! Hail, Lord of heaven !
(264)

LXVII. Adoration.

Hail, Lord ! Hail ! Thou King of heavenly saints !
Partner of the Queen's graceful form, Hail ! Wearer of the
sacred ash !
Hail ! Worthy Prince ! Hail ! Thou of Tillai's sacred court !
Hail! ! King of heaven ! My only Ruler, Hail ! (268)

LXVIII. Take me

Hail !, only Deity ! Incomparable Father, Hail !
Hail ! Guru of the heavenly ones ! Hail ! ! Tender Branch !
Hail, bid me come, receive me ! grant Thy Foot to gain;
And thus remove my lonely friendless woe ! (272)

LXIX.

Hail, to those who love with perfect love, Giver of love
surpassing theirs !
Hail ! Greatness that oft my falsehood pardon'd, granted
grace, and made me Thine !
Hail ! Prince, Who drank the outpoured poison,-to the
heavenly ones ambrosia gave !
Hail ! Thy perfect Foot on me, a wretch, in grace bestow !
(276)

LXX. The Universal Lord.

Hail ! Thou Who art earth, water, fire, wind, ether too !
Hail ! Thou, all life's phenomena,-Thyself invisible !
Hail, all living beings' End,-Thyself without an end !
Thyself reaching through all, by senses five unreached !
(280)

DECAD VIII.

MYSTIC UNION.

LXXI. Sinking in rapture.

Sire, as IN UNION strict, Thou mad'st me Thine; on me
didst look, didst draw me near;
And when it seemed I ne'er could be with Thee made one,-
when naught of Thine was mine,-
And naught of mine was Thine,-me to Thy Feet Thy love
In mystic union joined, Lord of the heavenly land !-'Tis
height of BLESSEDNESS. (284)
LXXII. All bliss in God.

For BLESSEDNESS I seek; not Indra's choice delights, nor
those of other gods;
Thou Only-One, I live not save with Thy Feet twain ! Our
Lord,my breast is Riven,
With trembling seized; my hands in adoration join;
And from my eyes a ceaseless stream pours down, as of a
river, O MY SAGE !(288)

LXXIII. Prayer for consummation.

MY SAGE, save to Thyself there's none to whom I cling;-in
me, deceitful one
No part from mingled falseness 'scapes; I'm falsehood's
self !Partner of Her whose dark
Eyes gleam, come Thou to me ! the love Thy true ones
feel,-
Who at Thy jewell'd Feet in love commingling rest,-mine
be it too, I PRAY ! (292)

LXXIV. Give me essential oneness.

I PRAY for love of Thine own jewell'd Feet; remove the
false; Thine own

Make me in truth; dog though I am,O bid me come, in grace
join to Thyself
For ever more Thine own ! So let me ceaseless praise,
Thro' every world returning ever come; my King, that I
may WORSHIP THEE ! (296)
LXXV. Thou art sole actuality

THEE WORSHIP both the earth and heaven, with shouts of
joy, and fourfold mystic scroll:
They yearning pine for Thee. For they who gain Thee
know naught true exists but Thee.
Ah ! since we vow to quit Thy service never, come
And grant Thy grace,Thou Partner of the lovely Queen !
Pausingwhy PONDER so ?(300)

LXXVI. He transcends thought and speech.

WHEN PONDERING Thee the thought goes forth, to reach
the bound desired by fitting word
Is not a whit attainable; nor are these things one hears
through forms of speech.
Thee, Who art all the world, the senses five know not.
How GAIN the Father's Foot that rests in all that is and
every sphere beyond? (304)

LXXVII. Pity me !

To me, a guileful soul, who thought to GAIN Thee, Lord,
salvation save by Thee
Is none. No other Being truly is, save Thee ! Lest pining
sorrow come,
In mercy to my sin, my soul vouchsafe to guard.

'Tis pitying grace like this alone RULER SUPERNE ! Thy
glory doth beseem. (308)

LXXVIII. My soul clings to Thee.

' RULER SUPERNE, there's none butThee, or here or there,'
and thus I ever spake,
Fool though I was, there was no difference ! Our Lord:
Thou Spotless One,
Who didst
Make me, an outcast wretch, Thine own, my Teacher Thou,
The THOUGHT, that other god exists than Thee the One,
my mind shall never THINK !(312)

LXXIX. Old days of ignorance.

BY THOUGHT, by deed, by hearing, or by speech, or by
these wretched senses five
I failed in days of old Thy truth to reach;- I, low and foolish
one.
I passed not through the fire, my heart burst not with
shame.
To Thee, O Father, even yet may I attain ! May I yet dwell
with Thee ! (316)

LXXX. Strange command: 'Tarry yet below.'

Me iron hearted and deceitful one, Thine own Thou
mad'st; Thy foot's sweet bliss
Filled me with joy; with me Thou didst commingling join.
The fire was there and I

Was there: that was which was ! Though this was so that
day,
There was in Thee desire for me, in me for Thee;-what
ignorance was mine? (320)
DECAD IX.

ECSTASY.

LXXXI. Falsehood lingers yet.

'The seed of lies is not destroyed ;'-so saying, Thou hast
placed me here !-
All those that were to Thy desire have come, and reached
Thy sacred Foot ! -
In depths of fear I sink O God, Who didst in ArUr ask for
alms,
What shall I do ? SPEAK Thou to me ! (324)

LXXXII. Resignation.

Thou SPAK'ST to me, amid Thy saints with sacred ash I
was besmeared;
By men on earth as Thy poor slave I've been abused;
henceforth, if what
I suffer pleases not, 'tis what my soul desires, because I am
Thy SLAVE, whom Tho~ didst make Thine own ! (328)

LXXXIII. Yet I know not why I'am left.

And am I not Thy SLAVE ? and didst Thou not make me
Thine own, I pray

All those Thy servants have approached Thy Foot; this
body full of sin
I may not quit, and see Thy face,-Thou Lord of Civa-world!-
I fear,
And SEE NOT HOW TO GAIN THE SIGHT ! (332)

LXXXIV. Tell me the hindrance to my instant freedom.

I SEE NOT HOW THY SIGHT TO GAIN; though Thee THAT
DAY I saw ! Speak Thou
In music say what 'tis that weighs my spirit down,-O Light
Superne !
Male, Female, rare Ambrosia, Sire ! I die, a dog, of power
bereft,
By what may I rise up, my Lord ? (336)

LXXXV. Falseness keeps me out.

Thou Partner of the fawn-eyed Queen; Thou Word, whose
end the Word
knows not;-
Ambrosia sweet, to thought unknown; King, faults of
wretched me Thou bear'st
I babbling tell my woes. Thy saints have reached the city
blest. OUTSIDE
I and my FALSENESS wander here ! (340)

LXXXVI. But O, the pity of it.

OUTSIDE We go, FALSENESS and I !True love to gain I've
lost the power.

This is my gain! Thy saints to Thee who utterly are joined now,

Know nothing else but Thee; in acts all glorious on their way they go !

O Civan, they have reached Thy FOOT ! (344)

LXXXVII. Failure !

O Master, give Thy slave to love Thy FOOT; Thy servants now have gained

The world from which they come not back; outside I have remained, I've tried

'To crown the village cow, and so have crowned the blind !' From love, of

Thy twain Feet

Estranged, a slave I 'wildered WEEP ! (348)

LXXXVIII. I am unworthy to be numbered with Thy saints.

I WEEP ! With loving mind towards Thee, like wax before the fire were they.

Thy gleaming, golden, jewelled Foot have they beheld, and worshipping

Have followed Thee; not following on with them, in vain have I been born !

Wherewith shall I before Thee bow? (352)

LXXXIX. At least, take my sin away.

In grace Thou hast put far all ills of those that bowed; on ancient saints

Thou didst bestow Thy Foot adorned ! If that's too great
for me, my guilt
(Who'm like a tough bambu) destroy; come swiftly, give
Thy healing Foot
Thou only True, from FALSEHOOD free ! (356)

XC. Teach me Thy way.

All FALSE am I; FALSE is my heart; and FALSE my love;
yet, if he weep,
May not Thy sinful servant Thee, Thou Soul's Ambrosial
sweetness, gain ?
Lord of all honied gladness pure, in grace unto Thy servant
teach
The way that he may come to Thee ! (360)

DECAD X

THE OVERFLOW OF RAPTURE.

XCI. The true ones blest - but I!

O Flood of mighty changeless grace ! They came,
who gain'd erewhile the gift immutable
Of station 'neath Thy twain flow'r-wreathed Feet.
They, LOVING THEE IN TRUTH, HAVE REACH'D THE TRUE
!
Thee, Endless One, benignly manifest,
diffusing light,-as Man, I saw Thee come !
Yet I, a dog, of heart by fate unblest,-
lie at the gate, ah me ! in low estate. (364)

XCII. Deny me not Thy truth.

O Half of Her with eyes of glist'ning jet,
Thou cam'st and mad'st me Thine, with tender hand
As feeding me from golden cup, since when
hard of access I deem Thee never more;
Thou on Whose Body gleam the ashes white !
They, LOVING THEE IN TRUTH, HAVE REACH'D THE TRUE
!
But, tell me, is it MEET that Thou should'st go
and leave me here, in falsehood thus to fall ? (368)

XCIII. Take 'deeds' away.

MEETNESS I'd none,-the false I took for true;
but when with loving glance Thou had'st me come,
Afflictions ceased ! Yet now deceit seems truth.
I have not died, O blooming lotus Foot !
Thou with Thy loving ones-to whom Thy grace
was given, O roseate Form,-on high
Hast gone, and left me here. Lord, hear my plaint:
there is no end of deeds for worthless me ! (372)

XCIV. No limit to Thy power.

There was no love in me towards Thy FOOT,
O Half of Her with beauteous fragrant locks !
By magic power that stones to mellow fruit
converts, Thou mad'st me lover of Thy Feet.
Our Lord, Thy tender love no limit knows.
Whatever sways me now, whate'er my deed,
Thou can'st even yet Thy Foot again to me

display and save, O Spotless Heavenly One ! (376)

XCV. My course laid out by Thee.

Thou Whom the lords of heaven themselves know not !
Thy source and end the VEdas cannot trace !
Tlou Whom in every land men fail to know !
As Thou hast sweetly made me Thine hast called
This flesh to dance on stage of earth,-
me to enjoy Thyself with melting soul,-
In mystic drama, too, hast caused to move,-
pining on earth, Thou Lord of magic power ! (380)

XCVI. 'I am Thine, save me!?

Without a seed, the fruit Thou causest spring;
th' entire of heaven and earth, and all therein
Thou didst ordain, and wilt destroy ! Me too,
deceitful, mean, within Thy temple gates
Thou fill'd'st with frenzy; mad'st to join the band
of Thy great loving ones ! Ev'n should the tree
They plant yield poison, men destroy it not;-
and thus am I, MY OWNER AND MY LORD ! (384)

XCVII. Devotion.

OWNER AND LORD, all hail! Besides Thyself
support to cling to hath Thy servant aught ?
I serve Thee, hail ! Transcendent Being, Lord
of those in heavenly courts who dwell, all hail !
Lowest of all have I become, all hail !
Giver.to me of every grace, all hail !

Thou Who didst make me Thine own servant, hail !
the First Thou art, and Last, my FATHER, hail ! (388)

XCVIII. Earnest appeal.

My FATHER ! unto me Ambrosia Thou !
O Blest Supreme ! Thou art to honey like
That flows abundant, thrills the soul with bliss I
Thy loving ones enjoy Thee as their own !
Helper Thou art ! with glist'ning glory crowned,
in weary anguish of Thy worshippers.
O Treasure ! tell me, wilt Thou leave me here,
in this poor world to pine away, our KING ? (392)

XCIX. Come !

O KING, our Lord, come Thou to me, to me !
Who art before the four-faced One and MAl,
And all the gods. Our Lord, come Thou to me, to me !
After the day when all things have their end
Thou art ! Our Lord, come Thou to me, to me !
I at Thy jewell'd feet would utter praise
With loving tongue ! Our Lord, come Thou to me, to me I
that I, Sin's-slayer, may Thy glories SING ! (396)

C. Longing desire.

THY PRAISE TO SING I long, all hail ! Thee sing !
while all my being sinks and melts in love.
I long to dance, all hail ! in Thy blest courts,
before Thy flow'ry dancing Foot ! A dog,-
I long to join, all hail ! Remove me from

this nest of worms, all hail ! The false I long
To leave, all hail ! Grant me Thy home, all hail !
Hail Thou who art to THY TRUE SERVANTS TRUE !
HYMN VI - neethal viNNappam (prapanja vairakkiyam)
'FORSAKE ME NOT'

This title, which forms the burthen of the poem, is given to
one of the Sage's most interesting compositions. It consists
of fifty quatrains, constructed in a beautiful metre (see my
Second Grammar 192) which is in fact epichoriambic (as is
explained in the notes to the Tamil text).

It is called AnthAthi poem. This means that it is
anaphoretic, the last word of a verse is to be repeated in
the beginning of each following verse, and very often
striking its keynote. Hymn V is the same). This has a
beautiful effect in Tamil, but the difference of Idiom often
forbids translator to attempt to reproduce it in English.

The poem throughout is a genuine human cry for Divine
help in the midst of a terrible struggle and is full of the
most vivid emotion. It was composed, according to
tradition, immediately after the wonderful cento that
forms the fifth poem, and gives expression to the youthful
devotee's feelings after his guru had finally departed, and
the company of the 999 (?) saints who attended him had
thrown themselves into the fire. He is said to have gone
round the Civan shrines in the PAndiyan Kingdom, and
first of all to have spent some considerable time in the
ancient city of Tiru-uttara-kOcamangai, which was at one
time a PAndiyan capital, situate eight miles south-west of
Ramnad, where the ruins of an important Civan shrine are

yet to be seen. There he suffered from the reaction naturally consequent upon the excitement produced by the wonderful events of the preceding months. He had been till now the petted, highly gifted favourite and prime minister of the PAndiyan Kingdom living in the midst of pomp and luxury, invested with almost absolute power; and was still in early manhood. He finds himself at once a Caiva mendicant, who has renounced everything subsists on alms, and must spend his days and nights in solitary meditation.

Meanwhile the circumstances in which he finds himself placed the lives of his companions, the whole environment of the temple, are not favourable to pure and high devotion. The lofty ideal is not realized here. Then, as now, the influences surrounding and emanating from the shrine itself were in many ways deteriorating. From the evidence of these verses, we conclude that there were two things from which he suffered. One of these was the allurements of the female attendants who, in bands pertained to the temple. We have noticed this elsewhere. Hindu commentators will often find mystic meanings, which are harmless, - if unfounded. Again and again in this and other poems he deplores the way in which he has been led to violate his vow. The other difficulty, often referred to was the way in which mere ceremonial acts had to be performed, affording no relief to his conscience. He thus fell into a desponding and well-nigh despairing state of mind, and sent forth this cry like that heard in the Psalter, and reiterated by the greatest Being that ever trod the pathway of this human life. Few things in literature have such a genuine ring as some of the verses in which young noble bewails his apparent desertion by his Master. Yet he never quite lost his confidence and love; and afterwards, as many of the lyrics show, exchanged for the 'spirit of heaviness the garment of praise'.

I do not think that any one can be found who will withhold his sympathy from the Sage. It may be noticed, though it is in connection with the Tamil text that the matter must be more fully discussed, that there is a great difference, as it seems to me, between the style of the first twenty stanzas (where indeed it may be conjectured that the poem originally ended) and those that follow. Notably in verses 21-50 there is only reference to Uttara-kOca-mangai, which city in verses 1-20 is a part of the perpetual refrain. These latter verses, too, are more ingenious and subtle, and are more ful of poetic fancies. Sometimes, indeed, they may seem to be even more beautiful than those that are the undoubted composition of the Sage. Their language, rhythm, and manner seem to me, however, to be different. But I readily acknowledge the difficulty that lies in the way of all merely subjective criticism, especially by a foreigner. Yet the exceedingly uncritical way in which these texts have been hitherto handled necessitates and justifies the attempt.

The writer did a great part of these translations at beautiful Lugano, not unfrequently relieving the toil by the enjoyment of an hour in the church of S. Maria degli Angoli, before the marvellous frescoes of Bernardino Luini; and could not help wishing oft times that the Tamil Sage and Seeker after God could have stood there, or haply knelt by his side. Could Manikkavacagar have traced that

history of the Great Master, of His passage from
Gethsemane to the glory of His heavenly dwelling place,
how would he have been affected?. One wonders!. It may
be that he, and the weaver of MailApUr, and the wandering
sages of the NAladiyAr, and others whose legends we
recall, have since, freed from the flesh, visited that spot.
Certainly they know those histories now! Shall we not in
regard to our poet-sage, wherever his ashes are scattered,
say hopefully and tenderly, Requiescat in pace?

Metre: kaTTaLaikkaliththuRai

I. The foresaken one's petition

Me, meanest one, in mercy mingling Thou didst make
Thine own,-
Lord of the Bull ! Lo, THOU'ST FORSAKEN ME! O Thou
Who wear'st
Garb of fierce tiger's skin ! ABIDING UTTARA-KOCA-
MANGAI'S KING
Thou of the braided lock ! I fainting sink. Our Lord, uphold
Thou me ! (4)

II.

The crimson lips of maidens fair, in ripeness of their
charms,
I press no more; yet, Lo ! THOU HAST FORSAKEN ME;
though in,
Not out Thy worthy service, UTTARA-KOCA-MANGAI'S
KING,

I am ! Thou mad'st false me Thine, why dost Thou leave me NOW ? (8)

III.

A tree on river bank of dark eyed maiden's senses five
I rooted stand ! LO, ME THOU HAST FOKSAKEN; Thou who dwell'st
In ArUr's shrine renowned; O UTTARA-KOCA MANGAI'S KING !
Half of her form, the beauteous one ! Thou FOSTERER of my life ! (12)

IV.

Thou took'st me in Thy gracious FOSTERING hand; and then, withdrawn,
LO ! THOU'ST FORSAKEN me lost here; Thou Whose lofty crown
Bears the pale crescent moon, O UTTARA KOCA-MANGAI'S KING !
Thou radiant Beam as lightning seen 'mid sheen of GLISTENING gold ! (16)

V.

Like moth in GLISTENING flame, to those of gentle speech, long time
I fall a prey ! LO, THOU'ST FORSAKEN ME! In Thy flower-crown
Sweet bees sip fragrant honey; UTTARA KOCA-MANGAI'S KING !

Since with ambrosia of Thy grace to feed me I REFUSED !
(20)

VI.

Through ignorance I have Thy grace REFUSED; and Thou,
my Gem !
Hast loathed me ! Lo, THOU'ST FORSAKEN ME ! My throng
of 'deeds '
Suppress, and make me Thine, O UTTARA-KOCA
MANGAI'S KING !
Will not the great-soul'd bear, though little curs are FALSE
? (24)

VII.

FALSE me Thou mad'st Thine own, as though some worth I
had; didst mend
Me, O Thou True ! LO, THOU'ST FORSAKEN ME! Thy throat
is black
With swallow'd poison ! STATELY UTTARA-KOCA
MANGAI'S KING!
O roseate One, Civan, who PUTT'ST AWAY my mortal
pains ! (28)

VIII.

What is Thy way of glorious grace that PUTS AWAY my sin
?
I ask with awe; THOU'ST LEFT ME, UTTARA-KOCA-
MANGAI'S KING;

Before whose jubilant Bull flower-crown'd foes fearing
fled !
The senses 'five' and fear in ways DIVERSE draw guilty me
! (32)

IX.

Like ant on firebrand lit at DIVERSE ends, sever'd from
Thee,
Distraught, Lo ! ME THOU HAST FORSAKEN, Thou the only
Lord
Of the vast triple world, strong UTTARA-KOCA-MANGAI'S
KING !
Whose BRIGHT right hand uplifts the warrior's triple-
headed spear ! (36)

X.

I gained access to Thy BRIGHT Feet, freed from this mortal
frame !
Yet me who pine, THOU'ST LEFT; O UTTARA-KOCA
MANGAI'S KING,
Around Whose beauteous flowery groves the swarms of
beetles hum;
Thou Who with bow of might didst burn the city of, Thy
FOES ! (40)

XI.

MY FOES, 'the five' deceived me; from Thy jewelled flower-
like Feet
I parted; LO! THOU HAST FORSAKEN ME ! Thou honey of

My sinful soul ! O UTTARA-KOCA MANGAI'S KING !
O WORTH, Whose golden form gleams 'neath the hallowed
ash ! (44)

XII.

O WORTHY ONE, Thou mad'st me Thine; by senses ' five '
deceived,
I worthless left Thee ! UTTARA-KOCA MANGAI'S KING !
And Thou
Hast left me ! Thou Whose mighty javelin slays Thy
trembling foes;
Great SEA of clear Ambrosia given for worthless me to
taste ! (48)

XIII.

As dog laps water from the lake, my soul Thy mercy's SEA
Quits not; me THOU'ST FORSAKEN, UTTARA-KOCA-
MANGAI'S KING;
Who dost as in a home abide in those who leave Thee not,
Wine of the palm ! Ambrosia ! Gem ! My FLOOD of bliss !
(52)

XV.

Like one whose tongue amid the FLOOD is parched I gain'd
Thy grace,
Yet sorrow springs; ME THOU'ST FORSAKEN; UTTARA-
KOCA-MANGAI'S KING;
Who ever dwellest in Thy servants' hearts that Thee desire
!

To me in guile immersed grant grace ! My joy is JOYLESS all ! (56)

xv,

With JOYOUS thought I saw Thy Foot, drew near, and gained Thy grace;
Yet am not free ! ME THOU'ST FORSAKEN, UTTARA-KOCA-MANGAI'S KING,
Whose flowery jewell'd Foot is Light of all true lights that gleam !
Father accessible ! Lord, Who didst make me all Thine own ! (60)

XVI

I wandered weary, none to say 'Fear not !' Like lightning's flash
Behold, THOU HAST FORSAKEN ME ! Thou Truth beyond compare;
Great UTTARA-KOCA-MANGAI'S KING, that like Thyself abides:
Like Mother Thou, like Father Thou, my soul's most precious WEALTH ! (64)

XVII.

O WEALTH ! Sole Refuge of my lonely heart ! By those who spurn
Thy glories fear'd ! Lo, THOU'ST FORSAKEN ME; O Grace by eager heart

And true enjoyed; THOU KING OF UTTARA-KOCA
MANGAI'S SHRINE,
With fair groves girt ! Darkness and light, this world and
that, Thou art ! (68)

XVIII.

'Be with me ! Govern, use, sell, pledge me,' thus I cried,
Yet me, erewhile Thy guest, THOU HAST FORSAKEN, Who
didst drink
The poison as ambrosia; UTTARA KOCA-MANGAI'S KING !
Thou healing Balm for those bowed down by 'changeful
birth's' disease ! (72)

XIX.

Fire of Thy 'biding grace my sins' thick springing wood
burns up,
Vidangan ! THOU'ST FORSAKEN ME; O UTTAR-KOCA-
MANGAI'S KING;
Who dost destroy the root of human 'birth,' and make me
Thine;
The hill-like elephant didst flay, and fright the Vanji-
BOUGH ! (76)

XX.

Like climbing plant with no-supporting BOUGH, I
wavering hung !
Lo, Tender One, me-tremblulg THOU'ST FORSAKEN; Thou
Who dwell'st

Where heavenly ones come not; strong UTTARA-KOCA-
MANGAI'S KING;
Thou Who art Ether, Earth, and Fire, and Wind, and watery
FLOOD ! (80)

XXI.

Like little shrubs where elephants contend, by senses five
I've been sore vexed; lo, THOU, my Father, HAST
FORSAKEN ME !
To sinful me commingled honey, milk, sweet cane,
ambrosia,
LIGHT of my soul, thrilling my flesh and inmost frame,-
Thou art ! (84)

XXII.

The LIGHT Thou art: the White One, gleaming bright. with
sacred ash
Besmeared. Lo ! THOU'ST FORSAKEN ME; Thou to Thy
servants true
Art near; from others ever distant; hard to know;
The Feminine, the ancient Male, the neutral One art Thou !
(88)

XXIII.

The form Thou gav'st I wore, in faults abounding, scant of
love,.
Me, worthless slave, THOU HAST FORSAKEN, see ! But, if
Thou leave,

I perish; none but Thee upholds Thy slave; Source of my being's bliss;
This clear perception hath Thy servant gained, Indwelling Lord ! (92)

XXIV.

Things true abiding, folly-stirred, for vanities I burn'd;
And THOU'ST FORSAKEN ME; Thou Who as robe dost wear the hide
Of fiery mighty-handed elephant !-I joys of sense
Seeking gain not, like ANTS that noiseless round the oil-jar swarm. (96)

XXV.

Like worm in midst of ANTS, by senses gnawed and troubled sore,
Me, utterly alone, Lo ! THOU'ST FORSAKEN; Thou Whom fiery death obeyed;
Whose fragrant flowery Foot the heavenly ones attain, and they
Who know; O MIGHTY One, Who from Thy servants partest not ! (100)

XXVI.

'When the GREAT waters fail, the little fishes faint; ' so reft of Thee
I quake. Lo ! THOU'ST FORSAKEN ME ! The moon's white crescent borne
On Ganga's wave, like little skiff on mountain stream,

Is hidden in Thy braided locks, O CHOICEST GEM of
heaven ! (104)

XXVII.

CHOICE GEMS they wore, those softly smiling maids; I
failed, I fell.
Lo ! THOU'ST FORSAKEN ME ! Thou gav'st me place 'mid
Saints who wept,
Their beings fill'd with rapturous joys; in grace didst make
me Thine !-
Show me Thy Feet, even yet to SENSE revealed, O spotless
Gem ! (108)

XXVIII.

While SENSES made me quake, I trembling swerved to
falsehood's way.
Lo ! THOU'ST FORSAKEN ME ! While heaven and earth the
poison feared
From out the mighty sea, Thou madest it ambrosia; Home
of grace !
Thy servant I, O Master, stand distraught; sole Worship of
my heart ! (112)

XXIX.

Thyself from every fetter free, Thou freed'st me from all
fault, O Sire,
Whose bow victorious is the mighty mount ! Lo, THOU'ST
FORSAKEN ME !

Thy lotus-form the cassia's gold wreath wears; O
matchless One !
By fivefold-evil am I stirred like milk by CHURNING STAFF.
(116)

XXX.

The senses' fire burns fierce; I'm stirr'd as the cool curds
by CHURNING'STAFF,
Lo ! ME THOU HAST FORSAKEN I Thou Who wear'st
chaplet of skulls
And clustering wreaths of flowers, and the long entrails'
twine; and dost Thyself
Adorn with ashes, and sweet sandal-paste, O ESSENCE
PURE ! (120)

XXXI. Thou art with all ! - but me !

PURE ESSENCE Multiform, Who art cool flood, sky, wind,
earth, fire;
THOU HAST FORSAKEN ME ! White, black, and azure art
Thou seen !
Roseate Thy form ! Thy girdle is the glistening hooded
snake !
O WARRIOR ELEPHANT, with dripping brow and mighty
foot ! (124)

XXXII. Sensuality was my bane.

Those WARRING ELEPHANTS, the senses five, I feared,-
was lost.

THOU HAST FORSAKEN ME, Thou, hard to leave,-hard to attain,

Save by Thy worthy saints, bright Gem ! While fierce fire raged,

Poison hard won from out the sea, Thou mad'st Thy food,

O Azure-throat! (128)

XXXIII. Pardon my waywardness !

That I wished to do I did,-wine of Thy grace I drank,- rejoiced;-

Then swerved ! THOU HAST FORSAKEN ME ! Thy fragrant flowery Foot,

As in the days of old Thou gav'st, command and bid me serve !

Take me, my Father ! O remove this wayward FOND DESIRE ! (132)

XXXIV. I was fickle and self-witted

Sitirred by no strong DESIRE I did my will, nor clung to Thine !

And, lo ! THOU HAST FORSAKEN ME ! When wilt Thou yet as wine

Of joy meet me, and all my mind with fragrant sweetness fill,

As of the plantain fruit,-TRANSCENDENT LORD of Kailai's hill ? (136)

XXXV. I am, though faulty, Thine !

TRANSCENDENT LORD, with Thine own ancient saints, me
faulty one
Thou didst desire ! O Aran, yet LO ! THOU'ST FORSAKEN
ME !-
Thou didst me place near Thee, like the hare spots thou
wear'st,-
O mighty Warrior 'gainst birth's five-mouth'd snake, my
soul would shun! (140)

XXXVI. Quench sensual fires.

Like flames in forest glade sense-fires with smoky glare
burn fierce !
I burn ! LO, THOU'ST FORSAKEN ME ! O conquering King
of heaven,
The garlands on Whose braided lock drip honey, while the
bees
Hum softly 'mid MandAra buds, whence fragrant
sweetness breathes. (144)

XXXVII. Is there no pity?

O King, to me poor ignorant, 'Fear not for faults,' Thou
didst
Not say, but HAST FORSAKEN ME, O Thou with fragrance
crowned !
Spouse of the sea-born maid with sparkling gems and jet-
black eyes !
Bhuyangan ! Golden Foot ! My 'deeds' PRESS round like
clustering hills. (148)

XXXVIII. I have erred through weakness.

By senses PRESSED, fearing I left Thee, weak to quit the
charms
Of sweet-voiced maids. Lo ! THOU'ST FORSAKEN ME !
Thou radiant Beam
King of the burning ground; Ambrosia to Thy worshippers;
Hard to be gained; sole HELP, removing loneliness of
lonely me ! (152)

XXXIX. Help me in this conflict with flesh.

SOLE HELP, whilst Thou wert there I wandered wanton,-
'deeds' my help !
THOU HAST FORSAKEN ME, Thou Helper of my guilty
soul;
Thou Source of all my beings bliss; Treasure that never
fails !
No whit bear I this grievous body's mighty NET ! (156)

XL. The pain of sensuality.

Caught by those eyes whose timid glance is like fawn's in
the NET,
'Wildered I grieved. Lo ! THOU'ST FORSAKEN ME ! Thou
on Whose head
The pale moon's crescent thin is seen ! Ocean of grace !
Thou Lord
Of Kailai's hill ! Spouse of the mountain Maid ! Source Of
my being's joy ! (160)

XLI. Woe is me, in this vile fleshy prison.

In the hot flood of lust for those of ruddy lips, like crocodiles,-
I eager plunged. Lo ! THOU'ST FORSAKEN ME ! This body foul,
Ant-eaten, I endure not; Civan, list to my complaint !
Thou Bridegroom of the beauteous Bride; my joyous Goal of bliss ! (164)

XLII. Grace once given, now withdrawn.

Thou gav'st indeed to me in grace to gain my goal, Thy Feet;-
Yet THOU'ST FORSAKEN ME, not fated to shake off this flesh !
The moon beheld the serpent bright in skull-cave hid, and feared;-
Then plunging hid his swelling crest within Thy braided lock, O KING ! (168)

XLIII. I adore Thee, though forlorn.

O KING, to wretched me, who know not any path, the Light
Of joy ! THOU HAST FORSAKEN ME !-Thou the true VEdic Lord
To me didst speak, Who passed speech ! To steadfast worshippers,
Thou art the First, the Last too,-Thou this universal Whole !(172)

XLIV. Tormented by lust.

Like oil was I poured in fierce fire of glancing dartlike
eyes,-
LO ! THOU'ST FORSAKEN ME! Whose word erst joined me
to Thy saints,
Who ever worship at Thy fragrant flowery Feet; my Lord !
My Master, faulty though I am, forsake me not ! Thee will I
SING. (176)

XLV. Spiritual desertion

I SANG Thee not, nor worshipped Thee, O hidden Gem,-nor
left this flesh.
LO ! THOU'ST FORSAKEN ME ! All wonderment I wept, yet
sought Thee not,
Nor, 'Where is Civan,' 'Who hath seen Him?' did I haste to
ask.
I lay supine, my soul no raptures knew;-I suffered sore !
(180)

XLVI. Still will I adore the mysteries of Thy nature.

Like fly in jack-fruit caught, I fell a prey to fawn-eyed
maids !
LO ! THOU'ST FORSAKEN ME ! But if Thou leave, I'll utter
loud reproach !
I'll call Thee 'Black-throat,' 'Who ate poison from the sea,'
'The Unqualified,'
'The man,' 'Crowned with the waning moon,' 'The mighty
God gone wrong.' (184)

XLVII. Various wanderings.

The ancient worship of Thy blameless Feet I gained; then fell;
Reviled Thee; woke once more; and, LO ! THOU HAST FORSAKEN ME !
Greatness, that heavenly Ganga stirs to shed bright gems and pearls !
Thy WREATH'S the crescent in the water seen, caught in Thy braided lock ! (188)

XLVIII. I will boast Thy name.

Hero, Who wear'st the fiery snake-WREATH on Thy starlike head !
Lo I THOU'ST FORSAKEN ME; But if Thou leave when others ask
'Whose servant Thou ?' 'Slave of the glorious slaves
Of Uttara-kOca-mangai's King,' I'll name myself, and cause them SMILE at Thee. (192)

XLIX. Ever praising.

I'll make them SMILE, unfolding faults and service to the Lord !
Lo! THOU'ST FORSAKEN ME; but if Thou leave, I shall ABUSE Thee sore !
'Madman, clad in wild elephant's skin;' 'Madman, with hide for his garb
'Madman, that ate the poison;' 'Madman of the burning-ground-fire
'Madman, that chose even me for His own !' (196)

L.

ABUSING Thee or praising,-crushed by sin, and grieved am
I !
LO! THOU'ST FORSAKEN ME, Thou Brightness on red coral
hill !
Thou madst me Thine; didst fiery poison eat, pitying poor
souls,
That I might Thine ambrosia taste,-I, meanest one ! (200)
HYMN VII - thiruvempaavai
(Cattiyai viyantatu)
THE MAIDENS' SONG OF THE DAWNING
The mystic 'Song of the Maidens' forms a pendant to the
'Morning Hymn' (XX). It has always been attributed to
Manikka-vACagar without any hesitation, though in many
respects it is certainly unlike most of his other lyrics. It is
said to have been composed for the use of the women at
ArunACalam, among whom it is, and was, the custom to
celebrate with great demonstrations of joy a festival in
honour of the god Civan and the goddess Catti in the
month of Margazhi, which corresponds to the second half
of December and the first half of January. At that time the
females of the city of all ages for ten successive days rise
before dawn, and perambulate the precincts, arousing
their companions from house to house, and proceeding to
bathe (in rigidly decorous manner) in the sacred tank.
There are passages in this poem which I have been obliged
somewhat to veil, and modify, carefully preserving,
however, the full and exact meaning of the original, as I
conceive it. There is, however, connected with the Caiva
worship, it must be said, a series of rites which is
sometimes called the tantric, and sometimes the Cakti
system. No doubt, in connection with this, many

unspeakable abominations have been, and are at times perpetrated; and every thoughtful Hindu is sincerely anxious that all trace of these corruptions should be swept away. In all nations Similar things have existed, and it would be quite superfluous to enumerate the ancient rites of a similar character that have been enthusiastically celebrated. From such things the Caiva system must sever itself absolutely, which it can the more decidedly do, because they have no real root in the Caiva Siddhanta philosophy itself.

In one edition of these poems there is the introduction to the 'Maidens' Reveille,' which gives a mystic interpretation to a large portion of the lyric. According to this author, from the month of Adi to the month of Margazhi (i.e. from July 15th to January 15th) is the night season; the other half of the year being the daytime; the whole year forming a single day of the Gods. The former half of the year, in which there is rain with black clouds, is the representative of the secular period of involution or destruction, when all things have been re-involved in the ripple veils of darkness, which period precedes that of the recreation, or evolution. The other half of the year represents the period of creation, i.e. the time during which the phenomenal universe is re-evolved from its eternal elements as the sphere of the activities of all things that have life. The month of Margazhi is then the symbol of the awaking of the universe from its slumber of involution. It is the dawn of the new creation,Ñ of secular evolution. [NOTE XIII]. Now this creation is the work of Catti, the manifested energy of Civan:Ñhis wife, who is the author, not of life indeed, but of the whole phenomenal system in which and by which life exerts its energy, and achieves its destinies.

Civan himself can come into no personal relation with matter and its veiling delusions and darkness. It is, therefore, Catti that accomplishes the work; she is an energy of activity, of knowledge, and of desire; and through her alone the Supreme evolves all things. But this tantric system, like the gnostic systems of old, does not permit Catti as the Partner of the Supreme, to accomplish directly the work of evolution. This would be far too simple and direct for Hindu philosophy. There is a long chain of feminine manifestations (aeons evolved in succession, each coming into a relation to the Supreme that constitutes a distinct stage in the process; and it is only at last that BrahmA and Vishnu are evolved, to be respectively the fashioned and the maintainer of the cosmic world. The writer here enumerates nine of these Cattis amongst whom are numbered the chief female divinities that, under various names and epithets, are worshipped or propitiated in various parts of India. Among them is the dreaded KAli. No doubt there are hints of all this in this poem, but its plain and obvious interpretation is the only one known to the majority of those that use it, and I imagine the composer himself was innocent of anything like the gnosticism and mysticism that his interpreters have given him credit for. As the hymn stands it is a beautiful composition, but in some parts it will seem to be somewhat obscure. I have tried to give a version that still be as literal as possible, but only the Tamil reader can feel how great a poet its author was; and only the student of the South-Indian Caiva philosophy can expect to enter into its spirit.

Metre: veNTanaiyAnvanta iyaRRavinaik koccackalippa

I. The temple worship
(The waits sing at the door)
The Splendour rare and great, that knows nor first nor
end,
we sing; Thou hear'st the song, yet still sleep'st on;
O lady of the large bright eye ! is thine ear dull
that it perceives not sound of praise that hails
The great God's cinctured feet ?ÑShe hears the strain
resound
through all the street, yet in forgetful sleep
On her flower-couch she muttering turns ! Ñ
See, here she nothing noting lies ! Why thus, why thus ?
doth this our friend beseem ?-OUR LADY FAIR, ARISE ! (4)

II. Trifle not.
'Hail to the heavenly Light,' thou ever say'st, as we,
by night and day. Now of this flowery couch
Art thou enamour'd, maid with faultless gems adorned ?
Shame I jewell'd dames, are these things trifles too ?
To sport and jest is this the place, when He in grace
Hath come to give the foot-flower, shame fast angels
praise ?
The Teacher, Lord of Civa-world, in Tillai's porch He rules.
Who are His lovers all ?-OUR LADY FAIR, ARISE ! (8)

III.
O thou whose smile as pearl is bright, arise, present
thyself before the Sire, the blissful One, th' Ambrosial,
And with o'erflowing sweetness speak ! Come, ope thy
doors !-

[She joins them. They enter the temple porch]
'Ye men devout, the Ruler's ancient saints, ye reverend men,
Will't be amiss if ye our weakness aid, us novices admit ?'
[in the temple]
No cheat is this know we not all Thy wondrous love ?
Who sing not what they beauty deem ? Our Civants form
ev'n so we yearn to see.-OUR LADY FAIR, ARISE ! (12)

IV.
[They all henceforth sing their morning song to the goddess,
imploring HER to arise in grace]
O thou of radiant pearl-like smile, is't not now dawn ?
have not the sweet-voiced come, like parrots many-hued ?
Thus thinking, as is meet, we speak; meanwhile in sleep
close not Thine eye; let not thy time in vain be spent ! -
Sole Balm of heaven, the VEda's precious Sense, the Dear
to eyes that see, we sing, our melting minds
In rapture all dissolved; nor deem thou should'st remain
for ever thus asleep !-OUR LADY FAIR, ARISE ! (16)

V. Say not, 'Civan is unknowable!'
The 'Mount' that MAI knew not, and Ayan saw not,-we
can know; so Thou dost utter falsities,
O guileful one, whose mouth with milk and honey flows,
ope thy door! He Whom earth, heaven, and other realms
know not,
In glory makes us His, cleanses our souls in grace.
His goodness sing ! 'O Civan, Civan,' hark ! they cry.
Thou understandest not; thou understandest not !-

So's she with perfumed locks !-OUR LADY FAIR, ARISE !
(20)

VI.
O fawn, but yesterday thou said'st, 'At dawn I come
to rouse you up;' but now, all unabashed
Tell us, what quarter didst thou seek ?-is't not yet dawn ?
He Who is sky, and earth, and all things else, to men
unknown:
Himself will come, will guard, and make us His; to us
who coming sing His-heavenly cinctur'd Foot, speak thou !
In rapture melt I The King of thee, of us extol;
of all the worlds ! -OUR LADY FAIR, ARISE ! (24)

VII.
Mother, are these too trifles? Many heavenly ones
know not, the One, the mighty glorious Lord.
Hearing His signals, ope thy mouth, and 'Civan ' cry,
Cry Southern-One.' Like was before the fire
Melting,-'My own, my King, Ambrosia,' we all
have sung! Hear thou ! apart from us yet dost thou sleep ?
Dost thou yet speechless lie, like the hard-hearted silly
ones ?
What grace is in this sleep ?-OUR LADY FAIR, ARISE ! (28)

VIII.
While cocks are crowing, small birds chant on every side;
while trumpet sounds, sound out the conch-shells
everywhere;
The heav'nly Light without compare, the Grace without
compare,-
the Being great without compare, we've sung; hear'st not ?

Bless thee, what slumber's this ? Thou openest not thy
mouth ?
is such the recompense for our King's love we bring ?
Th'Eternal, First of Beings; Him Who'bides the Only-One;
the Lady s Partner sing we all !-OUR LADY FAIR, ARISE !
(32)

IX.
Ancient of days, existing ere the ancient world!
Whose nature shares the newness of created things!
Thy worshippers devout, who've gained Thee for their
Lord,
adore Thy servants' feet.-to them give reverence due.---
And these alone shall be our wedded lords; joyous
ev'n as they bid, due service will we render meek.
Thus, if Thou grant to us this boon, our King, no lack
Thy handmaids e'er shall know!-OUR LADY FAIR, ARISE !
(36)

X,
Beneath the sevenfold gulf, transcending speech, His foot-
flower rests;
with flowers adorned His crown of all the universe is
crown !
The Lady's at His side !-His sacred form dwells not alone !
The VEdam, heavenly ones, and earth, praise Him; and yet
He's our one Friend, Whose praise ne'er dies; within His
saints He dwells;
pure He sustains the 'clan '; ye temple-ladies, say
What is His Town ? His Name ? His kin ? and who His foes
?
And how sing we His praise?-OUR LADY FAIR, ARISE! (40)

XI.

[In the temple tank]

Entering the broad, frequented tank with joyful cries,
and hands outstretched, we plunge and plunge, and sing
Thy Foot
O Guru, see, Thy faithful worshippers are blest! As fire
Thy'hue is red; Thou wear'st white ashes; Blessed One!
Thou Bridegroom of the Lady lithe, with broad, black eyes
!
O Guru, make us Thine in grace. In this our sport,
What those who would be saved perform, we've done, as
they;
guard that we weary not!-OUR LADY FAIR, ARISE! (44)

XII.

Lord of the sacred stream, where we, that thronging
mortal woes
may cease, acclaiming bathe ! Dancer in Tillai's sacred
court
'Midst waving fire ! This heaven, this flowery earth, us all,
in sport Thou guardest, formest, dost enshroud;-
Thou say'st the word !-Bracelets tinkling, jewels rattling
with a merry sound, tuneful beatles humming round our
locks adorned,
Plunge in the tank, where flowers are glistening; praise the
Masterts golden Foot,
and in the fountain bathe !-OUR LADY FAIR, ARISE ! (48)

XIII.

There burn dark crimson flowers of Kuvalai, here the red
lotus blooms;

there the bright race of small birds utters songs;
Here those who wash away their sin are gathered round !
This swelling tank is Like our Queen and King!
We ent'ring plunge and plunge again, our shells resound;
our anklets tinkling sound; our bosoms throb with joy;
The wave we plunge in swells. Plunge in the lotus crowned
flood
and joyful bathe!-OUR LADY FAIR, ARISE ! (52)

XIV.
While ear drops swing; while golden jewels wave;
while flow'ry locks are dancing; swarms of wing'd things
flit;
Bathe in the cool flood, sing the sacred court!
sing the mystic VEdas; sing their inner sense!
Sing glory of the Light, sing Him the cassia-wreath Who
wears !
Sing ye the power of Him, the First, sing Him the Last!
Sing ye the glory of Her Foot, Who armlets wears,
Whose guardian care we own !-OUR LADY FAIR, ARISE !
(56)

XV. The Lady of KArai-kAl.
Once on a time, 'our PerumAn,' full oft cried she.
His glory any time to speak she ceased not
With gladsome mind, while tears in ceaseless stream
flowed forth.
Once on a time, this woman came to earth, nor bowed
Before the heavenly ones,-by the great King with fretizy
filled.
Who like to her ? Of this mysterious One,
O lovely damsels, sing the Foot, and bathting plunge

beneath the flow'ry flood !-OUR LADY FAIR, ARISE! (60)

The word 'time' is Kal, so there is a play on the word
Karai-kAl. It may be that the poet in another passage
alludes to her beautiful prayer(XI, Verse 8)
'He gave me grace, tho' I all else forget, ne'er to forget
His foot, whose mighty dance we sing!.'

The Mother of KaraikAl :
Some of the legends in the Tamil periya PurAnam relate to
the period between the first and second great revivals of
Caivism, and a few are anterior to both. It seems pretty
certain that, while the Jains and Buddhists were active and
apparently triumphant everywhere, there were a great
multitude of the faithful Caivites who, like the Covenanters
in Scotland, were rendered more zealous by the
persecutions to which they were exposed. Among these
was the 'Mother' of KArai-kAl, who was a poetess, many of
whose verses are still preserved. The legend gives a most
interesting picture of some phases of South-Indian life a
thousand years ago. The Mother 'was the wife of a rich
merchant of KArai-kAl', whose name was, Paramadattan
('Endowed with heavenly gifts'). Her own name was
PunithavathiyAr ('the pure'). She was very devout, and
especially careful to entertain all Caiva devotees that came
to her door. One day her husband received from some
persons who had come to him on business a present of
two mangoes, of a very superior kind, which he got home
to his wife. Soon afterwards, a holy devotee arrived at the
house as a mendicant guest but she had nothing ready to
offer him except some boiled rice. This she set before him,
and having no other condiment to present, gave him one of

the aforesaid mangoes At noon her husband returned, and
atter his meal ate the remaining mango, which pleased
him so much that he said to his wife, 'There were two;
bring me the other.' She went away in dismay; but
remembering that the god to whose servant-because he
was His servant she had given the fruit, never deserts
those who serve Him, she offered a mental prayer, and
straightaway found a mango in her hand, which she
carried to her husband. Being A divine gift, it was of
incomparable sweetness, and he said to her, 'Where did
you obtain this?' She hesitated at first to reveal the wonder
that had been wrought on her behalf, but reflected that she
ought to have no concealments from her husband and so
told him everything. He gave no credence to her words,
but roughly replied, 'If that is so, get me another like it.'
She went away, and said in her heart to the god, 'If thou
givest me not one more fruit, my word will be disbelieved'.
Forthwith she formed another fruit still more lovely in her
hand. When she carried this to her husband he took it in
astonishment; but behold ! it forthwith vanished. Utterly
confounded by these wonderful things, he came to the
conclusion that his wife was a supernatural being, and
resolved to separate at once from her. He revealed the
matter, however, to no one, but quietly equipped a ship in
which he embarked a great part of his wealth and then on
a lucky day, worshipping the god of the sea, with sailon
end a skillful captain, he act sail for another country,
where he made merchandise, accumulated a fortune, and
after some time re-embarking, came back to India to
another city in the PAndiyan land, where he married a
merchant'. daughter, and lived in great luxury. A daughter
was born to him, to whom be gave the name of the wife

with whom he had feared to remain, but for whom he retained exceeding reverence.

After awhile his return and prosperity became known to his friends In KArai-kAl, who resolved to compel him to receive again his first wife, their kinswoman, whom he had deserted. They accordingly proceeded to his new residence, carrying with them in a litter his saintly spouse, the 'Mother' of KArai-kAl. When he heard that she had arrived and was halting in a grove outside the town, he was seized with a great dread, and proceeded with his second wife and daughter to where the 'Mother' was encamped surrounded by her kindred. He at once prostrated himself with profoundest reverence before her, saying, 'Your slave is happy here and prosperous thorough your benediction. To my daughter I have given your sacred name, and I constantly adore you as my tutelary goddess'. Poor PunithayathiyAr, utterly confounded by this salutation and worship, took refuge among her kinsfolk, who all cried out, 'Why is the madman worshipping his own wife!' To this Paramadattan replied, 'I myself beheld her work as miracle, and I know that she is no daughter of the human race, but a supernatural being, and so I have separated myself from her, and I worship her as my tutelary divinity, and have dedicated this my daughter to her, and therefore have I worshipped her and call upon you to do the same.' But PunithavnthiyAr pondered the matter and prayed within herself to Civan the Supreme, saying: 'Lord, this is my husband's persuasion. Take from me then the beauty that I have hitherto cherished for his sake alone. Remove from this burthen of the flesh, and give to me the form and features of one of the demon hosts who evermore attend on Thee, and praise Thee.' That very instant, by the grace of the god, her flesh dried up, and she became a demoness, one of Civan's hosts, whom the earthly worth and heavenly world hold in reverence. Then the gods poured down a rain of flowers, heaveny minstrelsy resounded, and her relative fearing, paid her adoration and departed. So she had now become a demoness, and her abode was the wild jungle of AlankAdu; but through the inspiration the god she sang several sacred poems, which are preserved. Afterwards there came upon her an irresistible desire to behold the Sacred Hill of KailACam, and with inconceivable speed she fled northwards till she arrived at the foot of the Mountain, and reflecting that it was not right with feet to tread the heavenly ascent, she threw herself down and measured the distance with her head. The goddess UmA, Civan's bride, beheld her thus ascending, and said to her spouse, 'Who is that in this strange fashion draws near, A gaunt fleshless skeleton, sustained only by the energy of love? To which Civan replied, 'She that cometh is the "Mother" devoted to my praises, this mighty demon-form she has obtained by her prayers.' When she drew near he addressed with words of love, calling her by the name of 'Mother,' which she for ever bears. As soon as heard the word she fell at his feet worshipping, and ejaculating 'Father !' Civan then said to her What boon dost thou ask of me?' She worshipped and replied, 'Loni, to me your slave give love which is undying, and infinite blessedness. I would fain be born on earth no more; but if I must so born, grant me at least that I may never, in any form, at any time, forget Thee, my God; when thou dost perform thy sacred mystic dance, beneath thy feet in rapture may I stand and

sing thy praise', To which the God replied, 'In AlankAdu
thou shall see my dance, and with rapture thou shalt sing.'
Then the sacred 'Mother' of KArai-kAl returned,
measuring the distance still on head to holy AlankAdu,
where she beheld the God's sacred dance, and sang her
renowned lyric his praise.

This legend illustrates a remarkable feature in the Caiva
worship of the south, where devotees are not infrequently
adored as having become demons. Doubtless, this is
connected with pre-Aryan usages, and the poems
attributed to the 'Mother' of Karaikaal present the most
vivid picture demon worship with which I am acquainted.
It is not difficult to imagine the source of tradition. We
have the picture of a devout and enthusiastic worshipper
of Civan, who sacrifices everything to the performance of
her supposed duties to the god. She is misunderstood by
inappreciative husband, who forsakes her, and finally,
with scorn, repudiates her. She has herself a chapel in the
jungle, where she spends her days and nights in prayers
and austerities on her death is worshipped. The legends
would soon accumulate, and the poems represent
dramatic form the artistic view of all the circumstances.

XVI The Cloud*, an Allegory

Erewhile thou didst the sea diminish, rising like the
Queen;
didst glisten like Her slender waist Who rules my soul;
Didst like the golden anklets sound that on Her sacred foot

in beauty gleam; didst bend like to Her sacred brow
The bow. As she, mindful of those who love our King,
who like herself, our Mistress, never quit His side;
Mindful of us too, as our Queen, pours forth sweet grace,
even so pour down, O CLOUD ! OUR LADY FAIR, ARISE !
(64)

---

* Here there is a subtle comparison between Civan, Catti,
and a cloud that in the monsoon season rises from the sea.
The cloud drinks the waters of the sea, gleams in the sky
with lightning fires, sends forth the voice of the thunder, is
sometimes made beautiful with a rainbow, and then
spreading itself over the heavens, pours down fertilizing
showers on all the earth below. So Civan drank the poison
of the sea; dances in Cithambaram while His golden
anklets sound; wears a form of dazzling splendour; is
renowned for the victories He gained with His bow; and
pours forth blessings over all the earth. The comparison of
UmA or Catti is obvious. This closely resembles III, 66-94

XVII.

The red-eyed one', and He Whose face turns to each point',
and gods in every heaven, taste no delight like ours.
Thou of the fragrant locks didst make our beings pure;
and here in grace didst rise in every home of ours;
The Warrior gave in grace His golden lotus feet;
the King of beauteous eye; Ambrosia rare to us His slaves;
Our PerumAn ! Singing His gift, plunge we and bathe
in the clear lotus-flood ! -OUR LADY FAIR, ARISE ! (68)

XVIII.

AnnAmalai His form, His lotus foot heaven's host
adored, while lustre of their jewell'd crowns grew dim;
So when the bright eyed sun the darkness drives away,
the cool moon's rays are paled, the stars themselves
depart.
Thus stood He forth; was Female, Male, was Neither-one;
was Heaven with gleaming lights, was Earth, was all the
rest.
Ambrosia manifest! Praising His jewell'd Foot, O Maid
plunge in this flowery stream !-OUR LADY FAIR, ARISE !
(72)

XIX The Maidens' Vow

'The children of Thy hand are we; our Refuge Thou ;'-
thus that old word we say anew; in this our dread
Our Lord, to Thee one prayer we make; vouchsafe to hear
'let none but Thine own lovers true our forms embrace;-
Our hands no service pay save to Thyself alone;-
our eyes,-by night, by day,-let them see nought but Thee''-
Our King, if here this boon Thou grant, to us the sun
in perfect beauty shines!-OUR LADY FAIR, ARISE! (76)

XX.

Be gracicus Thou ! to Thy foot's flower be praise!
be gracious! To Thy rosy beauteous feet be praise!
The golden feet, the source of all that live, be praised!

The flow'ry feet, the bliss of every life, be praised!
The twain feet, Goal and End of every life, be praised!
The lotus-flower, unseen by MAl and the Four-faced, be
praised !
The golden flowers, that saving made us His, be praised!
In Margazhi-month we bathing praise!-OUR LADY FAIR,
ARISE ! (80)
HYMN VIII - THE SACRED AMMANAI.
RAPTUROUS JOY.

The remarks made in the introduction to VII will apply in
Some degree to this poem also, which is traditionally said
to have been composed at the same place and time by the
bard, who seeing women in great numbers enjoying their
favourite game of AmmAnai and accompanying it a simple
song, listened to their words, and then put the substance
into these verses. In some of them He relates his own
experiences: In others he puts words into their mouths In
the play the women, generally six in number, sit in a circle
and toss a number of little balls from one to another with
great dexterity and very swiftly. It is a pretty sight. They
accompany their game a simple song, the rhythm of which
is suited to the action of the players. In this case there are
twenty verses of six lines, each verse having but a single
rhythm. The subject of such verse .... generally some heroic
exploits, such as are popular among all classes; or the
great acts of a deity. Here the title of 'rapturous joy' has
been prefixed, as the editor seems to have conceived that
as the main idea of the verses.

I. His advent as Guru. The Foot

Great MAl, the fiery-eyed, delved down, but failed to reach
His foot's expanding flower! To earth that foot came down,
Our birth' cut off, made those like us His own.-Lord of
The south-landis clustering cocoa-groves, and Perun-
turrai's shrine,
And Tillai's sacred court,-a sage He came, call'd me in
grace'
And gave release. SING we His foot whence mercy flows !
AMMANAY, SEE ! (6)

1-6. Here there are four lending ideas:
1) Civan rising as the mountain ArunAchalam passed
above and below the roaring flight of BrahmA and the
delvings of Vishnu; 2) this same Caiva graciously
manifested Himself as a GURU to the humble, loving bard
in order to release him from further metempsychosis;
3) He is also worshipped in the temple of Perun-turai, His
great southern-shrine, where the saint first knew Him; and
4) in the sacred court of Tillai He dwells, a BrAhman, one
of the 3000 saints, the mystic Dancer and Dispenser of
grace. There the sage is to obtain his consummation.
These four ideas perpetually recur in these poems. This is
un unfailing topic treated with inexhaustible variety.

II. Manifestations

To men on earth, to heavenly ones, to those beneath,
To those beyond, He's scarce made known; to us
accessible !
The Name revered, the South-King, Perun-turrai's Lord

Entering our souls, with frenzy filled them, showed the
final way.
Unsating Nectar, - in the billowy sea He cast His net;
The Sea of full desire SING we ! AMMAANAY, SEE ! (12)
--

Civan cast His net, is a fisherman. This refers to a story in
the fifty-seventh of the ÔSacred sports'. PArvathi was one
day inattentive while Civan was expounding to her the
VEdic mysteries, for which she was condemned by her
angry husband and preceptor to be born on earth as a wife
of a fisherman. Accordingly one day she was discovered
lying as a tender infant under a Pinnai tree(or Punnai,
Calophyllam Inophyllam)by the headman of the Paravar, a
great clan of fisherman found everywhere along the coasts
of the Tamil lands. By him she was adopted, and grew up a
maiden of surpassing beauty. At this time Nandi the
Chamberlain of Civan, in order to bring about the
accomplishment of the god's purpose with regard to the
banished PArvathi, assumed the form of a monstrous
shark; and in various ways annoyed the poor fishermen,
breaking their nets and wrecking their boats. On this the
headman of the paravars issued a proclamation that
whoever should catch the sea-monster should be
rewarded with the hand of his beautiful adopted daughter.
Civan forthwith made his appearance as a youth of noble
aspect who had come from Madura, and at the first throw
of his net caught the shark and brought it to land. He
accordingly, having himself become a fisherman, received
the fisherman's daughter in marriage. The god now
assumed his ancient form, and restored pArvathi to hers,
and with many gracious words took the foster father with
Him to KailACham, the paradise of Silver Hill.

--

III. The Initiation in Perun-turrai

Inthiran, MAl, all the other heavenly ones,
Stood round in upper air; - Civan in grace to earth came down,
Made those like us His own. His arm the sacred ashes shows;
All-glorious Perun-turrai's Lord, who comes our hearts to thrill;
To loose our bonds He on a charger rode, and gave
Unending raptures; SING the bliss ! AMMAANAY, SEE! (18)

IV. He chose not the ascetics, but me !

The gods who filled the heavens, - MAl, Ayan, Indra too,
Sore penance did, like anthills stood, yet know Him not !
To me a cur He came, with mother-love He lent His aid;
In flesh He came, with trembling rapture thrilled me through -
Honied ambrosia's Essence pure; the jewell'd foot
That trends the skies in gleaming light SING we !
AMMAANAY, SEE ! (24)

V. His grace to me all unworthy.

The Mighty One, the South-King, Perun-turrai's Lord,
Me vilest cur, of mind untaught, with frenzy filled;
Kneaded the stone, made it sweet fruit; plunged in the flood

Of mercy; all my sin destroyed. To Him, the Sage,
Who Tillai's city entering, in the sacred court abides,
The ancient Rider of the Bull, SING we ! AMMAANAY, SEE !
(30)

VII Civan, a 'false' mendicant

And hast thou heard, my friend, how-one with falsehood
came?
The Lord of Perun-turrai's southern shrine begirt
With storied walls, showed things ne'er shown before,
showed bliss,
Showed us His lotus foot, and honey of His grace; -
While rustics laughed, - that we the heavenly home might
gain,
He made us His; SING we this grace ! AMMAANAY, SEE !
(36)

VII. Civan's ten epithets.

Indweller in the heart of those who ceaseless ponder Him;
The Faroff-One; the Warrior; ever-loving habitant
Of Perun-turrai's southern shrine; the Sage; half of Whose
form
The Lady shares; the Love'd-One Who made me, mere cur,
His own;
With mother-love Who visits men; the sevenfold world
Whose essence is; Ruler of souls; SING we ! AMMAANAY,
SEE ! (42)

VIII. Seven aspects of Civan.

Half of the Queen, whose grace accepts our melodies,
The mighty Lord, the King of Perun-turrai's shrine; -
He rules the expanded sphere of renowned of upper heaven;
The Godwith eye in midmost of His brow; in Madura
Distreat, He carried earth for hire; was smitten by the King, -
SING we His golden form that bore the wounds !
AMMAANAY, SEE ! (48)

IX. Ten mythic ideas of Civan

His the crescent; His the mystic word; Perun-turrai's King;
He wears the twisted thread; He rides the glorious bull;
Black is His throat; His body red; He smears the ashes white;
First in all worlds is He, the rapture without end
As in the days of yore to ancient saints in grace He gives !
That all the worlds may wonder, SING ! AMMAANAY, SEE !
(54)

X. Various praises, six topics.

The Sage above the gods that rule the heavens; Who stands
In majesty above the kings that rule this earth;
The pleasant PAndi-land, whose gift is Tamir's pleasant speech, is His;
The Bridegroom of the Queen; in Perun-turrai, His delight,
He showed His gracious feet, made me, a dog, His own;
AnnAmalai's His shrine, SINE we ! AMMAANAY, SEE ! (60)

XI. Praises.

The fair Queen's Half; of southern Perun-turrai Lord;
Whose Nature thrills the souls that cling around His feet;
The Sire who made that Paandi-land the Civa-world;
Adown Whose braided lock the waters flow; Whose
blissful jewell'd foot
Abides within their souls, who rightly render them to Him;
Beyond the furthest limits praise uplift ! AMMAANAY, SEE
! (66)

XII. The Supreme and Absolute.

Listen, O damsel with the jet-black eyes ! MAl, Ayan, IndrA
too,
Through every 'birth' sought Him, me, with sweet grace, in
this one births
He made His own; guards me that I may suffer 'births' no
more;
In all that's real, manifest; the true His biding-place;
The Self in all that is, is He; of everything the Home;
Our Civan, Who that essence is, SING we ! AMMAANAY,
SEE ! (72)

XIII. Praises, six epithets.

While bracelets tinkling around, - while ear-rings wave -
while jetty locks
Disheveled fall, - while honey flows, and beetles hum;
The Ruddy-One Who wears the ashes white, Whose home
None reach or know, who dwells in every place, - to loving
ones

The True, the Sage Whom hearts untrue still deem untrue,
Who in Ai-Aru dwells, SING we and praise ! AMMAANAY,
SEE ! (78)

XIV. The story of his conversion

As elephant, as worm, in human shapes, in forms divine,
In other births diverse, - I lived and died, - was wearied
sore;
He stood in flesh revealed, melted my soul; and joyous
drove
My sin away; with every sweetness filled; and as a king
In grace appearing, in His service me received;
That Heavenly One's foot-flower SING we, AMMAANAY,
SEE ! (84)

XV. Civan's triumph at Dakshan's sacrifice.

He made the moon grow dim in Dakshan's sacrifice;
He Indra's shoulder crushed; cut off the 'Ecchan's head;
Teet of the bright-beamed sun, that rides the sky, He
broke;
Dispersed the gods, and drove away to every point;
Lord of South Perun-turrai's shrine with flow'ry groves
Begirt; the Fragrant-garlanded, SING we, AMMANAAY,
SEE! (90)

XVI. The sweetness of His Presence.

His Presence mingled in my body, and thought;
As honey, rare ambrosia, every choicest sweet
He gave His grace, in ways the heavenly ones know not;

The Warrior crowned with cassia's honied flowers; as
glorious light
Of wisdom known, with souls in number infinite,
Their King He dwells, this tell we out! AMMAANAY, SEE !
(96)

XVII. Ectasy of adoration.

I'll wear the flow'ry 'cassia' wreath, and wearing join
myself
To Civan's mighty arm; and joining cling in rapture lost;
Then shrinking shall I melt with love of His red lip;
I'll seek Him,- seeking I'll ponder Civan's jewell'd foot;
I'll faint and droop, and yet again revive. The ruddy foot
Of Him who dances there 'mid fire SING we! AMMANAAY,
SEE ! (102)

XVIII. Civan appeared as a BrAhman

In light He gleams, Her Half whose words as Parrot's note
are soft,
The Sage whom MAl and Ayan coming forth could not
discern;
In glorious Perun-turrai's grove with honied fragrance
filled,
In mercy affable, and sweetest grace transcending thought,
In light He came, caused light within my soul to shine;
The BrAhman full of tenderness SING we! AMMANAAY,
SEE ! (108)

XIX. Praise with eleven epithets.

The Primal One, End of the Three, beyond the End
The After One, with braided lock, of Perun-turrai which He
guards
The King, the Heavenly-One, the Partner of the Queen;
Who dwells in southern Anai-kA, the southern PAndi-land
Who owns, Ambrosia sweet to those who call Him theirs,
To such as one, the Father, SING we praise ! AMMANAAY,
SEE ! (114)

XX. Clinging to the Guru.

The mighty Lord whose nature others know not, - Perun-
turrai's King
In grace upon victorious charger riding came;
His servant's faults removed; gave virtue, cleansed from
stain;
Severed the clinging cords of earthly ties ! His praises old
We cling to, - so may earthly bonds be loosed; the mighty
bliss
Of Him to whom we cling, SING we !, AMMAANAY, SEE !
(120)

HYMN IX - thiruppoRcuNNam (Ananthamanolayam)
THE SACRED GOLD DUST.
THE MERGING OF THE SOUL IN RAPTURE.
Metre : AruchIradi Achiriaviruttam

In the VAthaVurar PurAnam V, 63, we are told that the
Sage when in Tillai saw women pounding the gold dust
which, mixed with perfumes, is strewn on the heads of
distinguished visitors to the shrine, and on great occasions
is lavishly thrown over all things and persons connected

with the worship. As they pounded, they sung foolish
songs; and he composed these twenty verses, in a
somewhat loose metre, to be sung in time with the pestles.
The song is much admired, but is a little obscure, and
almost colloquial. I have tried to preserve the rhythm,-five
principal accounts in each half line.

I. Reverence to the various queens of heaven

The pearl-twined wreath and flowery garland raise;
the flower-vase place, incense, and sacred lamp !
To Catti, COmi Goddess-earth, and Queen
of speech, chaunt ye auspicious songs !
For ,itti, Gauri, PArppathi, and Gangai,-haste,
and coming wave your cooling fans !
The Sire, Lord of AyyAr, the Father-King extol,
and dancing, POUND THE SACRED DUST OF GOLD ! (4)

II. Devoutly do this service.

For our Lord of the flowing-crowned lock
we needs must POUND THE SACRED DUST OF GOLD !
Ye of the beauteous shapely eyes, come ye,
and coming all, with us in union sing,
Cry out, nor stand aloof from the devoted throng;
bow down, our King, our Dancer worshipping !
The Goddess and He coming shall we take us
for theirs: POUND WE THE DUST OF RUDDY GOLD ! (8)

III. Adorn the place as a sacred pavilion.

Adorn with beauteous ashes, cleanse the place;
sprinkle pure gold, the treasures spread ye out,
Plant Indra's sacred tree; lift everywhere
the banner, placing round soft gleaming lights !
For the King of the heavenly ones; the Lord of Ayan, the
Monarch;
the Lord, the Sire of VElan the good;
For the spouse of the Mistress who rules such as we:
POUND WE BEFITTING DUST OF GOLD ! (12)

IV.

Adorn each pestle with glistening gems;
the handle and mortar adorn ye !
The loving, lowly devotees, salute
and wish them lasting bliss !
The golden shrine of sacred Ekamban in Kachi,
whither all the land resorts,
Sing we. And, freed from deeds that bondage bring,
singing, POUND WE THE DUST OF GOD ! (16)

V.

Ayan and Ari shall their garlands bring!
not Indra, nor with him the deathless ones,
Nor all the perfumed hosts of gods, save after us,
the pestle suffer we to lift
Sing we the golden shrine of sacred èkamban
the Bowman Who smote three forts of his foes,
Ye of smiling roseate lips ! for the three-eyed Sire's
dance-POUND WE THE DUST OF GOLD ! (20)

VI.

Many a pestle would the great ones upraise;
that the world would not serve for a mortar,
To mix the fragrant dust the saints crowd round,
that the worlds suffice not to behold.
In favouring love He made us slaves His own;
and gave His flowery Feet to crown our brows,
To the mountains Son-in-law, joyous ever,
sing we and POUND THE DUST OF GOLD ! (24)

VII.

While the golden armlets tinkling sound;
while the saintly bands uprising chant;
While townsfolk greet us with loud acclaim;
while them we greet with answering shout;
The Partner of the Queen, on whose soft feet
the anklets tinkling sound,-our God,
The King, like mighty mount of purest gold,
To serve, POUND WE THE DUST OF GOLD ! (28)

VIII.

Ye simple maidens fair, with bright wide eyes,
while armlets tinkle, bosoms heave and swell,
While shoulders gleam with ashes pure,
proclaim ye ever praises of our Lord,
Who showed His bright flower-Foot, and in this world
made us, lower than very dogs His own !
His ways of grace, sing o'er and o'er, and Him
to serve, POUND WE THE SACRED DUST OF GOLD ! (32)

IX.

Let the whole earth be the mortar;
as pestle plant Meru the lofty;
Saffron of truth pour forth in copious stream.
Him Who in southern Perun-turrai dwells
His sacred roseate Foot sing evermore !
With right hand seize the pestle's ruddy gold.
The Sage, the glorious One of beauteous Tillai's shrine
to serve, POUND WE THE DUST OF GOLD ! (36)

X.

While our bosoms pearl-adorn'd beat high; while in our
clustering locks the honey-bees play;
While with Civan our minds are dancing; while bright
eyes with dew are gleaning;
While wild rapture from our Lord is thrilling;,
as others live, their changing lives we live;
With our Fathers mercy glad, ever
dancing, POUND WE THE DUST OF GOLD ! (40)

XI.

Rich jewels like the moonlight gleaming;
panting mouths and lips of coral quivering;
Sing ye the way He made us His; sing ye the way
our service He accepts;
Seek ye our PerumAn, and seeking, joy in heart,
then let your trembling minds grow bold;
Dance ye to Him who dances in the Court;

dance and POUND WE THE DUST OF GOLD ! (44)

XII.

Him in whose throats is the blackness, Balm of the
dwellers in heaven, the ruby Dancer Himself,
The Sage, the Lord of the sages, us who took,
and made us His, and all His rareness showed;
The False to the false, the Truth of the true,-
ye beauteous ones with eyes like opening flowers,
Who wear the golden armlets ye of lovely form,-
praising, POUND WE THE DUST OF GOLD ! (48)

XIII.

Damsels with slender waists and crimson lips,
black eyes, bright smile, and words like music sweet !
My rare Ambrosia; our Sire; our Lord of might;
to the daughter of Himavat
Her Husband, Son and Sire, and Brother too;
our Teacher's feet sing ye, whose bosoms gleam
With gold and gems, ye damsels beautiful,
sing and POUND WE THE SACRED DUST OF GOLD ! (52)

XIV.

While the shells aound, while the anklets tinkle,
while waving chaplets crown your flowing looks,
While your roseate lips like ripe fruit quiver,
bright jewelled ones, sing the Civa-world !
For His foot, Whose head is crowned with braided lock

where GangA's streams resound with serpent's hiss;
While our bosoms with swelling tenderness
heave, POUND WE THE SACRED DUST OF GOLD ! (56)

XV.

Essence of wisdom's sweetness exquisite;
honey unfailing, full of excellence;
Him who is savour rich of every fruit; the King
with power to enter sweetly every mind;
The Dancer Who cut off embodiment
and made us His, in swelling strains praise ye,
Ye maidens sweet, with eyes like purple lotus flowers,
singing, POUND WE THE SACRED DUST OF GOLD ! (60)

XVI.

Thus we too, coming with the loving ones,
shall sing the ways He makes us His,
He shows the roseate flowery feet, that gods
in Heaven who rule, e'en in their dreams, know not.
He bears aloft the flag of victory
in prosperous war. Praise Civa-PerumAn ! -
Singing the conquering Hero's names who took
the towns, POUND WE THE SACRED DUST OF GOLD ! (64)

XVII.

Sing we the cassia-flower with honey rife;
sing Civa-town; sing we the infant moon
Upon His sacred braided lock; sing we
the mighty Bull, the trident and the axe,

His warring right hand wields; that dwellers
in this world, and in other worlds might 'scape;
Sing how the poison for his food He ate,
that day, and POUND WE THE SACRED DUST OF GOLD !
(68)

XVIII.

He trundled Ayan's head like ball, - sing Him !
He broke the teeth of Arukkan, - sing Him !
He slew the elephant, and wore its skin, - praise Him !
The Lord of death He spurned with sacred Foot, - praise
Him !
He shot His arrows 'gainst the towns combined, - praise
Him !
Poor wretched slaves, He made us His, - praise we
That love ! Here stand, and ever dance and sing,
and for the Lord, POUND WE THE DUST OF GOLD ! (72)

XIX.

Sing ye the cassia-wreath of rounded flowers !
Sing ye His folly wild ! His wisdom sing !
Sing ye southern Tillai, the saints' abode !
Sing we the blest One of the 'sacred hall' !
Sing we the serpent girdle that He binds !
Sing we the armlets ! on His hollow palm
Sing how the serpent rears its folds, and for
the Ruler, POUND WE THE DUST OF GOLD ! (76)

For Him Who is the VEdam and the Sacrifice;
for Him Who is the Falsehood and the Truth;
For Him Who is the Splendour and the Gloom;
for Him Who is Affection and Delight;
For Him Who is the Half, Who is the Whole;
for Him Who is the Bond and the Release;
For Him Who is the First, Who is the Last;
dancing, POUND WE THE DUST OF GOLD ! (80)
Hymn X- tiruk kOttumpi
THE HUMMING BEE

Metre : Naladittaravu koccuk kalippA

Our poet-sage, like S. Anthony of Padua, and some other
mediaeval saints, had a great sympathy with the irrational
creation. This poem is addressed to the humming bee, or
winged beetles, which abound in all the topes and glads of
South India, and are especially numerous in the shady
groves that surround the temples;; having a great
preference for the fragrant and beautiful trees which are
sacred to the Hindu deities. The insect, here called
Gottumbi, is probably the dragon-fly Ruplea Spenders.
Here the SOUL is really addressed and exhorted to seek
Civa's feet.

I. Mysteriously great.

The King that crowns the flower; Purandaran;
the Lady blest, in beauty clothed,
That sits on learned tongues; and NAranan;
the fourfold mystic VEdic Scroll,
The Splendours, Riders in majesty; - with all

the heavenly ones too, know Him not:-
Go to His roseate foot who mounts the Bull;
AND BREATH HIS PRAISE, THOU HUMMING-BEE ! (4)

II. I am nought, yet made like to Him

Who am I? - Wisdom's lessons what are they
that fill my mind? - and me who'd know
Had not the Lord of heaven made me His own?
He of the temple court, Who erst
A mendicant with mind distraught asked food,
in broken skull with flesh impure !
Haste to Him lotus-foot, as honey sweet;
AND BREATHE HIS PRAISE, THOU HUMMING-BEE ! (8)

III. All sweetness is in Him.

Honey from any flower sip not, though small
as tiniest grain of millest seed !
Whene'ver we think of Him, whene'er we see,
whene'er of Him our lips converse,
Then sweetest rapture's honey ever flows,
till all our frame in bliss dissolves !
To Him alone, the mystic Dancer, go;
AND BREATHE HIS PRAISE, THOU HUMMING-BEE ! (12)

IV. His love gives to loveless me.

There was no love in me like Kannappan's;
when He, my Sire, saw this, me poor
Beyond compare, in grace He made His own;
He spake, and bade me come to Him.

With heavenly grace adorned He shines, and wears
white ashes, and the golden dust !
To Him, - of mercy infinite, - go thou,
AND BREATHE HIS PRAISE, O HUMMING-BEE ! (16)

The Legend of Kannappa Nayanaar, or the 'Eye-Devotee'.
The image of this renowned South Indian devotee stands
in the temple at KAlahasti (Calastri) near the Pulicat Hills.
He was a rAja of UduppUr, and of the Shepherd caste (a
vEdan or Hill-men, perhaps a Kurumban). The story
represents his ancient clan as possessing great wealth and
authority in a wild hilly district, where their whole
occupation was hunting. There is a ZamindAr, who lives
there now in feudal state. The old chieftain, the father of
Kannappan, whose name was NAgan (the Dragon-man) is
represented to us as moving about attended by fierce
hunting dogs, armed with every kind of rustic weapon; a
skillful archer, around whose mountain-dwelling
innumerable forest animals of every kind had their home,
and where the cries 'shoot' 'hurl' 'strike' were mingled
from morning to night with the howlings of wild beasts,
the barking of dogs, and the sound of the horns and drums
of the hunters. He had no son, and therefore he and his
wife went to the temple of Subrahmanyan (a son of Civan)
- the favourite deity of mountaineers, and probably a pre-
Aryan deity of the South, an object of worship, under many
names and forms, in every Tamil hamlet. To him they
offered cocks and peafowl, made good feasts with copious
libations of strong drink, performed wild dances; and in
fact, according to the legend, seem to have worshipped
much after the rude fashion of the demon worshippers of

the present day. The result was that by the favour of their
tutelary deity a son was born to them, who from his early
childhood shared in his father's pursuits, being brought
up, it is expressly said, like a tiger's cub. The proud, happy
father used to carry him about on his shoulder, but finding
him one day too heavy to be thus borne, gave him the
name of 'Tinnan' ('the sturdy man') which remained his
pet household name. He was erewhile to bear a more
honourable and enduring title! Soon after this the old
chief, finding himself unable any longer to conduct the
hunting expeditions of the tribe, made over his authority
to his son, with whom alone this history is concerned.
Henceforth our young hero is ever in the dense jungle with
his veteran huntsmen. One day a wild boar, of gigantic
size, that had been caught in their nets, escaped and made
off with prodigious speed to the mountain side. Tinnan
pursued it with two faithful attendants, but it let them a
weary chase and did not stop till, exhausted with fatigue, it
fell down in the shade of a tree on the slope of a distant
hill. There Tinnan with his sword cut it in two. His
attendants came up and were astonished and delighted at
his success and said, ' We will roast the boar here, and
refresh ourselves'. But there was no water at hand, so they
took up the carcase of the boar and carried it some
distance onward, till they came to sight of the sacred hill of
'KAlahasti'.
At the view of the mountain one of the attendants cried
out, that on that mountain summit there was an image of
the 'God with flowing hair' (Civan). 'If we go thither we
may worship him' added he. Hearing this the young giant
Tinnan again shouldered the boar and strode on,
exclaiming, 'with every step that I advance towards the

mountain the burden of the boar diminishes. There is
some miraculous power here; I must find out what it is'. So
saying he rushed on with great eagerness till he came to
the bank of a river, where he deposited his burden, bade
his companions make a fire and prepare the feast, while he
himself hastened onward till he beheld on the slope of the
hill, on the further bank of the stream, a stone lingam, the
upper part of which was fashioned into a rude image of the
head of the god. The moment he beheld it, as the magnet
draws the iron, it drew his soul, which had been somehow
prepared by the merit of good deeds and austerities
performed in some former birth; and his whole nature was
changed, every feelng being swallowed up the intense love
for the god, whom for the first time he now beheld. As a
mother, seeing her long lost son return, tarries not, but
rushes to embrace him, as he threw himself upon the
image, tenderly embraced it, and fervently kissed it. With
tears of rapture, his soul dissolving like was n the
sunshine, he cried out, 'Ah, wondrous blessedness! to me a
slave this divinity has been given! But how is that the god
remains here alone in a wilderness where lions, elephants,
tigers, bears, and other wild beasts dwell, as though he
were some rude mountaineer like me?'.

Then, examining the image more closely, he saw that
water had been recently poured upon it and green leaves
strewn over it. 'Who can have done this?' said he. His
attendant, who had in the meantime has come up, replied:
'In the olden time, when I came here on a hunting
expedition with your father, a BrAhman, I remember
came, poured water and placed leaves upon this image,
repeating some mysterious words;- perhaps he is still
here. So it dawned upon the mind of Tinnan that these and

other services, which he himself could render, might be acceptable to the god. 'But,' said he, 'there is no one here to supply him with food. He is alone, and I cannot leave him for an instant, yet I must perforce go and bring for him some of the boar's flesh cooked for our feast'. So, after much hesitation and unwillingness to lose sight for a moment of his new found treasure he went back, crossed the stream, where he found the food already prepared and his servants wondering at the delay in his return. Tinnan regarding them not, took some of the boar's flesh and cutting off the tenderest portions, roasted them on the point of an arrow; tasted them to ascertain that they were savoury; carefully selected the best, putting them into a cup of teak leaves which he had sewn together; and prepared to return to the woodland deity with his offering. The servants seeing all this, very reasonably concluded that their master had suddenly gone mad, and hastened off home to take the news, and to ask the priestess of their tribe to return with them and exorcise the evil spirit that they supposed had taken possession of their lord. Tinnan unconscious of their departure, hastened back with the food in one hand, and his bow and arrow in the other. As he crossed the river, he filled his mouth with water, with which coming before the image he besprinkled it. He then took the wild jungle flowers from his own hair, and put them over it, and presented the coarse boar's flesh he had brought, saying: 'My Lord, I have chosen for thee the daintiest portions, have carefully prepared them with fire, have tasted them, and softened them with my own teeth. I have sprinkled thee with water from the stream, and have put on thee flowers thou mayest love. Accept my gifts!' [This presentation of the food to the lingam and other images is often referred to in these stories, and the impression is given that the worshippers believed that the idol itself consumed the offering; but it is never expressly said that the food disappeared before the shrines, though this is sometimes implied.] Meanwhile the sun went down and during the whole night Tinnan with his arrow on the strung bow kept watch and ward around the god and at dawn went forth to the mountain to hunt, that he might provide for the daily wants of his new master.

While he was gone on this errand the BrAhman in charge of the lingam, who was a learned ascetic of renowned virtue and holiness, CivagOchariyAr, came at daybreak, and having performed his own ablutions in the river, provided himself with a vessel of pure water for the purification of the divine image, and a basket of sacred flowers and fresh leaves for its adornment and uttering the mystic Five Syllables, devoutly drew near. A scene of unutterable pollution met his horrified gaze. Flesh and bones were strewed around, and the image itself had been defiled with filthy water and common wild flowers! With trembling horror he sprang aside, exclaiming, 'Oh, god of gods!what an unhallowed impious hands of mountaineers have brought these pollutions here. How didst thou permit them thus to profane thy presence?'. So saying, he wept, fell down, and rolled in anguish before the god. But, reflecting that at any rate it was wrong to delay any longer the sacred service, he carefully removed the unhallowed things from the precincts, and proceeded to perform worship according to the Vedic rites: and having sung the appointed Hymn, and many times gone round the right image, and prostrated himself in adoration, departed to his hermitage.

Meanwhile the servants, having taken the news of
Tinnan's madness to old NAgan, his father returned with
him and the priestess of their demon temple. They both
attempted to reason with the young enthusiast, and to
recall him tot he worship to which he had been
accustomed; but its wild orgies delighted him no more. His
whole affection was centered upon the new found Civan so
they regarding him as hopelessly mad, returned sorrowing
to their village.

[One object of this legend seems to be the reconciliation of
the orthodox Civa worship and the ruder forms of demon
worship then in use. The contrast is exceedingly striking
when the refined and thoroughly instructed BrAhman,
with his scrupulous attention to all the minutiae of vEdic
worship, who regarded the slaying of animals as a crime,
and the eating of their flesh as an unspeakable
abomination, and considered that whatever had touched a
man's mouth was polluted and that the wild human
inhabitants of the jungle were a lower order of creation is
brought face to face with the youthful chieftain of an
almost savage tribe, whose chief delight is how to hunt
down, slay and devour the birds and beasts of the forest;
who brings boar's flesh for the unpolluted Civan to eat,
and carries water in his mouth wherewith to besprinkle
the image; who actually uses his leathern slippers to brush
away the refuse leaves from the head of the god, who
know no sacred texts; and who worships the same god,
indeed, but has nothing to commend him save a rude
uninstructed though zealous devotion.]

Meanwhile the mountaineer guards the god by night,
returns at eventide to Offer his gifts and perform his rude
service, and spends the day in providing flesh of beasts for

the god's repast.At dawn, when the young woodman has departed, duly comes the pure and exclusive BrAhman having scrupulously made his own ablutions, cleanses the precincts, and performs his ceremonious worship. These men so different serve by turns before the same lingam, which they both regarded with equal reverence! But this cannot long continue so. The BrAhman makes a passionate appeal to Civan to guard himself from these pollutions, the author of which he cannot trace. He then return to his hermitage sad and utterly perplexed. But in the night the god appears to him, and then addressed him: ' That which thou dost complain of is to me most dear and acceptable! Thy rival ministrant is a chieftain of the rude foresters. He is absolutely ignorant of the VEdas and the Caiva texts. He knows not the ordinances of worship. But regard not HIM, regard the spirit and motives of his acts. His rough and gigantic frame is instinct with love to me, his whole knowledge - in thine eyes craze ignorance - is summed up in the knowledge of Me! His every action is dear to me; the tougch of his leathern slipper is pleasant to me as that of the tender hand of my son Skanda. The water with which he besprinkles me from his mouth is holy to me as the water of the Ganges. The food he offers me - to thee so abominable - is pure love. I regard not the externals of worship. He utterly loves me, even as thou dost; but come to-morrow when thou shalt see his worship, and I will give thee proof of his devotion to me'.

The BrAhman slept no more that night, but at daybreak was put in hiding behind the lingam by the god himself. And now Civan, who knows the hearts of worshippers, in order that Tinnan's truth might be manifest, caused blood to trickle down from the right eye of the image. The young worshipper drawing near beheld this, and exclaimed : ' Oh, my master, who hath wounded thee? What sacrilegious hand, evading my watchfulness, has wrought this evil?' Then seizing his weapons he proceeded to scour the neighbourhood to see if any mountaineer or wild animal could be detected as author of the mischief. Finding none, he threw himself on the ground in despair; but at length reflected that he had heard of remedies which would staunch the flow of blood. So he went and sought out in the jungle some herbs of virtue, and applied them; but the wound bled all the more copiously. Then a happy idea struck him; ' for a wounded eye the remedy is another eye applied,' said he; and pausing not an instant, with his arrow he scooped out his own right eye, and applied it to the bleeding eye of the image, from which at once the blood ceased to flow! At this his rapture knew no bounds. He sang and danced, and poured forth uncouth expressions of ardent thanksgiving; but on looking at the image once more, alas! blood was seen issuing from the other eye. After a moment or two of bewildered sorrow, his countenance was lit up with a radiant light of gladness; for he has still one eye left, and the efficacy of the remedy has been tried already; so he raises himself up, puts his one foot close up to the image's suffering eye, that he may be able to feel, when he no longer can see, where to apply the remedy; and proceeded to scoop the other eye. But this last sacrifice is too much for Civan to permit to be consummated; from out the lingam he puts forth a sacred hand, and grasps that of the youthful enthusiast, who still holds the arrow ready to accomplish his pious intention, and says: 'Stay, Tinnan, stay thine hand, my loving son! Henceforth the place for ever shall be at my right hands,

on my holy mount'. CivagOchari had learnt the lesson that
LOVE AND SELF-DEVOTION AND MORE THAN
CEREMONIAL PURITY, and fell prostate; while the choirs
of heaven chanted the beatification of the Saint, who is
from age to age adored while his title of Kann-appan - the
devotee who gave his eyes for the service of his God.

V. The only god.

Those gods are gods indeed, - These others are
the Gods, men wrangling say, and thus
False gods they talk about, and rant and rave
upon this earthly stage. And I
No piety could boast; that earthly bonds
might cease to cling, to Him I clung !
To Him, the God of all true Gods, go thou,
AND BREATHE HIS PRAISE, O HUMMING-BEE ! (20)

VI. He elevates, calms and purifies the soul-

In this mad world, 'mid stress and strife confused,
from birth and death, that ceaseless spring, -
Where hoarded treasure, women, offspring, tribe,
and learning's store, men prize and seek; -
He calms the storm of mental changing states,
and clears from error's mists the soul.
To mystic wisdom's mighty God go thou,
AND BREATHE HIS PRAISE, O HUMMING-BEE ! (24)

VII. Nothing shall draw me from Him !

On Cankaran the soul's embrosia, who thinks,

shall he fare ill? The sacred Foot
That aye endures shall I a prodigal forget?
But those who cleave not to that Foot,-
A sinful fellowship in worship vain,-
their very forms we will not know!
To Him, supremely Excellent, go thou,
AND BREATHE HIS PRAISE, O HUMMING-BEE ! (28)

VIII. His grace to me and mine

Unique it spring, rose up, sent forth its boughs
that none can count, - a tree of grace !
Right well He cared for me, - a cur - and called,
and caused in state aloft to ride,
He is my Sire ! To sirs and house and race
the mighty PerumAn is He !
To Him, the Fount of bliss unfailing, go;
AND BREATHE HIS PRAISE, THOU HUMMING-BEE ! (32)

IX. His self-forgiving compassion.

His throat is black; His nature passes far
all powers of thought that men possess !
I went, drew near, took refuge at His feet;
and He, straightaway, delusions all
From changing deaths and births that ceaseless rise
within my being caused to cease.
To Him, Who is compassion's sea, go thou,
AND BREATHE HIS PRAISE, O HUMMING-BEE ! (36)

X. His tender love has followed me.

Pain I endured, - grew old, - again waxed like
a weaning calf, - in ceaseless change;
And here I dwelt, desiring evermore
enjoyments that a dog might share, -
In folly's every guise. With mother-love,
He came in grace, and made me His !
To the rich Lord of mercy's store go thou,
AND BREATHE HIS PRAISE, O HUMMING-BEE ! (40)

XI. He gave grace without upbraiding

Thou didst not call me 'stony-heart,
'deceiver', 'obstinate of mind';
But Thou didst cause my stony heart to melt,
and in compassion mad at me Thine;
Thou Lord of Tillai's sacred temple-court,
in beauty rich, where swans disport !
Go, hasten to the golden beauteous Foot;
AND BREATHE HIS PRAISE, THOU HUMMING-BEE ! (44)

XII.

The loving Lord, Who taught, wretch as I am,
my lip to sing. His jewell'd Feet;
The Teacher great, Who pardon'd all the faults
of me, a very fiend in sooth;
He still in grace accepts my services,
nor spurns my worthlessness !
To Ican go, as tender mother known,
AND BREATHE HIS PRAISE, THOU HUMMING-BEE ! (48)

XIII. His love demands my all

Devoid of love for Him in sooth was I.
I know it, and He knows it too !
And yet He made me His, this too all men
on earth shall surely see and know.
He there appeared, in all His grace revealed.
He only is my being's King !
Come thou, and joyous join thyself with me
TO BREATHE HIS PRAISE, O HUMMING-BEE ! (52)

XIV. He came to me as my Guru

Germ of all being, far beyond this world, -
yet in this world too, seen;
With Her, whose flowery locks breathe sweet perfume,
in mercy manifest, He came;
A sacred Sage, versed in the mystic scroll,
He stood revealed, and made me His.
Go the God, in sacred form displayed,
AND BREATHE HIS PRAISE, THOU HUMMING-BEE! (56)

XV. Only His mercy brought me near.

How far away had I and all my thought
from Him the loving Lord remained,
Had not the Wearer of the flowing lock,-
He with the Lady,- made me His !
The Lord, Who is the heaven, Who is each realm
of earth and of the mighty sea !
Go to the roseate Feet that sweets distil
AND BREATHE HIS PRAISE, THOU HUMMING-BEE ! (60)

XVI. The thought of Him is joy.

Soon as I thought upon His sacred form
which every thought of man transcends,
The Lord of mercy's flood of purest joys,
that ne'er delude, swept o'er my soul.
My Lord revealed Himself that He might make
me ever fully His alone.
To Him, the Lord of Lords Supreme, go thou,
AND BREATHE HIS PRAISE, O HUMMING-BEE ! (64)

XVII. He saved me from senses' bondage

In pleasures false I plunged, and sank deep down,-
each day of earthly prosperous joy,
I thought it true, and thus enslaved I lay;
in grace revealed, He made me His !
Call Him 'my Teacher' 'precious Life', 'great Lord,
of Tillai's sacred temple-court;
And seek those selfsame roseate flowery Feet,
TO BREATHE HIS PRAISE, THOU HUMMING-BEE ! (68)

XVIII. Civan as depicted in ancient myths.

The tiger's skin, the robe, the pendants rare,
the ears' round golden ornaments,
The ashes white as milk, the sandal paste
so cool and sweet, the parrot green,
The trident, and the armless linked: this pomp,
and ancient fair array He owns,
Regarding well, with joyous soul go thou,
AND BREATHE HIS PRAISE, O HUMMING-BEE ! (72)

XIX. Visited me, nor despised my unworthiness

'Deceiver' ' sinner vile' 'rebellious one,'
all this to me He did not say;
The Generous One came oft to visit me,
nor took His Presence from my mind !
Of all the pains that fill'd my soul, no one
in any wise was left with me !
So to His gleaming jeweled Foot go thou,
AND BREATHE HIS PRAISE, O HUMMING-BEE ! (76)

XX. His grace to the lowly

Ayan, who crowns the lotus flower, and MAl
were grieved - for He was hard to reach !
But I, His lowly slave, all jubilant
fulfilled of exultation stood !
To me, mere cur, He gave a lofty seat,
endued right well with worthiness !
To Him, Whose form is fiery flame, go thou,
AND BREATHE HIS PRAISE, O HUMMING-BEE ! (80)

(Part II - Hymns 11 -51)

Hymn XI- tiru Tellenam
THE TAMBOUR SONG or REFUGE WITH CIVAN

Metre : Naladittaravu koccuk kalippA

Arunachalam.- The name of Rudra is scarcely ever applied to
Civan in the south, yet it would seem as if the idea of Civan
had been mainly developed from the Vedic Rudra, the god of
Storms, the father of the Maruts, of whom so many stories
are told which now are the accepted legends of Civan. It may
safely be said indeed that all the Vedic Rudra's acts and
attributes are given in the modern Caiva system to Civan.
One of these is connected with the legend of Arunachalam,
so often referred to in Tamil Caiva poetry. According to the
legend contained in the Linga Puranam, it is related that
Brahma and Vishnu disputed regarding their respective
claims to superiority, and thence a terrific fight arose. At this
time to quiet their contention, Civan, or Mahadeva, appeared
as luminous lingam , a pillar of fire, 'equal to a hundred final
mundane configurations, without beginning, middle or end,
incomparable, indescrible, undefinable.' Hari determined to
examine the source of this fiery appearance, and took the
shape of a boar whose description is very wonderful.
Speeding downwards for a thousand years he beheld no base
at all of the lingam. Meanwhile Brahma took the form of a
swan purely white and fiery eyed, with wings on every side,
rapid as thought, and went upwards to see the lingam's top;
but both failed, and at length united in a hymn of praise to
Civan as supreme; which so pleased the god that he offered
them a boon. They asked that they might both obtain an

eternal devotion for him, which was granted. 'Thenceforward the worship of the lingam has been inaugurated in the worlds. The pedestal is Mahadevi, and the lingam itself is the visible Mahecvara.'

I. Civan as a Guru.

Mal's self went forth a boar; but failed His sacred Foot
To find, that we His form might know, a Sage He came,
And made me His! To Him, Who hath nor name, nor form,
A thousand sacred names SING WE, AND BEAT TELLENAM!
(4)

II. I saw Him; thenceforward my soul worships Him unseen.

The Lord in Perun-turrai's ever-hallowed shrine
Who dwelt, my birth with all its germs destroyed; since when
I've none else; formless is He,- a form He wears,
The Lord of blest Arur SING WE, AND BEAT TELLENAM! (8)

III.

To Hari and to Brahma and to other gods
Not manifested, Civan came in presence there,
Melted our hearts, received our service due; that all
The world may hear, and smile, SING WE, AND BEAT
TELLENAM! (12)

IV.

From sinking in the vain abyss of worthless gods,-

From birth's illusions all,- the LIGHT SUPERNAL saved
And made me His. Soon as the new, pure Light, was given
How I in Bliss was lost: SING WE, AND BEAT TELLENAM! (16)

V.

To wildered gods, to Ayan, and to Mal unknown,
Civan assumed a form, that men on earth should joy.
That germs of birth consumed might die, with gracious
glance,
How to my soul He came, SING WE, AND BEAT TELLENAM!
(20)

VI.

The Lord, Who shakes the serpent dancing round His waist,
With His Hill-partner, came to earth, made us His own;-
Say thus, soul-lighted, eyes like full bright lotus flowers,
Pouring forth floods of tears, and SINGING, BEAT TELLENAM!
(24)

VII.

Civan unknown to Hari, Ayan, heavenly ones,
On earth drew even me; 'come, come,' said He, and made me
His!
When imprint of His flow'ry Feet was on my head impressed,
How grace divine was mine, SING WE, AND BEAT TELLENAM!
(28)

VIII.

Like rustling palm-leaves is this frame! Its births and deaths,
With dread of good and ill, He swept away, and made me His;
He gave me grace, though I, all else forget, ne'er to forget
His Foot; Whose mighty dance SING WE, AND BEAT
TELLENAM! (32)

IX.

As though some stone were made sweet fruit, the Lord in
grace
Gave ev'n to me His golden Foot, and made me His.
O ye with slender waist, red lips, and winsome smiles!
'Lord of the Southern-Land,' call Him; AND BEAT TELLENAM!
(36)

X.

Even in a dream His jewelled Feet 'tis hard for gods to see,-
With Her like laurel tree with jewelled arms,-entering in
grace,
In waking hour He took, and made me His! With loving souls
Your art-like eyes be filled with tears, AND BEAT TELLENAM!
(40)

XI.

When He, Her spouse whose eyes shine bright, mixt with my
soul,
And made me His, deeds and environments died out;
Upon this earth confusion died; all other mem'ries ceas'd;

141

How all my 'doings' died, SING WE, AND BEAT TELLENAM!
(44)

XII.

Ascetic bands sore languish'd, longing for release.
Grace to the elephant he gave, made me His own;
The light suprene deep plunged me in devotion's sea!
How sweet His mercy is, SING WE, AND BEAT TELLENAM! (48)

XIII.

Not those on earth, nor in th' abyss, nor heavenly ones,-
To none beside, so near He drew; He made me His!
To sing His advent, or Him, th' only Great, conceive
Is hard, His glory-song SING WE, AND BEAT TELLENAM! (52)

XIV.

Mal, Ayan, all the gods, and Sciences divine,
His essence cannot pierce. This Being rare drew near to me;
In love He thrilled my soul! WIth this remembrance moved,
Let your bright eyes with tears o'erflow, AND BEAT
TELLENAM! (56)

XV.

The spreading sea of grace superne that melts and swells,
From which 'tis sweet to draw and drink, we gather round.
The Feet of the bright southern Lord call we to mind,

His slaves, praise we His sacred grace, AND BEAT TELLENAM!
(60)

XVI.

Buddhan, Purandaran, the primal Ayan, Mal, praise Him,
The One-distraught, Who dwells in Perun-turrai's shrine, -the
Sire
Who made births cease,-Lord of fair Tillai's porch, His
gracious Feet
How in my soul they entered, SING, AND BEAT TELLENAM!
(64)

XVII.

I lay bewildere'd in the barren troublous sea
Of sects and systems wide discordant all;-
My care He banished, gave in grce His jewelled Feet;
Praise we His gracious acts, AND BEAT TELLENAM! (68)

XVIII.

Though Ether, Wind, Water, Earth should fail,
His constant Being fails not, knows no weariness!
In Him my body, soul, and thought, and mind were merged.
How all myself was lost, SING WE, AND BEAT TELLENAM! (72)

XIX.

Prime Source of heavenly ones, the Germ of those beneath,
Earth's Balm; Mal's, Ayan's Treasure, open eyed

We saw, SING YE, His gracious feet, Who dwelt with us!
Call Him 'Lord of the Southern-Land,' AND BEAT TELLENAM!
(76)

XX.

Sing His race; sing the heron's wing; Her beauty sing
Who wears bright gems; sing how He poison ate; each day
In Tillai's temple court He dances, where the waters play;
His tinkling anklets' music SING, AND BEAT TELLENAM! (80)

Hymn XII- tiru Caral
THE SACRED CARAL
THE SPORT OF CIVAN'S GRACIOUS 'ENERGY.'

I. Objections to 'ashes,' the snake, and the mystery of His
teaching.

Obj. What He smears is 'white ash'; what He wears is an
angry snake;
What He speaks with His lips divine is the mystic word, it
seems; MY DEAR!
Ans. What He smears, what He says, what He wears are the
means by which He,
As my Lord, rules me; and of all that hath life the Essence is
He! CARALO! (4)

These are the words used by Dakshan to his daughter Umai in
the Kaci Khandam,:-

His body he smears with ashes; a serpent he wears as
adornment;
Poison from the sea he eats; a skull he carries
He rides a white bull that rages with anger. Such an one,
O damsel, is he fit to come to our sacrifice?'

The ashes, the serpent, the poison, the skull, and the bull are
matters of praise in all Caiva poems.

II. Objections to His mendicant gruise.

Obj. 'My Father, Embiran, to all indeed is Ruler Supreme;
Yet He wears a clouted kovanam;' and why should this be so,
MY DEAR?
Ans. The Vedas four, the meaning with which all lore is
fraught, as the great thread
Himself alone as kovanam He spreads; behold, CARALO! (8)

An ascetic mendicant wears a very scanty cloth, suspended
by a string round the waist; but why should He, who often
appears in such stately majesty, wear this unseemly pretence
of decent clothing! The answer is ambiguous in the original,
but seems to say: 'All mysteries are contained and hidden in
Him, and the Vedic revelation is the link between Him and
the souls of men.' Strange symbolism!
Kaman, the 'Bodilcss." - The story of the destruction of
Kaman (or the god of Love) by Civan is very curious, and
should be read by the Tamil scholar in the Kamba-
Ramayanam. It seems that Civan resolved to enter on a
course of very strict devotion (Yogam) with the intention of
increasing his powers! The lesser divinities fearing this,

145

instigated Kaman to endeavour to distract the mind of the devotee. Accordingly the archer sallied forth with his arrows composed of the nine most fragrant flowers, and having fitted one on to the string, took aim at Civan's sacred breast. But the god suddenly opened his third eye in the centre of his brow, from which he darted a wrathful flame that instantly reduced Kaman to ashes. At the intercession of all orders of creation Kaman was restored to life, but not to a visible substantial form, and he still pervades the world riding on the chariot of the soft south-wind, working his mischief unseen. Ancient European mythology made him blind: he is here 'bodiless.' The legend may remind us of the story of Echo. The allusions to this myth in these lyrics are endless - and wearisome.

III. The objection that Civan is a homeless ascetic.

Obj. His shrine's the burning ground; fierce tiger skin His goodly garb;
All motherless and fatherless is He; all lonely dwelleth; see,
MY DEAR!
Ans.Motherless is He and fatherless; dwelleth all aone; but though'tis thus,
If He be wroth, the worlds to powder crumble all; behold,
CARALO! (12)

IV. The punitive indications of Bhairavan.

Obj. Ayan, the 'Bodiless,' with Anthagan, and Canthiran,
In divers ways He wounded sore, yet slew not; see, MY DEAR!

Ans. He Whose eyes are three, the Ruler great, if He shall punish,

Is't not a triumph to the heav'nly ones, O thou with flowing locks? CARALO! (16)

V. Dakshan's sacrifice.

Obj. Of Dakshan He smote off the head, off Eccan too; the hosts of gods

That flocking came He sent to nothingness; why this, MY DEAR?

Ans. Them who thronging came to nothingness He sent; 'twas grace!

In grace to Eccan too He gave one head the more; see CARALO! (20)

VI. Arunachalam.

Obj. Him the flow'ry god and Mal knew not; in fiery form He came

From earth that stretch'd to lower worlds; wherefore was this, MY DEAR?

Ans. From earth to realms beneath had He not reach'd, they twain

The insolence of self-esteem had not cast off; behold, CARALO! (24)

VII. Parvathi lives in His side, Ganga on His crest.

Obj.Soon as the mountain maid as part of Him He placed, another dame

In watery form upon His braided locks poured down! Why
this, MY DEAR?
Ans. Upon His braided locks in watery form had she not
leaped, the world
To cavernous destruction rushing ruined must have lain!
CARALO! (28)

VIII. The poison.

Obj. He ate halalam from the sounding sea, that day arisen
With mighty din; what means this wondrous act, MY DEAR?
Ans. Had He not eaten on that day the posion fierce, Ayan
and Mal
And all the other gods of upper heaven had died; behold,
CARALO! (32)

The Hala-hala Poison, the churning of the sea, the blackness
of Civan's Throat, and the epithet 'Ambrosia.'-
Among other things in these lyrics that require explanation to
the English reader, the subjects referred to in the above title
are of the most frequent recurrence, and are apt to weary
and even disgust.
It is most necessary however to understand once for all how
essential they are to the South-Indian concept of Civan, as
the great and beneficient Being Who is to be approached in
prayer and gratefully adored. It will hardly be possible for the
reader to do anything like justice to the Poet and religious
Teacher, unless he deem it worth while to make the attempt
to view these things candidly and dispassionately in the light

in which they are viewed by the more devout and intelligent of the Caiva community.

The legend is simply this: the lesser deities were in sore affliction and came to Civan for help. He accordingly came forth from Kailaca, and using Mount Mandara as His churning-stick, with Vasu-deva as the rope which caused it to revolve, proceeded to churn the sea of milk. The result was the appearance of the Ambrosia or food of immortal gladness. But before this a stream of fiery poison black and deadly, the Hala-hala poison, rushed forth. This the deity himself drank up, and hence his throat is for ever black, a glorious memorial of his voluntary sufferings. The cup of ambrosia He gave to the grateful gods. Another version of this story may be read in Wilson's Vishnu Puranam. It is also to be found in various form in Tamil verse, but is essentially a Sanskrit and northern myth. The question occurs, was this regarded as literal fact, or was it put forth as a parable? It may be said that three classes of Hindus are to be met with in the South: those to whom this and similar histories are wonderful stories and nothing more. They take no more interest in them than we should in the Arabian Nights' Entertainments.

A second class believe the legends devoutly, and regard them as capable of a mystic interpretation to which however they do not attach any surpassing importance, nor are they at all agreed as to its details. The third class think that under the veil of such legends ancient sages concealed mysterious teachings which they were unwilling to expose to the vulgar gaze. And they say that they alone possess the secret of the esoteric meaning of the myths, which they themselves regard as more or less antiquated and uncouth.

Whether the Upanishads and Sanskrit literature in general lend any countenance to this last idea is exceedingly doubtful. I incline to think that these mystic interpretations are only to be found in later, and chiefly in South-Indian, authors. It is very ceratin that the Caiva Siddhanta philosophers have made it their especial business to give to all such legends a more elevating, and at the same time distinctly Caivite, interpretation. The south of India has from the earliest time been more open than the rest of the east to western influences and teaching, and I feel convinced that this is one of the results. Whether in any way the chasm between western and eastern ideas can be bridged over by any such explanations is of course a most interesting question.

It is quite permitted us to say that, the truth supposed to be concealed (rather too carefully!) under these symbols is that, the Supreme Being has condescended to come to earth to taste the bitter cup of suffering, retaining ever the glorious signs of that agony, while to men He presents the draught of immortal blessedness. However this may be, the epithets of 'Black-throated' and 'Ambrosia' as applied to Civan need not be, must not be, simply grotesque, but associated with the pathos of sufferring and the tenderness of unselfish love. The idea of this is expressed in the first poem of the Purra-Nannurru, which is by Perundevanar, the translator of the Bharatam:-

'He wears th'adornment of a throat with poison black; that stain
The chaunters of the mystic scrolls are wont to praise.'

Of course there are many things which are said and sung by the devout of all systems in all lands that require to be explained, and it will generally be found that a mystic meaning is at the root of the uncouth phrase. This has been more or less lost sight of: the symbol is apt to supersede the real thought.

IX.

Obj. The Lord of Tillai's court, Who in the southern land delights, and dances there,
A mighty maniac, delighted in the female form, behold, MY DEAR!
Ans. had He not delighted in the female form, all in the wide world
Would have obtained heaven's bliss and earth had failed; behold, CARALO! (36)

X.

Obj. He is the endless One; and me, a dog, who came to Him,
He plunged in tide of rapturous bliss unending; behold, MY DEAR!
Ans. The sacred Feet that plunged me in rapture's flowing tide
are treasure rich to gods in upper heaven that dwell; behold, CARALO! (40)

XI.

Obj. Lady! what's this ascetic rite? Sinews and bone He wears,
A bony circlet on His arm He loves to bear; behold, MY DEAR!
Ans. The way of the bony circlet hear! In the end of the age
When the two had reached their fated hour, He put it on;
hehold, CARALO! (44)

XII.

Obj. His garb is the skin of the forest tiger; He eats from a skull;
The wild is His city; to Him here who will service pay? MY DEAR!
Ans. Yet, hear thou! Ayan and sacred Mal, and the King
Of them of the heavenly land, are His humble and faithful
ones; CARALO! (48)

XIII. His marriage.

Obj. The mountain monarch's golden Daughter bright of brow, the Lady blest,
He wedded with the fire as all the world doth know; what's that? say, MY DEAR!
Ans. Had He not wedded Her for all the world to know, the world entire
Had in confusion lost the import true of every lore; behold, CARALO! (52)

XIV. The dance.

Obj. The Lord of Tillai's court, by cool palms girt, whence honey drips,

There entering does a mystic dance perform; what's that, MY DEAR?

Ans. Had He not enter'd there, all the wide earth had quick become

Abode of demons armed with flesh-transfixing appears; CARALO! (56)

XV. The bull.

Obj. On stately elephant, swift stead, or car it pleased Him not to ride;

A bull He pleased to mount! Explain me this that I may know, MY DEAR!

Ans. The day He burnt with fire the triple mighty walls,

Mal divine a bull became to bear Him up; behold, CARALO! (60)

XVI. Civan a guru and an avenger too.

Obj. Well to the four, the fourfold mystic scrolls' deep sense,

That day, beneath the banyan tree, and virtue He reveal'd; behold, MY DEAR!

Ans.That day, beneath the banyan tree, though virtue He revealed,

He utterly destroyed the cities three; begold, CARALO! (64)

XVII. A mendicant.

Obj. In the sacred hall He dances, and wanders abroad to beg
for alms;
This homeless mendicant shall we approach as god? How so,
MY DEAR?
Ans. Hear thou the nature of this sacred mendicant! Him
Vedas four know not;
But they've invok'd Him Lord and Ican, praising loud; behold,
CARALO! (68)

XVIII. The disc.

Obj. When He smote down Jalandharan, the monster of the
sea, that disc
To Naranan, the good, in grace He gave; how's that, MY
DEAR?
Ans. Since Naranan, the good, dug out an eye, and laid at
Aran's foot,
As flower, to him in grace the disc He gave; behold, CARALO!
(72)

IX.

Obj. His garment is the spotted hide; His food the fiery poison
dark.
Is this our Peruman's great skill? Expound that I may know,
MY DEAR!
Ans. Our Peruman,- whatever He wore there,- whate'er He
ate,-
The greatness of His Nature none can know; behold,
CARALO! (76)

X. Virtue and true philosophy must be divinely taught.

Obj. To saints of goodness rare, beneath the Al, virtue and all
the Four He taught;
Explain to me the grace He showed, seated with them, MY
DEAR!
Ans. Had He not taught that day in grace, the worthy saints
virtue and all the Four,
To noble souls this world's nature had ne'er been known!
Behold, CARALO! (80)

Hymn XIII- tiru puvalli
THE SACRED LILY-FLOWERS
or
TAKING THE VICTORY FROM MAYA

I. Renunciation of other help.

His sacred Feet,- the twain,-soon as upon my head He placed,
Help of encircling friends,- the whole,- I utterly renounced;
In Tillai's court begirt with guarded streams, in mystic dance
He moves. That Raftsman's glory SING, AND PLUCK THE LILY-
FLOWERS! (4)

II. Further experiences in Madyarjunam.

From father, mother, kindered, and all else that were to me
As bonds, He set me free; made me His own,- the Pandi-Lord!
In Idai-maruthu, His dwelling, rapture's honey flowed.

That sweet recess with song PRAISE WE, AND PLUCK THE
LILY-FLOWERS! (8)

III. Converting grace.

Us too, than dogs more vile, of worth and note He made to
be;
With greater than a mother's tenderness, our Peruman
Cut off 'illusive birth,' made us His own; our 'deeds' so strong
Laid prostrate humbled in the dust; PLUCK WE THE LILY-
FLOWERS! (12)

IV. The Rebel-rout.

They praised not the king of Tillai's town, 'mid well-tilled
fields,
Dakshan renown'd, and Arukkan, and Eccan, Moon, and Fire!
By Vira-bhadra with his demon host that fill'd the sky,
Sing how that day they suffer'd wounds; AND PLUCK THE
LILY-FLOWERS! (16)

V. Perun-turrai and Tillai.

Civan, the Lord, who on His 'lock' the honied cassia wears,
Took fleshy rom, sought me, and entering came; before the
world
That I may dance, and utter triumph songs, in dance
He moves! For Him, King of heaven's sons, PLUCK WE THE
LILY-FLOWERS! (20)

VI. The Triads.

THREE fires He gave in gracious pity to the gods;
THREE heads to sever fire He sent from sacred brow, in grace;
THREE forms He wears, the Only-One, Incomprehensible;
THREE rebel towns He burnt; so PLUCK THE LILY-FLOWERS!
(24)

VII. His gracious work.

He made my head to bow; my mouth to laud His cinctured
Foot
He taught; gave me to join th'assemblage of His glorious
saints;
And with the Queen, in Tillai's court adorned, dances our
Peruman.
Sing we aloud His excellence, AND PLUCK THE LILY-FLOWERS!
(28)

VIII.

He taught the pathway to the golden Feet of His great saints,
Praise ye the Master's grace that made me His and gave the
sign!
'Old deeds' that made us wholly bond-slaves, sorely troubled
us,
Sing how He brought to naught; AND SO PLUCK WE THE LILY-
FLOWERS! (32)

IX.

That I might praise Him many a day, and service due perform,

The Mighty-One His fragrant foot-flower on my frame
impress'd;
A beauteous Light He shone, softened my heart, and made
me His!
Sing how those jewell'd Feet are gold, AND PLUCK THE LILY-
FLOWERS! (36)

X.

That this my frame, mere mass of fierce desires, might pass
away,
Great Perun-turrai's Lord placed on my head His glorious
Foot.
KABALI,- Who, well pleased, black poison ate from out the
sea, -
Sing we, amidst His warring foes, AND PLUCK THE LILY-
FLOWERS! (40)

XI.

The BEING INFINITE, with every varied sweetness filled;
The LORD, Who took my soul in joyous pomp; His sounding
Feet
All dwellers in the world shall praise! That is the way of good!
That way sing we His glory now, AND PLUCK THE LILY-
FLOWERS! (44)

XII.

Heaven's Lord, and Mal, and Ayan, and the other gods He
rules

As King, with attributes and signs that none may e'er attain;
The fiery poison from the vasty sea, He made His food
Ambrosia; and thus sing we, AND PLUCK THE LILY-FLOWERS!
(48)

XIII.

That day, beneath the banyan's shade, in grace the Vedas
rare
He gave; the heavenly ones and mighty saints, each day,
stood round,
And praised Him of the perfect Foot with cassia-flower
adorn'd;
Its golden petal's dust sing we, AND PLUCK THE LILY-
FLOWERS! (52)

XIV.

Fair pictured in my soul His Feet's twin flowers in grace He
gave;
The Lord, Who in Ekambam dwells, made here His chosen
seat;
In Tillai's sacred court, girt by wide walls, is now His home;
Sing how in mystic dance He moves, AND PLUCK THE LILY-
FLOWERS! (56)

XV. Dakshan's sacrifice.

Fire and the Sun, and Ravanan, and Andhagan, and Death,
With red-ey'd Hari, Ayan, Indra, and the Moon-god too,

And shameless Dakshan and the Eccan: these their honour
lost!
Singing His swelling glory now, PLUCK WE THE LILY-FLOWERS!
(60)

XVI.

The strong bull's Rider; Champion brave of those of Civa-
town;
In Madura, earth-carrier; in grace He ate the cakes;
Was smitten by the Pandiyan's staff, who claimed His service
there.
Sing the song of the wound He bore, AND PLUCK THE LILY-
FLOWERS! (64)

XVII.

The ancient Mal, Ayan, the heavenly ones, the Danavar,
Knew not His sacred golden Foot, but joined in praise!
Entering within my breast, He made me His! His ornament
The gleaming serpent SING WE THUS, AND PLUCK THE LILY-
FLOWERS! (68)

XVIII.

That with desire insatiate my soul might ever joy
At sound of tinkling anklets on His glorious sacred Foot,
In dance He moves,- the Lord of Perun-turrai's car-thronged
streets.
This mighty rapture chaunting loud, PLUCK WE THE LILY-
FLOWERS! (72)

XIX.

The Perun-turrai-Lord, Who wears the hide of elephant;
Who took a madman's form;- Who in this world became a
child;
Source of all heavenly bliss; great Uttara-koca-mangai's
Prince;
As in our minds He entering cam, PLUCK WE THE LILY-
FLOWERS! (76)

Hymn XIV- tiru unthiyar
THE UNTHIYAR
or
SACRED VICTORY

CIVAN'S TRIUMPHS

Tamil scholars give different interpretations of the word
Unthiyar. It seems to mean 'the players at a game resembling
battledore and shuttlecock.' The word Unthi is, I imagine,
used for the shuttlecock or ball which the players cause to 'fly
aloft.'
In this lyric FIVE GREAT TRIUMPHS OF CIVAN are celebrated.
I. The first of these (I-4) is the destruction of the three towns,
in Tami and Sanskrit Tripura, which is curiously enough made
to be the name of a giant overthrown by Civan. I give an
abstract of this story from Muir:-

'There were in the sky three cities of the Asuras, one of iron, another of silver, and a third of gold, which Indra could not demolish, with all his weapons. Then all the great gods, distressed, went to Rudra as their refuge, and said to him, after they were assembled: "Rudra, there shall be victims devoted to thee in all sacrifices. Bestower of honour, destroy the Daityas with their cities, and deliver the worlds." He, being thus addressed, said, "So be it;" and making Vishnu his arrow, Agni its barb, Yama, the son of Vivasvat, its feather, all the Vedas his bow, and the excellent Savitri (the Gayatri) his bowstring, and having appointed Brahma his charioteer, he in due time pierced through these cities with a three-jointed three-barbed arrow, of the colour of the sun, and in fierceness like the fire which burns up the world. These Asuras with their cities were there burnt up by Rudra.'

II. The second of these triumphs is the destruction of Dakshan's sacrifice. The story of this is told with many variations, and is evidently, as Professor Wilson pointed out long ago, of some great struggle between the followers of Vishnu and Civan: but it is neither possible to give any full interpretation of it, nor to reconcile the discrepancies in the various accounts of it. The account given below is that of the Kaci Khandam, which every student of Tamil should read.

In the Kaci Khandam, the account of Dakshan-his sacrifice, punishment, forgiveness, and penance in Benares - occupies chapters xxxviii-xc inclusive, and fills 148 stanzas. It sums up, with some inconsistencies, the whole story as given in the Sanskrit books. Dakshan (- the Intelligent) is represented sometimes as the father, and sometimes as the son of Aditi; and at other times the two are curiously said to have been reciprocally producers and produced. He is identified with

Prajapati, the Creator. This almost seems like a statement that the whole universe is developed from intelligence, and might appear like a very symbolical acting forth of Hegel's system. Dakshan had many daughters married to the great saints, and especially Kacyapa(Kaciban) is said to have been the husband of twelve of them. One of his daughters was Durga, or Uma, who was subsequently born from the mountain after her voluntary death, and so received the name of Parvathi. So Civan, the Supreme, was a son-in-law of Dakshan, the Intelligence from which the Universe was developed. It is rather entangled.

On one occasion all the gods and saints made a visit to the silver mountain Kailaca. They were there received with great kindness, by the mighty one upon whose head is the Kondral wreath, whose throat is black with the poison he swallowed to save the world, and from the centre of whose forehead a third eye shines resplendent. But the deity did not recognize his father-in-law, nor rise to receive him. This fills Dakshan with disgust, and he proceeds to indulge in the most extravagant abuse of Civan. It will be seen that everything with which he reproaches Civan is used by Manikka-Vacagar as praise. Of course a mystical meaning is given to each circumstance! The following is a summary of his language:-
'He has no mother, no father, and no relatives!
He is a maniac who dances with demons on the burning-ground.
He has an eye in his brow from which devouring fire blazes forth.
He wears the skin of a fierce tiger, foul and fetid.
Race, family, caste, quality hath he none.

He wears as an ornament the skin of a serpent that causes deadly ill.

He has discarded the anointing of himself with flowery essences,

And besmears himself with foul ashes of corpses in the burning-ground.

His food is poison from the billowy sea;

As conveyance he has an ancient bullock;

He wears the skin of a black elephant;

His ruddy hand grasps a skull bereft of flesh.

If you say he is a Brahman, he has changed all rules of ordered life;

If you say he is a merchant full of wealth, he goes about begging;

He has no skill in any mystic lore.

Nor is he a Brahmacari, for a large-eyed damsel is part of his body;

He bears an implement of war, and so is not a worthy ascetic;

He wanders amid the hot desert sands, and so is no seemly householder;

He cut off the head of the flower god,

So knows not the laws of excellent justice;

The lady with gleaming brows is half of his frame,

So he is not male, or female, or sexless one.

In the day when he destroys all worlds,

Having worn as a garland the skull of flowery Ayan,

And whirling the three-headed gleaming lance

Everywhere he kills, Is it possible to call him a saint?'

After thus relieving his mind by abuse to punish Civan's discourtesy, he resolves to perform a mighty sacrifice (magam), and so gain additional powers. Civan must be dethroned or slain. All the gods are invited, and there is a very magnificent assembly on Dakshan's mountain. Then comes forth a sage Dadici, who protests that no sacrifice can be of efficacy to which Civan has not been invited; such a place of worship must become 'a burning-ground, where goblins, demons, and dogs prowl around.' His protest is answered by additional abuse, and so the devotees depart, leaving the gods and goddessess to joint with Dakshan in the unhallowed offering. And now the great mischief maker in all such legends, whose name was Naradar, the sweet lutist of the holy mount, hurries to Kailaca to tell the goddess Umai of her father-in law's projected offering. She longs to be present, and implores her spouse to permit it, but he rejects her request. Somehow or other she does however go, and with every token of filial piety meets her father and mother; and after the first greeting enquires why the great god, the lord of all, is not invited:

'It seems as though you had forgotten the greatest of guests.' To this, abuse of Civan is the only answer.

She at once dies, puts off the body which owns Dakshan as father, and is reborn as the daughter of Himavat, whence, Civan afterwards takes her as Parvathi, 'the mountain maid.'

III. The third triumph is his bestowal of the milky sea on the son of Vasishtha. For this it is sufficient to refer to the Koyil Puranam. It is a rather confused and somewhat meaningless story as it has come down to us.

IV. The fourth triumph is given at great length in the Kaci Khandam, and is connected with the god's manifestation as Vira-bhadra. For this it is only necessary to refer to chapter xc of the above work.

In regard to the Kaci Khandam, indeed, which is mainly a translation from the Sanskrit Skanda Purana, it must be noted that there is in it much didactic poetry of a more elevated character, which characterized as a collection of legends which are uterly unprofitable, and have been worked into the devotional poetry of the Caivites to its very great detriment. The legends of Dakshan's sacrifice, of the appearance and ferocity of Vira-bhadra as a kind of incarnation of Civan, and of the unseemly disputes between Vishnu and Brahma as to the pre-eminence, occupy large portions of the book and are utterly useless in these days. We may give a summary of chapter xxxi, entitled 'The Appearance of Bhairava."

Civan, the Supreme, envelopes the world in elusive mystery, so that none know him while He is all in all. Hence, even among the gods, disputes arose as to who was the greatest. 'I am the supreme Essence,' cried Vishnu. 'I am the Self-existent,' declared Brahma from his lotus-seat. The sacred Veda, the unwritten record of mysterious truth, was called upon to decide. The divine essences whose incarnation, or manifestation rather, is the fourfold Veda spoke out: The first Vedic genius declared that since Civan alone performed the three operations of creation, preservation, and destruction, he was the Supreme and unoriginated God. The second declared that since Civan had performed arduous sacrifices and penances, so as to merit praise from the whole universe, he was the supreme. The third announced the same conclusion, but based it upon the fact that Civan fills all things with light, and is adored by all the mystic sages as the giver of wisdom. The fourth Vedic mystery declared that since Civan revealed himself in various forms exciting emotions of joy and ecstatic devotion in the hearts of his worshippers, who beheld him crowned with cassia-wreaths, he was the greatest of the gods. [It is easy to see the arguments by which the supremacy of Civan is here upheld, and there are gleams of truth which Christianity emphasises and illustrates, but the legends connected with the statements are very wonderful, and certainly obscure and confuse, rather than illustrate, the truth concerning the supreme and absolute.] Vishnu and Brahma listen only to deride. 'Civan,' they cry, 'rides on a bull; he has a matted coil of hair; he dances in the burning-ground; he smears ashes; his throat is black with the swallowed poison; he wears as a girdle a hissing snake; he is the leader of a wild demon-host, and Umai is a part of his form. This being so, how can he be the life of the soul of all ?' [These are the arguments that were urged by Jains and Buddhists, and the wonder is that they did not everywhere and finally prevail.]

Roused by these insults, Civan suddenly appears. His aspect is described in the usual terms, and he sends forth a manifestaion or incarnation of himself, or of his destroying energy, to which the name of Vairavan (Vira-bhadra) is given. This anomalous being is of terrific appearance, and endowed with all the Destroyer's terrible energy. He is followed by a host of malignant demons. Civan calls him his son, and bids him destroy all his enemies. Vairavan accordingly seizes the fifth head of Brahma between his thumb and forefinger, twists it off and throws it on the ground, performing a terrific dance which throws the whole universe and every order of sentient existence into a paroxysm of terror. This subdues the opposing deities, and Vishnu worships at Civan's feet, praising him in the most extravagant terms. The whole ends

in a wild orgy, in which Civan and Brahma join. This is so
often referred to in Caivite poetry, and seems so incapable of
any edifying interpretation, that we have thought it
necessary to give the authentic summary from the Kaci
Khandam once for all.

V. The last is the victory over the Ceylon king, Ravana. This
legend is perpetually referred to in the south, and seems to
have a popularity among the poets somewhat in excess of its
apparent importance.

After his victory over Kuvera, Ravana went to Saravana, the
birthplace of Karthikeya. Ascending the mountain, he sees
another delightful wood, where his car Pushpaka stops, and
will proceed no further. He then beholds a formidable dark
tawny-coloured dwarf, called Nandicvara, a follower of
Mahadeva, who desires him to halt, as that deity is sporting
on the mountain, and has made it inaccessible to all
creatures, the gods included. Ravana angrily demands who
Cankara (Mahadeva) is, and laughs contemptuously at
Nandicvara, who has the face of a monkey. Nandicvara, who
was another body of Civan, being incensed at this contempt
of his monkey form, declares that beings, possessing the
same shape as himself, and of similar energy,-monkeys,- shall
be produced to destroy Ravana's race (Tasmad mad-virya-
sanyuktah madrupa-sama-tejasah utpatsyanti badhartham hi
kulasya tava vanarah). Nandicvara adds that he could easily
kill Ravana now, but that he has been already slain by his
own deeds. Ravana threatens that as his car has been
stopped, he will pluck up the mountain by the roots, asking in
virtue of what power Civan continually sports on that spot,
and boasting that he must now be made to know his danger.
Ravana then throws his arms under the mountain, which

being lifted by him, shakes, and makes the hosts of Rudra
tremble, and even Parvathi herself quake, and cling to her
husband (Chachala Parvathi, chapi tada clishta Mahecvaram).
Civan, however, presses down the mountain with his great
toe, and along wit it crushes the arms of Ravana, who utters
a loud cry, which shakes all creation. Ravana's counsellors
then exhort him to propitiate Mahadeva, the blue-throated
lord of Uma, who, on being lauded, will become gracious.
Ravana accordingly praises Mahadeva with hymns, and
weeps for a thousand years. Mahadeva is then propitiated,
lets go Ravana's arms, says his name shall be Ravana from
the cry (rava) he had uttered, and sends him away, with the
gift of a sword bestowed on him at his request.
[Metre: kavithal isai]

I. The three cities

Bent was the bow;- upsprang the tumult;
Perished three cities! Fly aloft, Unthi!
As they burnt straightway together,- Fly, &c. (3)

Two arrows we saw not- in Egambar's hand:
One arrow; three cities! Fly aloft, Until!
And one was too many !- Fly, &c. (6)

There was shaking of framework;- and as He moved His foot,
The axle was broken- say, Fly aloft, unthi!
Perished three cities! - Fly, &c. (9)

Those who won their escape- a triad of persons-He guarded.
To Him whose arrows fail not,- Fly aloft, Unthi!

Saying, He's the Tender-One's Spouse!- Fly, &c. (12)

II. Dakshan's sacrifice.

The frustrate offering thrown to the ground-the gods-
Sing how they fled!-Fly aloft, Unthi!
To Rudra the Lord,-Fly, &c. (15)

Aha! Mal divine got a portion that day of the offering;
And He died not!- Fly aloft, Unthi!
The Four-faced's father!- Fly, &c. (18)

The fierce one- Agni-to consume it collected
His hands of flame. He cut them away! - Fly aloft, Unthi!
Spoiled was the sacrifice! - Fly, &c. (21)

Dakshan, who raised the anger of Parvathi,
He saw and spared, what good? my dear!- Fly aloft, Unthi!
To the SPouse of the Beautiful, - Fly &c. (24)

Purandharan became a tender 'kuyil,'
And flew up a tree!- Fly away, Unthi!
King of the heavenly ones!- Fly, &c. (27)

The angry sacrificer's head-
Sing how it fell! - Fly aloft, Unthi!
That birth's chain may be snapt! - Fly, &c. (30)

The head of a sheep- to Vidhi- as his-
Sing how He joined!-Fly aloft, Unthi!
While you're with laughter convulsed!- Fly, &c. (33)

Sing how Bhagan, who cam to eat, 'scaped not,
He plucked out his eye!- Fly aloft, Unthi!
That germs of our birth may die!-Fly, &c. (36)

The Lady of the tongue lost a nose; Brahma a head;-
The Moon-god's face He smashed!-Fly aloft, Unthi!
That ancient troublous deed might die!- Fly, &c. (39)

The god of the Vedas four, the Lord of the sacrifice,
Fell; sing how he sought the way they went!- Fly aloft, Unthi!
And Purandharan, too, in the offering!-Fly, &c. (42)

The teeth in the mouth of the Sun-god
How He swept them broken away!-Fly aloft, Unthi!
The sacrifice came to confusion!-Fly, &c. (45)

Dakshan that day lost his head;
Tho' Dakshan's children stood round!-Fly aloft, Unthi!
Perished the sacrifice!- Fly, &c. (48)

III. Ubamanya.

Who that day to the son gave the sea of milk;
To the glorious Lord of the braided lock,-Fly aloft, Unthi!
To Kumaran's father, - Fly, &c. (51)

IV. Brahma.

The Four-faced's head, who sits on the beauteous flower,
Was quickly nipt off!-Fly aloft, Unthi!

171

By His nail was nipt off!- Fly, &c. (54)

V. Ravana.

His heads who stayed the car, and raised the hill,-
Sing how twice five of them perished!-Fly aloft, Unthi!
And twenty perished!-Fly, &c. (57)

Hymn XV- tiru tonokkam

Metre : Naladittaravu koccuk kalippA

There is an amusing illustration drawn by a native artist, of
this game as played in South India. Its name literally means
'aiming at the shoulder,' for it ends up with placing the hands
of each opposing pair on the shoulders of the other. In some
lines this is used as a symbol of the approach of the soul to
Civan's feet.

I. The cleansing from delusion.

The demon-car allures: 'a stream flowing from flowery lake,'
Men think, and rush to draw, in ignorance and folly lost!
Thou hast such fond delusions far removed, O Dancer blest
In shining Tillai's court! As we Thy roseate Foot would reach,

PLAY WE TONOKKAM! (4)

II.

The Lord of Tillai's court, whose glory never wanes;
Whom 'he who hurled the calf at fruit,' and Brahma could not
see;
Lest I in endless births and deaths should sink, made me His
own;
Praising His excellence, ye maids with thickly clusterig locks,
PLAY WE TONOKKAM! (8)

III. Kannappar.

As in the worship paid true ministrations HE discerned:-
The glorious slippered-foot, the chalice-mouth, the flesh for
food;-
Such gifts acceptance gained! He knew the woodman's pure
desire;
And as the saint stood there, with joyous mind, fulfilled of
grace,
PLAY WE TONOKKAM! (12)

IV.

So that my stony heart was melted, He all tenderly
Compassionate stood by, and came within my soul in grace,
Led me in way of good; and then, as all the country knows,
He here drew nigh, spake with me face to face; and thus
PLAY WE TONOKKAM! (16)

V. God manifold, yet One.

Earth, water, fire, air, ether vast, the wandering moon, the
sun,

And man, - to sense revealed: EIGHT WAYS He joined Himself
to me;
Throughout seven worlds, in regions ten, He moves: yet One
alone
Is He! As manifold He comes and 'bides with us; and so
PLAY WE TONOKKAM! (20)

VI. Various sectaries.

Buddhists, and others,- in their wisdom fools,- the men of
many sects,
All with their systems worthless and outworn, bewildered
stand;-
My every power He fills with bliss superne, makes all life's
works
Devotion true,-through His compassion, FATHER seen! And
thus
PLAY WE TONOKKAM! (24)

VII. Candecuvara Nayanar.

The Neophyte from evil free, cut off the feet of him
Who rashly overturned the work in Civan's honour done:
A Brahman he in caste, His father too! Through Ican's grace,
While gods adored, his crime was utterly consumed; and thus
PLAY WE TONOKKAM! (28)

The Legend of Candecuvara Nayanar: The Young Brahman
Cowherd.- In a town in the Cora country, called Ceynalur, a
Brahman boy was born, whose name was Vicara-carumar,
who from his earliest days instinctively understood the whole

Caiva creed; so that when the sages came to instruct him he met them with the recitation of the essential doctrines of the system, which he had grasped by a divine intuition. It may be permitted to repeat the articles of his creed, as these are summed up in the legend: 'All souls are from everlasting fast bound in the chains of impurity. To destroy that impurity, and to give to these souls infinite felicity and eternal release, He who is eternal is revealed. He performs the five Acts of creation, preservation, destruction, "envelopment," and gracious deliverance. He is the one Lord (Pathi), Who possesses the eight attributes of absolute independence, purity of form, spontaneous understanding, absolute knowledge, natural freedom from all bonds, infinite grace, endless might, and boundless blessedness. His name is Civan, the Great Lord. He performs his gracious acts by putting forth the energy (Catti), Who, as a person, is one with Him, and is therefore the divine Mother of all, as He is the divine Father, and must with Him be loved and worshipped. Nor can we say "we will do this in some future birth," for we are born here as human beings for this and no other purpose; and the human form in the infinite series of transmigration is hard to attain unto. Nor should we defer till to-morrow our dedication of ourselves, since we know not the day of our death. Therefore must we avail ourselves of Civan's gift of grace, studying the sacred Agamas and other works, without doubting, or commingling of perverse interpretation. This is the WAY of life!

One day, together with his school companions, he went down to the bank of the river where the village cows were grazing in charge of a man of the herdsman caste. This rustic, having no sense of right and wrong, beat one of the cows with a stick; but Vicara-carumar was vehemently stirred by this outrage, and rushing up to him in great wrath, restrained him from striking the sacred animal: 'Know you not,' said he, 'that cows have come down from the world of Civan to this earth? In their members the gods, the sages, and the sacred purifying stream dwell. The five products of these sacred creatures are the sacred unguents of Civan. And the ashes which are the adornment of the God and his devotees are made from their refuse!' Dwelling upon this idea he conceived a desire to devote himself entirely to the task of herding and caring for the troop of sacred cows; and accordingly sent away the rustic, who reverentially departed. And thus our hero became a self-dedicated Brahman. As such he easily obtains permission of all the Brahmans of the town to take charge of their cows, and daily along the bank of the beautiful river Manni, he leads forth his troop in the green pastures, allowing them peacefully to graze their fill, and supplying them with drinking water. When the fierce heat of the sun oppresses, he leads them into the shady groves, and guards them well, meanwhile gathering the firewood necessary for his household worship; and then at evening, leaving each cow at its owner's door, he goes to his home. While things went on in this manner, the cows increased daily in beauty, waxed fat, were joyous, and by day and night poured forth abundant streams of milk for their owners. The Brahmans found that they had more milk than formerly for their offerings and were glad. The cows, tended with such solicitude, were brisk and cheerful, and though separated for awhile from their calves that remained tied up in the houses, grieved not a whit, but with joy awaited the coming of their young herdsman, following him gladly, crowding around him like tender mothers, and lowing joyfully at the sound of his voice. The youthful Brahman, seeing the exuberance of their milk, reflected that this was a fitting unction for the head of the God; and conceiving a great desire so to employ it, constructed a lingam of earth on a little mound beneath the sacred Atti tree on the bank of the river, and built around it a miniature temple with tower and walls. He then plucked suitable flowers, and with them adorning the image, procured some new vessels of clay, and took from each of the cows a little milk, with which he performed the unction prescribed for the divine emblem (the Lingam); and Civan, the Supreme, looked down and received with pleasure the boy-shepherd's guideless worship. All essentials of the sacred service he supplied by the force of his imagination. Though this was done daily, the supply of milk in the Brahman's dairy was no whit diminished.

For a long time this continued, until some malicious person saw what was going on, and told it to the Brahmans in the village, who convened an assembly before which they summoned the boy's father, and told him that his son Vicara-caramar was wasting the milk of the Brahmans' sacred cows by pouring it idly on the earth in sport. The father feared greatly when he heard the accusation, but protested his entire ignorance of the waste and democration, and asking pardon, engaged to put a stop to his son's eccentric practices. Accordingly the next day he went forth to watch the boy's proceedings, and hid himself in a thicket on the bank of the river. He soon saw his little son ceremonionaly bathe in the river, and then proceed to his minutine of Civa-worship, and then pouring a stream of anointing milk over the earthern lingam. Thus convinced of the truth of the accusation, he was

greatly incensed, and rushing forth from his concealment
inflicted severe blows upon the boy, and used many
reproachful words. But the young devotee's mind was so
absorbed in the worship,- so full of the rupture of mystic
devotion,- that he neither perceived his father's presence,
nor heard his words, nor felt his blows. Still more incensed by
the boy's insensibility, the infatuated father raised his foot,
broke the vessels of consecrated milk, and destroyed the
whole apparatus of worship! This was too much for the
young enthusuast to bear; the god of his adoration was
insulted, and the sacred worship defiled. He regarded not the
fact that it was his father, a Brahman and a guru, who was
the offender; but only saw the heinous sin and insult to
Civan. So with the staff in his hands he aimed a blow at the
offender's feet, as if to cut them off; and, behold, the
shepherd's staff became in his hands the Sacred Axe of Civan,
and the father fell maimed and dying to the ground. The
enthusiastic boy then went on with his worship as if nothing
had occured, but the Lord Civan, with Umai, the goddess,
riding on the sacred White Bull, immediately appeared
hovering in the air. The young devotee prostrated himself
before the holy vision in an ecstasy of joy; when the Supreme
One took him up in his divine arms, saying, 'For my sake thou
hast smiten down the father that begat thee. Henceforth I
alone am thy father,' and embracing him stroked his body
with His sacred hand, and kissed him on the brow. The form
of the child thus touched by the divine hand shone forth with
ineffable lustre, and the God further addressed him thus:
"Thou shalt become the chief among my servants, and to
thee shall be given all the offerings of food and flowers that
my worshippers on Kailaca's mountain present.' His name

there upon became Candecuvarar ('the impetuous Lord'). The manifested God finally took the mystic cassia-wreath from His Own head, and with it crowned the youthful saint. And so he ascended to heaven with Civan, and was exalted to that divine rank. The father too, who had been guilty in his ignorance of such impiety to the God, and had been punished by the hand of his own son, was forgiven, restored, and with the whole family passed into Civan's abode of bliss.

VIII.

Our pride is gone, forgotten reason's laws; ye maidens fair!
We think but of the cinctured foot of Him, Lord of the south,
Whom heaven adores! The rapturous Dancer's grace if we obtain,
His slaves,- even so in rapture lost, we then shall dance; and thus
PLAY WE TONOKKAM! (32)

IX.

The Three in story famed, of giant race, escaped the fire,
And guardians stand before my 'Brow-eyed' Father's door; since when,
Indras beyond compute, and Brahmas (who can count the sum?)
Behold! And many Mals, too, on this earth have died; and thus
PLAY WE TONOKKAM! (36)

X. Vishnu's devotion and reward

From out a thousand lotus flowers one flower was wanting
still;-
His eye Mal straight dug out, and placed on Aran's foot, our
Lord!
To Him then Cankaran forthwith the mighty discus gave,-
A gracious recompense. Thus everywhere extolling Him,
PLAY WE TONOKKAM! (40)

XI. The Bhairava.

Kaman his body lost, Kalan his life, the fiery Sun his teeth,
The Goddess of the tongue her nose, Brahma a head, Agni his
hand,
The Moon his crescent, Dakshan, Eccan too, a head they lost.
These holy deeds in righteous wrath He wrought; and thus
PLAY WE TONOKKAM! (44)

XII. Arunacalam.

Brahma and Hari through their foolishness said each:
'The Deity! the Deity supreme am I;'
To quell their swelling pride, Aran in form of lustrous fire,
In grandeur measureless stood forth, the Infinite; and thus
PLAY WE TONOKKAM! (48)

XIII. A wasted life.

Poor servile worshipper,- how many, many a time
I've watered barren soil,- not worshipping the Lord Supreme!
The Eternal-First, th' imperishable flawless Gem, to me

Came down; and bar of my 'embodiment' destroyed; and
thus
PLAY WE TONOKKAM! (52)

XIV. Deliverance.

The inner Light, past speech, the Worthiest entered within
My soul, and brought me through lust's mighty sea that
knows no shore,
And then the craving senses' sateless vultures routed fled!
Sing how a royal path in glory was made plain; and thus
PLAY WE TONOKKAM! (56)
Hymn XVI- tirup ponnusal

THE SACRED GOLDEN SWING
or
PURIFICATION BY GRACE

I.

Let precious coral be the posts, strung pearls the ropes,
Pure gold the beauteous seats,- Mount we, and sweetly sing
The flow'ry Foot Narayanan knew not, to me
His currish slave in Uttara-koca-mangai given
As home, Ambrosial grace, that never palls, His feet impart.
Ye guileless, bright-eyed ones, MOVE WE THE GOLDEN
SWING! (6)

II.

Three gleaming eyes His face displays; His flow'ry feet

The gods that dwell in heaven and grow not old, see not;
In Uttara-koca-mangai seen, in flesh abides
The King, while honied sweetness of ambrosia flows.
Sing Idai-maruthu, His home! O ye like peafowl rare,
Whose walk hath swanlike grace, MOVE WE THE GOLDEN
SWING! (12)

III.

He Who no end and no beginning knows,- while saints
A multitude, and countless heavenly ones, stood round,-
His sacred ashes gave in grace; and mercy's tide
Flow'd there: sing Uttara-koca-mangai's gemlike home
Of palaces, with terrace high, where lightnings play!
Maids, bright with gems and gold, MOVE WE THE GOLDEN
SWING! (18)

IV.

His throat the poison holds; Lord of the heavenly ones;
To Uttara-koca-mangai's gemlike cloud-capped heights
He came, with Her whose words are music; fill'd the mind
Of us His slaves, ambrosial sweetness gave and grace
That cuts off 'death and birth'! His holy praises sing!
Ye who wear store of bracelets bright, MOVE WE THE
GOLDEN SWING! (24)

V.

The god, Whose form the Two might not discriminate;
In tender mercy, that the god's assembled band

Might not know shame, but 'scape, made them His own, and
poison ate
As food: He, Uttara-koca-mangai's Dancer, crowned
With crescent of the moon. Praise we His worth! O ye
With jewell'd bosoms fair, AND MOVE THE GOLDEN SWING!
(30)

VI.

The Lady's Half is He; His braided lock with flow'ry cassia
dight
In Utt'ra-koca-mangai 'midst his saints He dwells.
He freed my soul from sin; made me, a cur, His own;
From 'birth's old ill' His glorious coming saves.
His pendant ear-rings' swing sing we with melting love, O ye
With flower-crown'd bosoms fair, AND MOVE THE GOLDEN
SWING! (36)

VII.

He dwells in beauty, Lord of the great mystic word,
Of Utt'ra-koca-mangai shrine, past thought; His praise
Who sing, and worship, and bow down, He frees from bonds
of sin.
As gem-bright peafowl moving beauteous, on a swan,
My Father came, and made me His! His beauty sing,
Ye with gold adorned, AND MOVE THE GOLDEN SWING! (42)

VIII.

From glorious mountain height to earth He came,

Ate plenteous food, arose upon the lower seas,
In magic form upon a charger rode, and made us His;
In sacred Uttara-koca-mangai where His virtue shines,
With loud acclaim Him whom Mal could not reach we praise,
And while our full hearts melt, MOVE WE THE GOLDEN
SWING! (48)

IX.

In sacred Uttara-koca-mangai's groves of cocoa-palm
He came, in form unique a gracious light shone forth;
Our 'birth' He caused to cease, made such as us His own;
The Queen His Partner, and Himself, received our homage
due;
We sing His worth Whose crest breathes cassia's sweet
perfume;
Ye maids, whose jewell'd bosoms heave, MOVE WE THE
GOLDEN SWING! (54)
Hymn XVII- Annai pathu

THE MOTHER-DECAD
or
'SOUL'S PLENITUDE.'

Metre: kavi viruttam

I.

'His word is the Vedam; ashes white He wears;
Rose-red is His form; His drum is the Natham;
MOTHER!' SAITH SHE.

'His drum is the Natham; to the Four-faced,
And to Mal too, this Lord is the Lord;
MOTHER!' SAITH SHE. (4)

II.

'His eye gleams black; He is compassion's sea;
Within He dwells, He melts the soul,
MOTHER!' SAITH SHE.
'Within He dwells, and to the melting soul
Tears of undying bliss gives He,
MOTHER!' SAITH SHE. (8)

III.

'Th' eternal Bridegroom, He in minds devout
Abides with perfect beauty crown'd;
MOTHER!' SAITH SHE.
'In minds devout abides, the southern Lord,
Perun-turrai's Sire; the Blissful;
MOTHER!' SAITH SHE. (12)

IV.

'A dancing snake His jewel, tiger-skin His robe.
A form with ashes smeared He wears;
MOTHER!' SAITH SHE.
'The form He wears whence'er I see and gaze,
My soul within me faints, why this?
MOTHER!' SAITH SHE. (16)

V.

'Long are His outstretch'd arms; loose flow His locks;
Lord of the goodly Pandiyan land;
MOTHER!' SAITH SHE.
'Lord of the goodly Pandi land, He rules
My wandering thoughts, and shows His love;
MOTHER!' SAITH SHE. (20)

VI.

'Whose glory none may know in Uttara-mangai 'bides;
He in my heart and soul abides;
MOTHER!' SAITH SHE.
'He in my heart abides, Whom Mal and Ayan
Could not see! How wondorous strange!
MOTHER!' SAITH SHE. (24)

VII.

'White is His steed, and white His shaven head;
He wears the sleeper's mystic dress.
MOTHER!' SAITH SHE.
'Wearing the sleeper's dress, a prancing steed
He rides, and steals away my soul,
MOTHER!' SAITH SHE. (28)

VIII.

'He wears the twining-wreath; the sandal paste
He smears; He rules and makes us His,

MOTHER!' SAITH SHE.
'He makes us His; in lowly servants' hands,
Hark, how the lordly servants' hands,
MOTHER!' SAITH SHE. (32)

IX.

'The fair One's Half, ascetic's garb He wears,
Enters our homes an alms to ask,
MOTHER!' SAITH SHE.
'He ent'ring alms to ask, my inmost soul
In sorrow sinks; wherefore is this?
MOTHER!' SAITH SHE. (36)

X.

'Cassia, the moon, the vilva flower, and wild
Phrenzies crowd thick His head,
MOTHER!' SAITH SHE.
'The vilva flower that crowns His sacred brow
Wild phrenzy bringeth me to-day,
MOTHER!' SAITH SHE. (40)
Hymn XVIII- Kuyil pathu

THE KUYIL-DECAD

The Kuyil is often referred to in these poems. Our Sage, like
St. Francis of Assisi, was exceedingly fond of birds, and
indeed was filled with love for the whole creation. In this
poem he calls upon the Kuyil to join him in the praises of his
Master, recounting the chief themes on which he was wont

to dilate. The epithets applied to the Kuyil are skilfully varied; it is pictured to us as a diminutive bird haunting the leafy groves; of a dark azure hue with a golden tint; as uttering a sweet call of a peculiarly tender kind; as possessed of a beauty gladdening the eye; and as imparting pleasure to all that hear its inviting notes. Mystically the Kuyil is the human soul.

The Kuyil (or Kokila: Eudynamys indicus) is found in all parts of the peninsula of India, and is a great favourite with the people. Its somewhat monotonous cry is more appreciated by the natives of the East than by those of the West, yet it is not unpleasing, - in moderation. Its note is sweet and plaintive. It must not be confounded with the English cuckoo, though it is of the same species, and not unlike it in some particulars.

I. Civan's infinity.

O KUYIL, sweet of song, if thou dost seek our Peruman to know;
If thou would'st ask of His twain feet; they're planted'neath the sevenfold gulf.
Would'st hear of His bright jewell'd crown? 'Tis glory old that passes speech.
Nor origin, nor qualities hath He, nor end; CALL HIM TO COME! (4)

II. His grace to Mandodari.

Him the fair sevenfold world extols,- since every being's form
is His;-
In southern sea-girt Lanka He, the Lord Who Perun-turrai
owns,
Vandothari the beautiful, made glad with His abounding
grace!
KUYIL, the southern Pandi Chief, CALL HITHER with thy voice
divine! (8)

III. In His capital.

KUYIL with form of azure hue! In Uttara-koca-mangai's
shrine,
Where bright the sacred temple stands, whose storied
tenements rise decked with gems,
One with the graceful Lady's flower-like form in virtue
sweetly rich He dwells,-
The loving Lord by whom the world grows bright,- go thou,
and HITHER CALL! (12)

IV. His voluntary humiliation.

Thou KUYIL small, that dost frequent the grove with sweet
fruit rich, hear this!
The Gracious-One Who left the heavens, enter'd this earth,
made men His own;
The Only-One, despised the flesh, entered my soul, and fills
my thought;-
The Bridegroom of the Fawn-eyed-one that gently rules,- GO
HITHER CALL! (16)

V. His gracious appearing.

KUYIL, whose beauty is delight! Like sun with circling radiant
beams,
Through upper heaven come down, He frees His saints from
thrall of low desire;
The First, the Midst, the End is He;- the Three knew not His
sacred form;-
His feet are bright with crimson glow;-the mighty Warrior
CALL TO COME! (20)

VI. The manifestation in Madura.

KUYIL, glad pleasure give I Thee! the sevenfold worlds He
rules;-
The Loving-One ambrosia gives;- the Blissful-God came down
from heaven,
And on the goodly charger rode like jewel set in ruddy gold.
KUYIL, 'mid branches twittering, Gokari's Lord GO, CALL TO
COME! (24)

VII. The monarch of the Tamil lands.

KUYIL, I'll joy in thee, and be thy comrade, ever by the side;-
Him of the beauteous form Who shines, more choice than
gold, in glory bright;
The King, Who on the horse in splendour rode, in Perun-
turrai dwells!-
The Southern-One, the Ceran, Coran, great Buyangan, CALL
TO COME! (28)

VIII. Arunacalam.

O tender KUYIL, come thou here! Mal sought Him, and the
'Four-faced'-one,
Nor found, then ceased, and pondering stood. Cleaving the
heaven, in shining fire,
Beyond all worlds He rose that day, His body like the light
rayed out.
On prancing steed a groom He rode; CALL Him with
streaming lock TO COME! (32)

IX. The gracious initiation.

KUYIL, thy dark form gleams with gold; thou in the fragrant
grove dost joy!
The Blest, Whose glorious form is bright as splendour of the
lotus red,
On earth, showed us His feet; set free from every bond, and
made me His.
The beauteous cinctured golden Form,th' Ambrosial-One, GO
CALL TO COME! (36)

X. His manifestation as a guru.

Hear this, thou KUYIL, calling 'midst the grove whose shady
boughs enlace!
A Brahman here He came, revealed His beauteous rosy feet
to me.
'This man is one of us,' He said, and here in grace made me
His own!

The LORD OF GODS, Whose sacred form is as red fire, GO BID
TO COME!
Hymn XIX- tiruththa saangam

THE SACRED TEN SIGNS: THE ROYAL INSIGNIA

I. The Name of the King.

'Parrot fair and tender! soothly tell the glorious Name
Of Perun-turrai's King!'- 'Lord of Arur,- the ruddy Prince,-
The White-flower-god,-and he of the milky sea praised Him
thus:
Name we our Peruman, the PRINCE OF GODS!' (4)

II. King Civan's Land.

'O Emerald, whose blameless speech is sweet! The LAND
declare
Owned by the Lord of all the sevenfold world, Whose own we
are.'
'He rules His loving ones in love, and gives unfailing grace,
His LAND is aye the southern PANDI realm! (8)

III. The city of the King.

'O babbling bird, dweller in flowery grove with fragrance
filled!
What is the TOWN where dwells our Lord, the partner of the
Queen?'
'The CITY Uttara-koca-mangai named by men devout
And true, as Civa-town on earth is prais'd! (12)

IV. The King's River

'Red-mouth'd, green-wing'd bright bird! Tell us the RIVER of
the Sire
Who makes His home within our heart, great Perun-turrai's
King!'
'O maid, the Master's RIVER is the rapture sent from heaven,
Come down, the foulness of our mind to cleanse.' (16)

V. The Mountain of the King.

'O parrot purple-mouth'd! Tell me the ever-during MOUNT'
Of Perun-turrai's King, that hides its head in clouds.' -'O maid,
Behold and study well,-His MOUNT is bliss of sweet
"RELEASE";
Where the soul's darkness flees, and light shines forth.' (20)

VI. The King's Courser.

'Come hither, parrot mine! and tell, before thou sek'st thy
cage,
The Lord of matchless glory, what rides He?'-'He joyous rides
Upon the COURSES of the sky;- with honied thought the
maids
Divine attending chaunt melodious praise!' (24)

VII. The King's Weapon.

'Parrot whose words are honey from the bough! What
WEAPON pray

O'ercomes the foes of Perun-turrai's blameless King?'
'The triple WEAPON that He wields, transfixes threefold sin,
Causing the souls from malice free to melt.' (28)

VIII. The King's Drum.

'Parrot, whose words as milk are sweet, tell me the martial
DRUM
That awful sounds before our Perun-turrai's King!'-' In love
It bids the foe of "birth" confounded flee,- and makes arise
All bliss of heaven: the joyous NATHA-DRUM.' (32)

IX.The King's Garland.

'Parrot, whose word is music, say what is the GARLAND worn
By Perun-turrai's LORD, Who dwells in hearts where love
wells up?'-
'Who owns me, worthless cur, and daily wards off "evil
deeds,"-
He wears as WREATH the Tali-arrugu.' (36)

X. The King's Banner.

'Green parrot of the grove declare, what BANNER glorious
waves
Above the King of Perun-turrai's waters pure?'- 'Aloft
The stainless BANNER of the bull resplendent gleams
In beauty manifest, while foes flee far.' (40)
Hymn XX- tirupalli yezuchi

MORNING HYMN IN THE TEMPLE

or
THE ROUSING FROM THE SACRED COUCH

'THE FREEDOM OF THE UPLIFTED SOUL.'

I.

Hail! Being, Source to me of all life's joys! 'Tis dawn;
upon Thy flower-like feet twin wreaths of blooms we lay,
And worship, 'neath the beauteous smile of grace benign
that from Thy sacred face beams on us. Civa-Lord,
Who dwell'st in Perun-turrai girt with cool rice-fields,
where 'mid the fertile soil th' expanding lotus blooms!
Thou on Whose lifted banner is the Bull! Master!
Our mighty Lord! FROM OFF THY COUCH IN GRACE ARISE! (4)

The image of the god is laid upon a couch each evening, and
taken up in the morning. This reveille is the first business of
the day. This was composed in Perun-turrai, 'the great
harbour,' where the poet went to buy horses for his King, and
was made a disciple. The bull is Civan's emblem. He rides on
a white bull. It is also on his banner. The bull-headed Nandi,
whose image is everywhere in South India, is his Lord High
Chamberlain.

II.

The sun has neared the eastern bound; darkness departs;
dawn broadens out; and, like that sun, the tenderness
Of Thy blest face's flower uprising shines; and so,
while bourgeons forth the fragrant flower of Thine eyes'
beam,

Round the King's dwelling fair hum myriad swarms of bees.
See, Civa-Lord, in Perun-turrai's hallowed shrine Who
dwell'st!
Mountain of bliss, treasures of grace Who com'st to yield!
O surging Sea! FROM OFF THY COUCH IN GRACE ARISE! (8)

III.

The tender Kuyil's note is heard; the cocks have crowed;
the little birds sing out; sound loud the tuneful shells;
Starlights have paled; day's lights upon the eastern hill
are mustering. In favouring love O show to us
Thy twin feet, anklet-decked, divinely bright;-
Civa-Lord, in Perun-turrai's hallowed shrine Who dwell'st!
Thee all find hard to know; easy to us Thine own!
Our mighty Lord! FROM OFF THY COUCH IN GRACE ARISE!
(12)

IV.

There stand the players on the sweet-voiced lute and lyre;
there those that utter praises with the Vedic chaunt;
There those whose hands bear wreaths of flowers entwined;
there those that bend, that weep, in ecstasy that faint;
There those that clasp above their heads adoring hands;-
Civa-Lord, in Perun-turrai's hallowed shrine Who dwell'st!
Me too make Thou Thine own, on me sweet grace bestow!
Our mighty Lord! FROM OFF THY COUCH IN GRACE ARISE!
(16)

V.

'Thou dwell'st in all the elements,' 'tis said; and yet
'Thou goest not, nor com'st;' the sages thus have sung
Their rhythmic songs. Though neither have we heard nor
learnt
of those that Thee by seeing of the eye have known.
Thou King of Perun-turrai, girt with cool rice-fields,
to ponder Thee is hard to human thought. To us
In presence come! Cut off our ills! In mercy make us Thine!
Our mighty Lord! FROM OFF THY COUCH IN GRACE ARISE!
(20)

VI.

Thy saints, who sinless in Thy home abide and know,
have come, their bonds cast off; and now, a mighty host,
With beauteous garlands decked, and clothed in human
shape,
they all adore Thee, Bridegroom of the Goddess dread!
Civa-Lord, Who dwell'st in Perun-turrai's hallow'd shrine,
girt with cool rice-fields, where th' empurpled lotus blooms!
Cut off this 'birth', make us Thine own, bestow Thy grace!
Our mighty Lord! FROM OFF THY COUCH IN GRACE ARISE!
(24)

VII.

'The flavour of the fruit is that;' 'ambrosia that;'
'that's hard;' 'this easy:' thus Immortals too know not!
'This is His sacred form; this is Himself:' that we
may say and know, make us Thine own; in grace arise!

In Uttara-koca-mangai's' sweet perfumed groves
Thou dwell'st! O King of Perun-turrai's hallowed shrine!
What service Thou demandest, Lo! we willing pay.
Our mighty Lord! FROM OFF THY COUCH IN GRACE ARISE!
(28)

VIII.

Before all being First, the Midst, the Last art Thou.
The Three know not Thy nature: how should others know?
Thou, with Thy tender Spouse, Thy servants' lowly huts
in grace didst visit, entering each, Supernal One!
Like ruddy fire Thou once didst show Thy sacred form;
didst show me Perun-turrai's temple, where Thou dwell'st;
As Anthanan didst Thyself, and make me Thine.
Ambrosia rare! FROM OFF THY COUCH IN GRACE ARISE! (32)

IX.

The gods in heaven who dwell may not approach Thy seatt!
O Being worthiest! Yet us who at Thy foot.
Pay homage, Thou to earth descending, madest blest.
Dweller in fertile Perun-turrai's shrine! our eyes
Beheld Thee; honied sweetness made our being glad.
Ambrosia of the sea! Sweetest of sweets! Thou art
Within Thy longing servants' thought! -Soul of this world!-
Our mighty Lord! FROM OFF THY COUCH IN GRACE ARISE!
(36)

X.

Said sacred Mal and flower-born Ayan as they gazed
on Civan's form, 'This day in vain we spend and cry.
'Tis time we went to earth and there were born. 'Tis earth,
'tis earth alone where Civan's grace is wont to save.'
Thou King, Who dwell'st in Perun-turrai's hallow'd shrine,
mighty Thou wert to enter earth, and make us Thine!
Thou and the Grace, that flower-like blooms from forth Thy
form,
Ambrosia rare! FROM OFF THY COUCH IN GRACE ARISE! (40)
Hymn XXI- koyin muutha tirupathikam

THE ANCIENT SACRED TEMPLE-SONG
or
'ETERNAL REALITY.'

I.

The Mistress dwells in midmost of Thyself;
within the Mistress centred dwellest Thou;
Midst of Thy servant if Ye Both do dwell,
to me Thy servant ever give the grace
Amidst Thy lowliest servants to abide;
our Primal Lord, Whose Being knows no end,
Who dwellest in the sacred golden porch,
still present to fulfil my heart's intent!
(4)

II. I have not swerved

E'erwhile in presence here Thou mad'st me Thine;
and I even so to be with effort strain:

I follow Thee, and Thy behests fulfil;
but still I here behind am left, great Lord!
If Thou appear not now in grace, and bid
me come, will not Thy servants doubting say,
'And who was he that stood erewhile with Thee,'
Who joyest in the golden hall to dance? (8)

III.

'He joy'd erewhile in loving service done,'-
if I, with heart of feeling reft made hard
By grief, complain, for all the world to know,-
will they not say, 'This is no fitting thing?'
Thy faithful ones, the sacrifice performed,
now dwell in bliss with Thee, and Thou with them.
If Thou Thy face to me turn not, I die,-
life's SOurce, Who dwellest in the golden court! (12)

IV.

Thou Source of All! Guide to the senses five;
and to the Three; to me, too, in life's way!
Thine ancient servants' thronging multitude
is gathered now within the heavenly courts.
Fount of all brightness! Thou hast given them grace;
shall I not cry, 'To me show pity too?'
And so I weep,- what other can I do?-
Thou King of Tillai's sacred court of gold! (16)

V.

'King, Dancer in the golden court,
Ambrosia,' - looking for Thy grace,- I cry.
Like patient heron watching for its prey,
by night and day, I drooping 'bide and mourn
Thy saints have reached the shore,- in joy they shine;
to me if Thou deny that vision bright,-
Like butter hidden in the curdled milk,;(br>
still silent, will not they reproach? (20)

VI.

Even they will heap reproach upon my name,
revile, and scoffing point me out as Thine;
While others all will utter various speech;
but I will cherish yearnings for Thy grace.
Teacher!- that I amid Thy loving ones
may render service in the sacred hall,-
Faher!- Who dances in the golden court,-
henceforth, O ruler, pity show to me! (24)

VII.

'Show pity, Dancer in the golden court,'
with ever-yearning soul I pray. Of old,
Rare teaching didst Thou give, and mad'st me Thine!
Shall I become mere beast, with none to own?
Thy saints around Thee throng, where Thou and they,
in happy sport commingled, ever dwell.
That I may thither rise to join the band,
our only Bliss, in grace O bid me come! (28)

VIII. Whom have I save Thee?

Grace if Thou show not to Thy servant, who
is here to bid me cast away my fears?
All gold, Thou entering here, mad'st me Thine own,
as thing of worth; Dancer in court of gold!
Me, from Thee severed, with bewildered mind,
and troubled sore, ah! bid to come to Thee.
If Thou show not Thy glorious fellowhip,
I die; and then will not men scoff? (32)

IX. The joys of Civan's paradise.

They smile, they joy, honied delights they quaff,
in thronging crowds Thy words expound and hear,
And loud extol. Then each apart repeats
the saving mystery of Thy sacred Name.
'Our Head, Who dancest in the golden court,'
they cry. before these blessed ones, shall I
Like dog, that jackals chase and scare, remain?
My Teacher, even now bestow Thy grace!

X. Let not my trust be vain!

'He will not cease to pour on us His gifts,'-
thus have I raving named Thy Name,
My eyes with tears were fill'd,- my praising mouth
falter'd,- I bow'd, - in thought with melting soul
Many a time Thine image I recalled,-
and uttering praises named the golden court.
My Master, grant Thy grace to me, and oh!

have pity on the soul that pines for Thee! (36)
Hymn XXII- koyitr trirupathikam

THE SACRED TEMPLE-LYRIC.

[AN ANAPHORETIC DECAD.]
'THE CHARACTERISTICS OF SACRED ENJOYMENT.'

I. Show me Thy Face.

With changing wiles the senses five bewilder me:
their course Thou dost close up, Ambrosial Fount!
Come, Light Suprene, that ever springing fill'st my soul!
and give me grace to see Thee as Thou art.
Essential Sweetness pure! O mighty Civa-Peruman,
Who dwell'st in Perun-turrai's sacred shrine!
O Thou, the bliss all endless happy stations yield,
transcending far, my Pleasure and my LOVE! (4)

II. Praise for grace imparted

In LOVE, Thy servant's soul and body thrilling through,
and melting all my heart with rapturous bliss,
Thou hast bestowed sweet grace beyond my being's powers;-
and I for this have no return to give!
Thou art before! Thou art behind! Thou art the Free,
through all diffus'd! Thou First, without and end!
South--Perun-turrai's Lord! O Clva-Peruman!
Civa-Puram's ever-glorious KING! (8)

III.Inspire me to feel and utter the very truth regarding Thee.

O KING, the slave of Thine own loving ones am I.
Father! not soul alone but body too,
Thou enterest melting, and with sweetness fill'st each pore.
Thou dost disperse false darkness, O true Light!
Ambrosial Sea, whose clearness knows no ruffling wave!
Civan, Who dwell'st in Perun-turrai's shrine! Thou Thought
unique, thinking what passes word and thought!
teach me to KNOW the way to speak of Thee! (12)

IV.

Sages that KNOW all else; the heav'nly ones and all
the others, scarce can KNOW Thee, Being rare!
Life of all lives, with none confused! My healing Balm,
that from 'Embodiments' my spirit frees!
Pure Light, clear shining 'mid the darkness dense!
Civan, Who dwell'st in Perun-turrai's shrine!
O Bliss, of qualities devoid! Henceforth to me,
who have to Thee drawn nigh, what can there LACK? (16)

V.

Fulness, that knows no LACK; ambrosial Essence pure!
O unscaled mount of ever-blazing light!
Thou art the Veda,- Thou the mystic Veda's sense.
Within my mind Thou coming, 'bid'st its Lord!
As torrents burst their bounds, Thou rushest through my
soul!
Civan, Who dwell'st in Perun-turrai's shrine!
O King, my body hast Thou made Thine home; henceforth

what blessings shall Thy suppliant ASK of Thee? (20)

VI.

That I may ever ASK and melt, within my mind,
O Light, Thou dost arise! In beauty shines
On heavenly heads the lotus of Thy roseate feet!
Civan, who dwell'st in Perun-turrai's shrine!
The boundless ether, water, earth, fire, air;- all these
Thou art; and none of these Thou art; but dwell'st
In these conceal'd, O formless One! My heart is glad
that with these eves THIS DAY I've seen Thee clear! (24)

VII.

THIS DAY on me in grace Thou risest bright, a Sun,
bidding from out my mind the darkness flee!
That thought may cease upon Thy nature manifest,
I think. Beside Thee all that is is nought,-
Moving ever,- as atoms ever wasting,- Thou art One!
Civan, Who dwell'st in Perun-turrrai's shrine!
Thou art not anything; without Thee nothing is;
who are they that can know Thee as Thou art? (28)

VIII.

Expanse of light, that everywhere through every world,
o'er earth and heaven springs forth and spread alone !
Thou Fire in water hid! O Pure One, if of Thee
we think, Thou'rt hard to reach. Fountain of grace,
Upsprining in the thought devout, as honey sweet!

Civan, in Perun-turrai's sacred shrine
Who dwell'st,- who are my kindered here, and strangers
who?
my LIGHT. Thou changest all to rapturous joy! (32)

IX.

O Form, beheld in radiant LIGHT made manifest;
Thou only Mystic Ones Who wear'st no form;
Thou First! Thou Midst! Thou Last! Great Sea of rapturous
joy!
Thou that dost loose our being's bonds!
Thou sacred Hill of grace and good, from evil free!
Civan in sacred Perun-turrai's shrine
Who dwell'st! There is no way for Thee to part from me!
Come, GIVE to me worship at Thy feet! (36)

X.

What Thou hast GIVEN is THEE; and what hast gained is ME:
O Cankara, who is the knowing one?
I have obtained the rapturous bliss that knows no end;
yet now, what one thing hast Thou gained from me?
Our Peruman, Who for Thy shrine hast ta'en my thought!
Civan, Who dwell'st in Perun-turrai's courts!
My Father, and my Master! Thou hast made this frame
Thine home; for this I know no meet return! (40)
Hymn XXIII- sethila pathu

WEARINESS OF LIFE

(THE INFINITY OF BLISS IN CIVAN.)

I. Sever'd from Thee I cannot live.

I, false, am sever'd from the flowr'y feet that, entering here,
made my soul melt, distilling nectar sweet.
Yet I, poor wretch, die not as yet; but, in a waking dream,
the inner purpose of my soul I've lost.
O Teacher,- King, - Great Sea of grace, - Father,- Whose
roseate form
Ayan and Mal could never come to know,-
I know not what to do, O CIVAN, Thou Who didst draw near
IN SACRED PERUN-TURRAI'S SHRINE TO DWELL! (4)

II. Still I wander here.

Ant-hills were they, and trees were they; water and air
their food; thus heavenly ones, and others too,
Were sore distress, but none Thy flow'ry feet beheld,
O King! Me, mastered with a single word,
Thou held'st erewhile. I pant not now, nor melt in mind
subdued;
I feel no love devout; this loveless frame
I've not subdued; I wander yet, CIVAN, Who didst draw near
IN SACRED PERUN-TURRAI'S SHRINE TO DWELL! (8)

III. Where are my old joys?

Ev'n me, the meanest one, Thou didst as thing of worth
regard,
and gav'st Thy grace; and giving mad'st me glad.

I trod on air, O Rider of the Steed! _Author of good!
To all heaven's countless hosts the Dwelling-place!
Eternal One! Who atest poison from the billowy sea!
The cities of Thy foes Thou didst consume!
Bowman! -Command that I should die,- CIVAN, Who didst
draw near
AND DWELL'ST IN SACRED PERUN-TURRAI'S SHRINE! (12)

IV. Why didst Thou make me Thine?

Thy loving ones, and those who wrought hard deeds of
penitence,
Ayan and Mal too, joyous, melted then
Like wax before the fire, thinking on me; while many a one
here stood around! Why didst Thou make me Thine?
My mind was like the gnarl'd and knotted tree; like senseless
wood
my eye; harder than iron my dull ear.
Thou rul'st the south-shore! Lord of Civa-world, Who didst
draw near
IN SACRED PERUN-TURRAI'S SHRINE TO DWELL! (16)

V. I know no other gods but Thee.

I've left the law of 'sportive gods.' In love I neared Thee,
named
Thee 'Teacher';- in Thy gracious way I'll 'bide.
O Being rare,- Whom ev'n the 'earth-born gods' find out,-
that Thee
I may not quit, O Ruler, show me grace!
Show me Thy jewell'd feet, O God; body's illusions all

be by Thy grace for ever swept away.
Lord of the gods that rule the 'evolving gods'! CIVAN, our God
WHO DWELL'ST IN SACRED PERUN-TURRAI'S SHRINE! (20)

VI. I cannot endure this severance

I loose not body's bonds, nor enter fire to end the strife;
nor know the method of Thy sacred grace.
I cannot bear this 'frame'; yet way to 'scape I none discern.
Praise, praise, Thou Rider on the warlike bull!
I die not yet! sever'd from Thee what pleasure can I take?
In grace vouchsafe to bid me, 'This do thou!'
CIVAN, Who didst draw near where waters flood the fertile
fields,
AND DWELL'ST IN SACRED PERUN-TURRAI'S SHRINE! (24)

VII. I am not worthy, yet hear my voice!

Illusionst; Who at'st the poison from the refluent sea;-
heaven's Lord; our azure-throated Balm of life!
A cur, I cannot ponder Thee, nor bow me at Thy foot,
'Nama-Civaya' humbly breathing out!
Vile as a demon I, - show me Thy mighty way, Thou o'er
Whose braided lock wanders the crescent moon,-
Beseems it far from Thee I roaming weep? CIVAN, Who
cam'st
IN SACRED PERUN-TURRAI'S SHRINE TO DWELL! (28)

VIII. Can my sufferings be pleasing to Thee?

Ayan who in the lotus dwells, the Sleeper on the warring sea,

Purandaran, and all the rest, stood round.

From dregs of ill Thou mad'st me clean, showing Thy jewell'd feet;

didst give the sign, and with Thy servants join!

Then sore amazed I knew not what to do. Balm of my soul,

and is it sweet Thy servant suffer pain?

CIVAN, Who didst draw nigh where cooling waers flow around the fields,

AND DWELL'ST IN SACRED PERUN-TURRAI'S SHRINE! (32)

IX. Is there no place for me among Thy saints?

Indra, the Four-faced, and the heavenly Ones stood round,- on earth

with tender sweetness then Thou mad'st me Thine,-

Thou of the flow'ry Foot, that took the life from Death;

Ganga is Thine; the fire burns in Thy hand;

And Mal, in triumph-songs, to that same flower-foot sings;

command me too, whose eye sees not, to come!

Bright flow the flow'ry streams around the fields where CIVAN came.

IN SACRED PERUN-TURRAI'S SHRINE TO DWELL! (36)

X. I languish thinking on heavenly joys

In tender grace Thou cam'st and bad'st me come, didst banish fear;

then in Thy grace's mighty sea I plunged.

I drank, was sated; now I melt no more, - CIVAN, Who cam'st

IN SACRED PERUN-TURRAI'S SHRINE TO DWELL!

He who the armlet wears, and flowery Ayan know Thee not,

heaven's Lord, sole Partner of the Mountain-Maid!
I wilder'd stand, while rising swells the mighty joy, - O SEA
WHOSE WATERS REST ON KAILAI'S LOFTY HILL! (40)
Hymn XXIV- adaikalap pathu

THE REFUGE - DECAD

or

'THE ASSURANCE OF MATURITY.'

It seems probable that this song was founded upon the
Buddhist formula which required the devotee to utter nine
times the word saranam, three times to Buddha, three times
to the law or doctrine, and three times to the congregation
(=church, or order). This entire abandonment of self on the
part of the disciple was his initation into the Buddhist system.
Here our author takes 'refuge' at the foot of the loving
Master Who has called him, and will at last receive him to
Himself. This element of personal devotion to One Whom he
believes to have been the Supreme manifested in the flesh is
very striking, and gives a power that was wanting in the
Buddhist system. We must remember that all his life our sage
was brought into hostile contact with the Buddhists, and that
he fashions his poems so as to afford the strongest possible
contrast to that which he hated.

I.

Thy saints like clustering lotus-flowers have joined Thy
roseate foot;

Mature of mind, with Thee they're gone; while I, a sinful
man,
In body foul and vile remain, devoid of wisdom's lore,
Of mind impure. MASTER! THY SLAVE, I THEE MY REFUGE
MAKE! (4)

II.

My meanness only hateful things can do; Thy greatness still
Forgives!- The serpent-gem Thou wear'st; swells Ganga's
stream Thy crest;
Thou, by Thy sacred grace, the root of these my 'births'
Dost cut away, MASTER! THY SLAVE, I THEE MY REFUGE
MAKE! (8)

III.

Great Peruman, Thou who dost free from 'birth'! Thou frenzy
giv'st
O Peruman! - Within my mind, O Peruman the wise,
Thou com'st. The flow'ry One, and giant Mal too, knew Thee
not;
Rare Peruman! MASTER! THY SLAVE, I THEE MY REFUGE
MAKE! (12)

IV.

In floods from sorrow's pouring clouds that rise, Thy loving
ones
Sinking have seized the raft of Thy blest foot, and risen to
heaven.

Whirl'd amid trouble's sea, where women-billows' dash, and lusts's

Sea-monster wounds, I sink. MASTER! I THEE MY REFUGE MAKE! (16)

V.

Fall'n 'mid the circling troops of them of curling locks; Thy power

Forgetting; in this body dark I wearied lay. Thou Half

Of Her with wide balck eyes and glance like startled fawn! Heaven's Lord!

Give me Thy grace! MASTER! THY SLAVE, I THEE MY REFUGE MAKE! (20)

VI.

Broken by mighty churning-staff of those of jet black eyes,

Like cream in churn I bounded, suffered pain. O flow'r-foot, Hail!

When com'st Thou? When shall I whose deeds are 'mighty' worship Thee?

Lord of the Earth! MASTER! THY SLAVE, I THEE MY REFUGE MAKE! (24)

VII.

Caught in the net of hot desire for those of glancing eyes

And slender form, I writh'd and roll'd in sorrow sore; that I

Wallow no more, pit my fault, appear, pour sweetest balm!

Lord of the temple-court! MASTER! I THEE MY REFUGE
MAKE! (28)

VIII.

Thou Half of Her with beauteous eyes! unto Thy flowr'y feet
Thou call'st me,- then dismisses me to deepest depths; Thy
thought
I know not. Like pipe's changing tones now sinks, now swells
my soul.
Alas! I perish quite! MASTER! I THEE MY REFUGE MAKE! (32)

IX.

Thy loving ones beneath Thy jewell'd feet that grace confer
Abiding, gain the bliss that knows no refluent tide. No way
To worship Thee I find; in sooth I know not Thee, noe lore
That tells of Thee! MASTER! THY SLAVE, I THEE MY REFUGE
MAKE! (36)

X.

Eager I took ambrosia of Thy grace so freely pour'd;
I strove to drink; my sinful soul by evil fate was bound!
Give me to taste the rare stream gushing honey-sweet, and
save!
I sink in woe! MASTER! THY SLAVE, I THEE MY REFUGE MAKE!
(40)
Hymn XXV- aasai pathu

THE DECAD OF DESIRE

or
KNOWLEDGE OF 'SELF'

I. I long for Thy summons,

O flawless Gem, who gav'st the wealth of Thine own roseate
feet,-
By the kite-banner'd King unseen,- and here mad'st me Thine
own!
My darkness drive far off; say 'hither come'! The grace to
gain
That calls me there to dwell, BEHOLD, O SIRE, MY SOUL HATH
YEARN'D! (4)

II. Weary of the flesh

I not endure to wear this garment of the flesh,- of joints
And bones compact,- with fatness filled,-covered with skin! O
King,
Call me! To men of every sort, as fits their case Thou com'st
Ambrosia rare, ah, Thee to see, BEHOLD, O SIRE, I YEARN! (8)

III. Let me hear Thy call.

Call me, my King, that this poor frame, with vileness fill'd,
may die!
Thou 'Dancer,' Guru-gem, Who guarding makest me Thine;
O God by gods unreach'd! Civan! Look on my face awhile.
For Thee, to hear Thee call, BEHOLD, O SIRE, MY SOUL HATH
YEARN'D! (12)

IV. I wait in humble hope.

This walking cell, with loathy filth filled full, contemptible,
Clings to me, and afflicts my soul! Hail to Thee, mighty Lord!
Broken, subdued, and melted, looking ever for Thy light,
Thy blest feet's flower to gain, BEHOLD, O SIRE, MY SOUL
HATH YEARN'D! (16)

V. Where are the old joys?

Within this frame is loathsome; and without skin-covered
sores,
Sore grief! Thou Rider on the Bull! Bedeckt with ashes white,
Stooping to me, Thou cam'st, and mad'st me Thine; Ambrosia
rare!
For word of tenderness, BEHOLD, O SIRE, MY SOUL HATH
YEARN'D! (20)

VI. I long for the life of heaven,

Weary, mere dog, I cannot here abide. Take back earth's joys
Thou gav'st, O Thou whose roseate teet-flowers heaven's
sons know not!
Thou know'st no bond! Thy face's light, the gleaming of Thy
smile,-
To see, BEHOLD, O SIRE, HOW EAGERLY MY SOUL HATH
YEARN'D! (24)

VII. I long to praise Thee there

Thou Infinite, Whom earth and heaven extol, Thou Light
superne,-
Thou cam'st to make me Thine! Give me the world of final
bliss;
Thy thousand names I'd circling sing. Thee mighty Lord to
praise,
Th' Ambrosia ever new, BEHOLD, O SIRE, MY SOUL HATH
YEARN'D! (28)

VIII. My whole being worships Thee.

With hands Thee worshipping, embracing close Thy jewell'd
feet,
And placing still unwearied on my head, 'Our Lord, our Lord,'
I cry;-
'My Teacher,' with my mouth I cry. Like wax before the fire,
King of Aiyarr'! BEHOLD, O SIRE, MY MELTING SOUL HATH
YEARN'D! (32)

IX. When shall I join Thy saints?

To cast quite off this sinful frame; to enter Civan's home;
To see the Wondrous Light, that so these eyes may gladness
gain;
O Infinite, without compare! Th' assembly of Thy saints
Of old, to see, BEHOLD, O SIRE, THY SERVANT'S SOUL HATH
YEARN'D! (36)

X. Thy voice stills passion

Caught in the net of passion fierce by those whose eyes shine bright,

I languish'd,- I a cur,- O light of truth! and saw no help.

Thou Half of Her with gentle foot!- Thou only One! To hear

Thee say with coral lips, 'Fear not, 'BEHOLD, O SIRE, MY SOUL HATH YEARN'D! (40)

Hymn XXVI- athisiya pathu

THE DECAD OF WONDER
(RELEASE)

I.

With melting mind I said not, 'He is gold,' 'His is a ruby's light;'

I languish'd pondering charms of damsels young. Boon indescribable,

Mercies beyond compare, to me were given; He of the flowery foot,

THE FATHER, MADE ME HIS, AND JOINED ME TO HIS SAINTS: SUCH WONDER HAVE WE SEEN! (4)

II.

Of righteous deeds I had no thought, nor joined those who think on these;

To sorrows born and deaths, I wandered here. He said, 'This is my slave.'

He, the Supernal, stood in nearness manifest,- His half, the Queen.

THE FIRST ONE MADE ME HIS, AND JOINED ME TO HIS
SAINTS:
SUCH WONDER HAVE WE SEEN! (8)

III.

Aforetime, that my 'mighty deeds' might pass, the Father
tiple-eyed,-
Whom all find hard to know, to servant-bands abundantly
revealed,-
Who plac'd the crescent moon on 'braided lock' of more than
golden sheen,
THE SIRE,- HE MADE ME HIS, AND JOIN'D ME TO HIS SAINTS:
SUCH WONDER HAVE WE SEEN! (12)

IV.

Perpend the one sole cause for which the world a madman
nameth me:
I liv'd as others, knew no way to join me to His grce divine;
To deaths, to fallings into direful hells. I gave myself a prey.
THE FATHER, MADE ME HIS, AND JOIN'D ME TO HIS SAINTS:
SUCH WONDER HAVE WE SEEN! (16)

V.

I hasted not to join the choirs; I pluck'd no flowers nor
worshipped;
A slave to charms of those of perfum'd locks I squander'd
gifts of life.

By night our King dances midmost the fires,- the snake amidst
His braided hair!
HE MADE ME HIS, AND JOIN'D ME TO HIS SAINTS:
SUCH WONDER HAVE WE SEEN! (20)

VI.

Through my mere folly I the Letters Five forgot, that speak
His sacred Name;
I drew not near those wise in lore divine, longing to share
their virtuous deeds.
Born on the earth and dying there mere thing of earth, to
earth I gave myself!
THE MIGHTY MADE ME HIS, AND JOIN'D ME TO HIS SAINTS:
SUCH WONDER HAVE WE SEEN! (24)

VII.

This but untrue, whose walls are flesh, worm-stuffed,
decay'd, dripping with all that's foul,-
This did I take for true, whirled round in sorrow's sea. He
Who of rarest gem,
Of pearl, of ruby, adamant, and coral red,- the gleaming
splendour wears,-
MY FATHER, MADE ME HIS, AND JOIN'D ME TO HIS SAINTS:
SUCH WONDER HAVE WE SEEN! (28)

VIII.

Erewhile, that I no more might'bide with Him, He sent, and
plac'd me in this cell.

He look'd on me, spake gentlest words of mystery; brake off the yoke; His hand
Upraised, made former falesness cease, removed all fault, filled me with gleaming light:
'TWAS THUS HE MADE ME HIS, AND JOIN'D ME TO HIS SAINTS:
SUCH WONDER HAVE WE SEEN! (32)

IX.

Like fragrance hid within the blooming flower, the meaning of this frame
No mortal mind can reach: the Being infinite. That Being I knew not.
I trusted words of fools that pluck the fruit of deeds. From sensual snare to save
THE FATHER, MADE ME HIS, AND JOIN'D ME TO HIS SAINTS:
SUCH WONDER HAVE WE SEEN! (36)

X.

This hut, with darkness dense, the fruit of 'mighty deeds,' I took for wonderful,
Rejoiced, and so was falling into deepest hell. He gave my soul true light!
He that with angry foot and ruddy fire forthwith the triple walls threw down
The true way showed to me in grace, the false destroyed:
SUCH WONDER HAVE WE SEEN! (40)
Hymn XXVII- punarchi pathu

THE DECAD OF MYSTIC UNION
or
THE NATURE OF RELEASE

I. When shall I reach the Inaccessible?

The gleaming golden Hill, the flawless Pearl, the Shrine of
tender love
Who made me, last of man, His own, in speechless service
glad! He Whom
Dark Mal and Brahma baffled yet approach not,- gave
Himself, rare Balm!
When shall I dwell in MYSTIC UNION JOINED WITH HIM, MY
FLAWLESS GEM? (4)

II. My soul cries out for Thy rest.

Thy servant I endure not, O my king, upon this earth in mire
Of fivefold sense! In thought adoring Civan as my Lord,
With mind that melts, like sands where waters spring, with
cries of jubilee,
When shall I praise, in MYSTIC UNION JOINED WITH HIM, MY
FLAWLESS GEM? (8)

III. When shall I join the happy saints?

While lofty Mal and Ayan fear'd, a hill of fire Who rose, He
loveless me
Made His! Ambrosia rare! Amid His saints, whose souls gush
out with love,

To hearts' content, my praise outpouring, wreath'd with
fragrant flowers,
When shall I lie, in MYSTIC UNION JOINED WITH HIM, MY
FLAWLESS GEM? (12)

IV. His blissful presence.

With Ayan of the Lotus, Mal, and all the rest,- with the
Immortals's King,
Speak praises to Him name! The Light surpassing speech and
words' intent!
The Nelli's Fruit; Milk, Honey, Balm with sweetness fill'd;-
Ambrosia pure.
When shall I clasp, in MYSTIC UNION JOINED WITH HIM, MY
FLAWLESS GEM? (16)

V. Hidden from gods, to me revealed.

To see the foot and crown, that gleam with light, Ayan and
Mal, down deep,
Up high, they dug, they flew; but could not see His form!
While all this earth
Stood round, my service claimed, made me His own, and
bade me come! His love
When shall I praise, in MYSTIC UNION JOINED WITH HIM, MY
FLAWLESS GEM? (20)

VI. When shall I recover the old rapture?

In love He came, and rapture gave in olden days, to me His
slave!

And then He left me on this wide vast earth to wander
'wildered!
With floods of gushing tears, and frame with transport
thrilled, in joy and love,
When shall I stand, in MYSTIC UNION JOINED WITH HIM, MY
FLAWLESS GEM? (24)

VII. When shall I know Him?

Hard to others' thought, thou'rt fire, water, wind, earth,
ether; Him,
Sole One to whom none can compare; in joy beholding,
praising loud,
While tears in torrents flow, adoring hand out-stretched,
fragrant flower-wreaths
When shall I bring, in MYSTIC UNION JOINED WITH HIM, MY
FLAWLESS GEM? (28)

VIII. The heavenly re-union.

In bliss dissol'd, soul melted utterly, with every gesture meet:
Laughter and tears, homage of hand and lip,- with every
mystic dance,-
To see with joyous thrill, that Sacred Form, like ruddy evening
sky,
When shall I pass, in MYSTIC UNION JOINED WITH HIM, MY
FLAWLESS GEM? (32)

IX. Parvathi praised as one with Civan.

Sire and Mother of the seven worlds old; Who me, a dog,
mad'st Thine;
Thee only Balm for woes of life; Thee wisdom's honey-
dripping Gem,
For ever praising,- night and day. Thy beauteous foot with
flow'ry wreaths
When shall I deck, in MYSTIC UNION JOINED WITH HIM, MY
FLAWLESS GEM? (36)

X. His eternity.

Thou guard'st, creat'st, destroy'st; 'midst all that fill the
spacious heaven
The ELDER Thou, and First, Who knows no eld; Brahman,
Who mad'st me Thine;
Thou Infinite! For ever singing, bowing low, Thy foot's fair
flower
When shall I clasp, in MYSTIC UNION JOINED WITH HIM, MY
FLAWLESS GEM? (40)
Hymn XXVIII- vaazhap pathu

NO JOY IN LIFE

I. Longing for release.

Transcendent One, extending through both earth and
heaven,
THOU SEE'ST TO NONE BUT THEE I CLING!-
O Civa-puram's King! In glorious beauty bright,
Civan, in holy Perun-turrai's shrine,

Who dwell'st! To whom make I my plaint, whom blame, if
Thou
Who mad'st me Thine deny Thy grace?
THOU SEE'ST NO JOY have I upon this sea-girt earth;
BE GRACIOUS, BID ME COME TO THEE! (4)

II.

Me, worthless one, Thou mad'st in grace Thine own, great
Gem,-
THOU SEE'ST TO NONE BUT THEE I CLING!-
Whose form unique even those in yonder world know not,
past thought of both,- all piercing power
Thou art, the glorious Lord! O Civa-puram's King!
Civan, in Perun-turrai's shrine
Who dwell'st our mighty Lord, Thou Ruler of my soul,
BE GRACIOUS, BID ME COME TO THEE! (8)

III.

That foot alone I seek that Mal in songs extolled;
THOU SEE'ST TO NONE BUT THEE I CLING!-
Thou sought'st me, mad'st me Thine, O Civa-puram's King!
Civan, in Perun-turrai's shrine
Who dwell'st. Though I complain, in Thee my soul delights;
to gain anew Thy love my thought;
Thou see'st my heart is faint, I have no joy in life;
BE GRACIOUS, BID ME COME TO THEE! (12)

IV.

Thou Who the gleaming rebel-town didst swift consume,
THOU SEE'ST TO NONE BUT THEE I CLING!-
Dancer, Who bid'st in Tillai, Civa-puram's King!
Civan, in Perun-turrai's shrine
Who dwell'st, the three worlds' bounds that day the twain
pass'd through,
and saw nor first nor last of Thee,
In might so didst Thou rise! Thou see'st I joy not here;-
BE GRACIOUS, BID ME COME TO THEE! (16)

V. Absolute self-surrender.

Partner of Her whose words are sweetest melody!
THOU SEE'ST TO NONE BUT THEE I CLING!-
Surely Thou mad'st me Thine, O Civa-puram's King!
Civan, in holy Perun-turrai's shrine
Who dwell'st,- the whole: my body, mouth, nose, ears, and
eyes:-
all these in Thy control I place.
THOU SEE'ST THY SERVANT HATH NO JOYS UPON THIS
EARTH;-
BE GRACIOUS, BID ME COME TO THEE! (20)

VI. The sense's power.

Partner of Her with footfall downy soft,
THOU SEE'ST TO NONE BUT THEE I CLING!-
Thou mad'st me wholly Thine, O Civa-puram's King!
Civan, in Perun-turrai's shrine
Who dwell'st,- me trembling cur, Thou mad'st Thine own;
that grace

through senses' perturbation I forgot;
THOU SEE'ST THAT IN DECEPTION LOST, I JOY NOT HERE;-
BE GRACIOUS, BID ME COME TO THEE! (24)

VII.

Thou Light, that shin'st a Sun through all the spheres,
THOU SEE'ST TO NONE BUT THEE I CLING!-
Sacred, supremely glorious Civa-Puram's King!
Civan, in Perun-turrai's shrine
Who dwell'st, Thee I see; - my melting soul dissolves,
'wilder'd I know not any way in life to joy.
THOU SEE'ST I, FOLLY'S CHILD, CAN IN THIS LIFE PARTAKE NO
JOY,
BE GRACIOUS, BID ME COME TO THEE! (28)

VIII.

Partner of Her whose fingers jewels rare adorn,
THOU SEE'ST TO NONE BUT THEE I CLING!-
Thou art like ruddy flame, O Civa-puram's King!
Civan, in Perun-turrai's shrine
Who dwell'st,- endless Ambrosia,- Essence rare and great,-
Ambrosia rare,- Thy servant Thou didst save,
And mad'st me Thine, IN LIFE I CANNOT JOY THOU SEE'ST;
BE GRACIOUS, BID ME COME TO THEE! (32)

IX.

Thou'rt sin's Destroyer, save Thy healing foot alone,
THOU SEE'ST TO NOUGHT BESIDE I CLING!-

God of all gods, O Civa-puram's King! Civan,
in sacred Perun-turrai's shrine Who dwell'st
Through the three worlds passing, above below the twain,
as roaring flame Thou didst uplift Thy form.
Lord of the bull! THOU SEE'ST IN LIFE I CANNOT JOY;
BE GRACIOUS, BID ME COME TO THEE! (36)

X.

Partner of Her, Thy bride, of faultless old renown,
THOU SEE'ST TO NONE BUT THEE I CLING!-
Thou wear'st the crescent moon, O Civa-puram's King!
Civan, in sacred Perun-turrai's shrine
Who dwell'st,- shall I bow down to others? shall I praise?
or may think them aids for me? speak Thou!
Lord of the youthful bull! THOU SEE'ST I KNOW NO JOY;
BE GRACIOUS, BID ME COME TO THEE! (40)
Hymn XXIX- arut pathu

THE DECAD OF GRACE
or
'CLEANSING FROM DELUSION.'

The T.V.U.P states that this was one of the earliest of the
Sage's poems, and that it was sung at Tiru-perun-turrai. It
certainly bears the impress of youth, and in many respects is
inferior to some of his later poems. It is said to have for its
subject the purification of the soul from the great delusion
(Maha-maya). What this is can only be known by a careful
study of the Caiva Siddhanta philosophy.

The metre is the same as in XXII, and is very sweet. In each stanza, the two latter lines nearly correspond throughout the whole poem, an epithet or two being changed. Civan is addressed as the god who appeared in the Triclinia (Kuruntham) grove near Tiru-perun-turrai, and about thirty different epithets are applied to him, some of which are mere repetitions. The epithets applied to Tiru-perun-turrai are also varied. The last line in each stanza contains a Telugu phrase equivalent to 'and what is that'? so that the line literally reads: 'Save Thou in grace, saying "what is that"? or in other words, 'What is there to fear? fear not.' The poet is complaining of the power of earthborn delusions, and prays the god to take away his anxious fears. I cannot trace any sequence in the thought from stanza to stanza.

In the Siddhanta, very great stress is laid upon the idea that all embodiment, while it is painful and to be got rid of as soon as possible, is yet a gracious appointment of Civan, wrought out through Cakti, for the salvation of the human soul through the destruction of deeds, which are the root of all evil to mankind. Now the Buddhist formula represents suffering as being the whole account of the matter: 'Birth is suffering, old age is suffering, sickness is suffering, death is suffering. The origin of suffering is the thirst for pleasure, being, and power. The extinction of this thirst brings about the extinction of suffering.' The Caiva Siddhanta doctrine, on the contrary, gives to life and sufering a real significance. The present life is a probation,- a purgatory,- a preparation for endless fellowship and communion with the Supreme. Thus Grace is recognised where the Buddhist sees only suffering; and the instrument of man's release is that wisdom which understands the divine purpose, and adapts itself to that purpose. Our Sage dwells much upon the value of prayer, and of humble worship paid to the divine guru, while in Buddhism all is to be done by unaided human effort. At every point the two systems are in directest opposition!

I.

O Light! O Lamp girt with effulgent beams!-
the dame with curling locks and beauteous form
Is Thine, Supreme, Who wear'st the milk-white ash!
The Just, Whom Ayan of the flower knew not,
Nor Mal! In happy Perun-turrai Thou
'neath the Kuruntham's flow'ry shade didst rest.
Great First of Beings! when I craving call,
BID THOU IN GRACE THY SERVANT'S FEARS BEGONE! (4)

II.

O Dancer! Spotless One! O ash-besmear'd!
Thy brow hath central eye! Lord of heaven's host!
Sole Deity! through all the world Thyself
I sought lamenting loud, but found Thee not.
Thou, Who by Perun-turrai's pleasant lake
'neath the Kuruntham's flow'ry shade didst rest.
Great Source of Being! when Thy servant craving calls,
BID THOU IN GRACE THY SERVANT'S FEARS BEGONE! (8)

III.

Our Leader! Ruler of my life and soul!
Whom ladies twain, with perfum'd flowing locks,

Claim as their Spouse! Lord of the firy eye!
Whose glance caus'd sudden fire from Dakshan's frame to
spring,
And goodly Kaman's too! In sacred Perun-turrai Thou
'neath the Kuruntham's flow'ry shade didst rest.
Great Anganan! when I Thy servant craving call,
BID THOU IN GRACE THY SERVANT'S FEARS BEGONE! (12)

IV.

The Lotus-god, the four-fac'd, Kannan too,
dark as the azure sky, could not approach
Thee, Pure One! when They pray'd Thee to shine forth,
Father! thou wert as mighty flame display'd.
In Veda-echoing Perun-turrai Thou
'neath the Kuruntham's flow'ry shade didst rest.
Great Being spotless! when Thy servant craving calls,
BID THOU IN GRACE THY SERVANT'S FEARS BEGONE! (16)

V.

[These two lines are not translateable!]
....
....
....
....
Thou, Who in Perun-turrai's sylvan groves
'neath the Kuruntham's flow'ry shade didst rest.
O Teacher glorious! when Thy servant craving calls,
BID THOU IN GRACE THY SERVANT'S FEARS BEGONE! (20)

VI.

O Happy One and Pure! Thou like to gem
whose radiant beams 'mid pure white ashes shine!
In mind of those who think of Thee Thou giv'st
sweetness intense. Thou rare Ambrosia, Who
In sacred Perun-turrai's home of Vedic lore
'neath the Kurunthanm's flow'ry shade didst rest.
O Father glorious! when Thy servant craving calls,
BID THOU IN GRACE THY SERVANT'S FEARS BEGONE! (24)

VII.

Thou True One changing oft Thy form; Meru Thy bow,
Thy foemen's cities three Thy HAND consumed!
Thy FOOT burnt up death's king! O ruddy One,
Whose FORM was as a fiery column seen!
Thou, Who in Perun-turrai's happy home
'neath the Kuruntham's flow'ry shade didst rest.
O glorious Teacher! when Thy servant craving calls,
BID THOU IN GRACE THY SERVANT'S FEARS BEGONE! (28)

VIII.

The Free, the First, the Triple-eyed, the Sage,-
Thou giv'st the heavenly goal to those,
Who off'ring flowers with clustering buds adore,
devoutly pondering praise; consummate One,
Thou, Who in Perun-turrai's happy home
'neath the Kuruntham's flow'ry shade didst rest.
O Sire, all glorious! when Thy servant craving calls,

BID THOU IN GRACE THY SERVANT'S FEARS BEGONE! (32)

IX.

Regarding me distraught, Thou bad'st confusion cease,
destroying thought of this world and the next,
Thou very God, Thou Holy One, upon Thy crest
the swelling lustrous snake and Ganga bide.
Thou, Who in Perun-turrai's home of lucid Vedic lore
'neath the Kuruntham's flow'ry shade didst rest.
Glorious in mercy! when Thy servant craving calls,
BID THOU IN GRACE THY SERVANT'S FEARS BEGONE! (36)
X.

In Perun-turrai girt with ordered stately groves,
'neath the Kuruntham's flow'ry shade,
I call to mind Thy glories all, and pondering yearn,
and as my mighty Lord Thee oft invoke
Ascetic rare! when I, Thy servant, craving call,
struggling amid the billowy sea,
In grace declare the fitting path to reach
the silver hill, and BID ME COME! (40)
Hymn XXX- tiru kazhukundra pathicam

THE LYRIC OF THE 'EAGLE-MOUNT.'

THE SIGHT OF THE 'GURU.'

This is one of the places which the Sage is said to have visited
before seeing Cithambaram. It would appear that here he

had some peculiar manifestation of the god, who had revealed himself to him in Perun-turrai. It is open to conjecture that the Guru, whom he regarded as Civan manifested in the flesh, resided there, or at least was a constant visitant. The place itself is a renowned Caiva shrine, and has its own legend, a considerable poem of 832 quatrains. This is of recent origin, and, I should suppose, of small authority. It states that the original name of the hill was Veda-giri, or the hill of the Veda. It is said to have four hills clustered together, each being one of the four Vedas, while the central peak, which is of basaltic formation, is Civan Himself in the form of the Lingam. It is curiously stated that 'in Arur the god dwells for the first watch of the night, and in Cithambaram for the midnight watch; but in Veda-giri he is always to be formed.' The name of the hill of the Veda was changed to that of the hill of the Eagle, because two eminent persons, having disputed an order of Civan, were sentenced to perform penance there.

I.

O peaceful Perun-turrai's mighty Lord!
to those whose talk is of Thy thousand names
One even stream of matchless pleasure flows.
My Lord, Who once didst wipe away sore griefs,
When good and evil deeds were balanced,-
(for aftermath of ill no living seed),-
In sacred glories countless didst Thou come,
AND SHOW THYSELF UPON THE EAGLE'S HILL (4)

II.

Thou Who for hire of cakes didst carry earth!
Thou madman great, of the great haven's shrine!
While I, who knew no law of right, to Thee,
through ignorant delusion drew not near,
O Best of Beings, Lord of Civa-world,
me, lower than the meanest cur, a man
Of evils sore, Thou cam'st to make Thine own,
AND SHOW'DST THYSELF UPON THE EAGLE'S HILL (8)

III.

In wilderment I strayed from Perun-turrai far,
where tears were changed to joy, and foulness purged;
By sinful deeds to ruin brought, henceforth
I sinner knew not what should after grow.
Reft of the home where Thy bright feet once stood,
a prey to dire perplexity, I dwelt.
To save me from confusion sore Thou cam'st
AND SHOW'DST THYSELF UPON THE EAGLE'S HILL (12)

IV.

That I the matchless ornament might wear
of love unique,- draw nigh, and daily praise,-
Abashed with awe of reverence,- the shame
that knows no shame,- sinking amid the sea;
Of Perun-turrai, dear beyond compare,
the glorious ship I seized and climbed theren;
Straightway, in splendour no eye sees, Thou cam'st
AND SHOW'DST THYSELF UPON THE EAGLE'S HILL (16)

V.

In glorious form displayed, Thou teeming cloud
of perfect good, in Perun-turrai seen!
O matchless Gem, Who putt'st Thyself within
the thought of me, who naught of virtue knew!
The world itself shall witness bear that I
desired Thee eagerly, and then Thou cam'st,-
That when I called Thee, then Thou cam'st,-
AND SHOW'DST THYSELF UPON THE EAGLE'S HILL (20)

VI.

Great flood of Perun-turrai's shrine, Thou didst
the love that knows no change bestow;
When foes with many an impious speech stood round,
what didst Thou unto me before them all?
Thy Foot shall be my only refuge still,
from every death, and every various ill,-
And, therefore, when in love I called, Thou cam'st,
AND SHOW'DST THYSELF UPON THE EAGLE'S HILL (24)

VII.

O Ican, Who the four and sixty demons mad'st
to share the eightfold qualities divine,-
When I had sunk in evil deeds,- the fruit
of triple foulness that confusion brings,-
Thou didst the bands of clinging sorrow loose;
mad'st me Thine own; gav'st me Thy feet's pure flower;

In presence of Thy servant-band didst come
AND SHOW THYSELF UPON THE EAGLE'S HILL (28)
Hymn XXXI- ganda pathu

'MINE EYES HAVE SEEN.'

THE SIGHT OF THE MYSTIC DANCE
or
THE UNSPEAKABLE VISION.

Tillai.- In the legends of the Sage it appears that he did not
visit Tillai till he had seen the other shrines of Caiva worship,
and had become renowned both as a devotee and as a poet.
It almost appears as if there existed some rivalry between the
great temple of the Pandiyan land in Madura, and the
famous shrine of he Cora land in Cithambaram. It is quite
certain that this latter in great measure superseded the
former. It does not appear, indeed, that Manikka-Vacagar
ever revisited Madura after his formal renunciation of his
position there. It may almost be inferred that he was never
heartily forgiven by the king for the misappropriation of the
cost of the horses. Of the fifty-one poems about a half were
composed in Tillai, and these may be divided into two
classes: the lyrics that express his own feelings and illustrate
his life; and those which were composed (as is believed) for
the use of others. I wish that it had been possible to re-
arrange the poems.
Among the Tillai lyrics are to be found his most impassioned
utterances. With this poem (XXXI) must be compared (XL),
both of them expressing his enthusiastic joy at being

permitted at length to behold the greatest shrine of his
Master.

Tillai in the time of the Sage was to the devotees of Civan
what Jerusalem was to the Jews of old; and many of the
expressions in these two lyrics will remind the reader of
Psalm cxxii; and not a few of the expressions are identical
with those in the rhyme often attributed to Bernard of
Morlaix. One is frequently reminded of 'Jerusalem the
Golden, with milk and honey blest.'

I.

In senses' power, sure cause of death, I erewhile 'wildered
lay,-
Oft wrapt through realms of boundless space, then plunged
in dismal hells!
He gave perception clear, made me all bliss,- made me His
own!
I'VE TILLAI SEEN that holds the Gem, which endless rapture
yields! (4)

II.

Enmeshed in grievous memories of deeds and fated births
Outworn I lay; nor knew my soul one faintest thought of Him,
The Matchless One, Who cuts off 'birth'; Who made me His
with power!
HIM HAVE I SEEN IN TILLAI'S COURT, where worships all the
world! (8)

III.

His form I knew not,- even then He fixed His love on me,
Planted Himself within my thought and flesh,- so made me
His!
The Lord of sacred Turutti, I, currish slave, with joy
HAVE SEEN IN TILLAI'S FANE ADORNED, the sweet and blissful
seat! (12)

IV.

To me, untaught, most ignorant, the very lowest cur,
In mighty grace He came, with heavenly beauty me to clothe,
And loosed my 'servile bonds of sense' in sight of many men;
His form I'VE SEEN IN TILLAI'S TEMPLE COURT, where all bow
down! (16)

V.

Me whirled about 'mid 'caste' and 'clan' and 'birth', and sore
perplexed,-
Vile helpless dog,- He made His own, all sorrow rooting out;
Destroyed all folly,- alien forms,- all thought of 'I' and 'mine';
Ambrosia pure, HIM HAVE I SEEN IN TILLAI, where the saints
consort! (20)

VI.

From birth itself, from sickness, age to 'scape; earth's ties to
loose;
I went,- I SAW the 'Only-First-One,' Owner of the world,
Who dwells, while Vedic sages, hosts of heavenly ones adore,

IN TILLAI-CITY'S SACRED COURT, girt round with leafy groves. (24)

VII.

My servile bonds of sense in grace He loosed,- me loveless mean,-
Fast tied He to His sacred Feet by willing mind's stout bonds,
That never part; made me a fool in sight of men; and now
I'VE TILLAI SEEN, where sportings of the wondrous Mage are known. (28)

VIII.

Sunk here midst infinite conceits, all ignorance was I;
I lay, poor empty soul, unwetting aught that might spring forth;
Now Him who made me His, bestowing raptures infinite,
I'VE SEEN IN TILLAI, where the guileless heavenly ones bow down! (32)

IX.

To me, a dog, who knew not anything of seemly right,
He gave His heavenly grace, took me and cut off actions' guilt;
He gave unfailing love: light high and higher shone; Him I
IN TILLAI'S COURT HAVE SEEN, where the four mystic scrolls are conned! (36)

X.

The elements, the senses five, He is; and substance too.
All diverse forms He, mighty, wears: knows no diversity.
The gleaming Light that rules, and ill destroys; the Emerald;
HIM HAVE I SEEN IN TILLAI BRIGHT, where Vedas worship and
extol! (40)
Hymn XXXII- praththanai pathu

THE SUPPLICATION.

I. Alternations of feeling.

Mingling with Thy true saints, that day in speechless joy I
stood;
Next day, with dawning daylight trouble came, and there
abode.
My soul grows old. Master! to seek the gleam of fadeless
bliss
Wand'ring I went. In grace to me, Thy slave, let loye abound!
(4)

II. Impatience.

Some of Thy saints have gained through plenteous love Thy
grace. Grown lod,
All vain my griefs, - of this vile corpse I see no end.
Remove from sinful me my deeds of sin; let mercy's sea
o'erflow!
O Master, to Thy slave give ceaseless soul-subduing grace! (8)

III. Fortitude-strong in love-needed.

Deep in the vast Ambrosial sea of grace Thy perfect saints
Have sunk. Lo, Lord, I wearied bear this frame with darkness
filled!
Men see, and cry, 'A madman, one of 'wildered mind is here.'
Master, that I may fearless live, true live I NEEDS must gain!
(12)

IV. Craving for consummate bliss

I NEED!; I NEED! Midst Thy true faithful ones, in grace
desiring me,
Thou mad'st me Thine, my grief's expell'd, - Ambrosia!
precious peerless Gem,
Like gleam of quenchless lamp! And I, Thy servant too, shall I
Reach Thee, and ne'er again know NEED? Thou all-abounding
Love! (16)

V. Shall I get free from Self?

Thou Partner of the bright-eyed maid! To dwell among Thy
saints,
Desiring Thee in truth, shall it be giv'n to sinful me
By Thine own grace, gaining the ancient sea of bliss superne,
To rest, in soul and body freed from thought of 'I' and 'mine'?
(20)

VI. Longing desire of the Infinite Bliss

Thy loving ones have gained 'cessation' absolute; but here
My spirit ever melts, outside I lie,- base dog, and mourn!

O Master mine, I would attain true love's vast sea of bliss,
That cahnge, surcease, oblivion, sev'rance, thought, bound,
death knows not! (24)

VII. Cut short Thy work!

They've seen the sea-like bliss, have seized it, and enjoy! Is't
meet,
That I, low dog, with added pains and pining sore should
bide?
Master, do Thou Thyself give grace, I pray! I faint! I fail!
Cut short Thy work! O light! let darkness flee before Thy
mercy's beam! (28)

VIII. Come quickly

Enter'd amongst Thine own, to whom true melting grace
abounds,
I stand with soul like tough bambasa stem, and wear away.
O Civan, grant the love Thy crowned servants bear to Thee!
O swiftly come, and give to me Thy tender beauteous Foot!
(32)

IX. Was I not made Thine own?

Thine own stood round, and all declar'd: 'No grace withheld,
all grace
Is given,' - and I, Thy servant, shall I mourn as aliens wont?
Thou King of Civa-world, by glorious grace didst change my
thought,

An make me Thine,- I pray Thee, Lord, place me in changeless
bliss! (36)

X. Is aught gained by delay?

Thou Partner sole of the Gazelle! Sweet fruit to them that
worship Thee!
Teacher! If I am like an unbor'd gourd, doth thus Thy glory
live?
O King, when comes the time that Thou wilt grant in grace to
me
A soul that melts and swells in knowing Thee, Who cam'st in
flesh? (40)

XI. Must I langusih here?

In concert joining shall Thy saints, there bending smile and
joy?
O Master, drooping, all forlorn, like withered tree, must I
Stand sullen while they mingle, melt, souls swelling, lost in
bliss
In rhythmic dance? Grant bliss of sweet communion with Thy
grace! (44)
Hymn XXXIII- kulaitha pathu

THE DECAD OF THE BRUISED HEART
or
'SELF-DEDICATION.'

It would be hard to find a more touching expression of
absolute mystic self-renunciation than these verses contain.

I. Useless suffering

If cruel pain oppress from 'deeds of old,' guard Thou
Who ownest me! If I, a man of 'cruel deeds'
Suffer, from this my woe doth any gain accrue?
O light of Umai's eyes, take Thou me for Thine own!
And though I err, ah! should'st not Thou forgive,-
Thou on whose crest the crescent rests? If I appeal,
Wilt Thou withhold Thy grace, Father, from me Thy slave? (4)

II. Why is the affliction of embodied existence prolonged?

Thy slave's afflictions all to drive far off I deem'd
Thou mad'st me Thine, erewhile; Thou Partner of the Queen,
Whose form is like the slender creeping plant! Our King;
bidding me come, why didst Thou not in grace destroy
This body vile? Our Lord, Who dwell'st in you yon blest
world!
Thou called'st,- if my service not accepting now
Thou dost afflict, Master, will any gain accrue? (8)

III. Pardon my offences.

Thy mercy given to save one void of worth,
a dog like me, hath it this day pass'd all away?
Thou Partner of the Tender One, our Mighty King,
ev'n faults that like a mountain rise, to virtues turn,
If Thou but say the word! If Thou didst take me once

for Thine, why dost Thou not- though ruined- pity take
On me? our Lord,- Thou of eight arms and triple eye! (12)

IV. When wilt Thou call me back to Thee?

Bridegroom of Her with fawnlike eyes! Our King! If Thou
hast caused me Thine abiding glory to forget;
If Thou hast thrust me out in fleshly form to dwell;
if Thou hast caused Thy slave to wander here forlorn;
Knowing Thy servant's ignorance, O gracious King,
when comes the day that Thou Thyself wilt show Thy grace?
Ah! When, I cry, when wilt Thou call me back to Thee? (16)

V. All is Thyself!

The tongue itself that cries to Thee,- all other powers
of my whole being that cry out,- all are THYSELF!
Thou art my way of strength! The trembling thrill that runs
through me is Thee! THYSELF the whole of ill and weal!
None other here! Would one unfold and truly utter Thee,
what way to apprehend? Thou Lord of Civa-world!
And if trembling fear, should'st Thou not comfort me? (20)

VI. Desires.

Thou know'st what to DESIRE is meet,- when we DESIRE
Thou'rt He that wholly grants! To Ayan and to Mal
DESIRING Thee, how hard to reach! Yet me Thou didst
DESIRE, my service claim! DESIRING what didst Thou
Bestow Thy grace? That and naught else do I DESIRE!
And if aught else there be that stirs in me DESIRE!

That too, in sooth, is Thy DESIRE,- is it not so? (24)

VII. I am wholly Thine

That very day my soul, my body, all to me
pertaining, didst Thou not take as Thine own,
Thou like a mountain strong! when me Thou mad'st Thy
slave?
And this day is there any hindrance found in me?
Our mighty One! Eight-arm'd and Triple-eyed!
Do Thou to me what's good alone, or do Thou ill,
To all resigned, I'm Thine and wholly Thine! (28)

VIII. My destinies are in Thy hand.

Me dog, and lower than a dog, all lovingly
Thyself didst take for Thine. This birth-illusion's thrall
Is plac'd within Thy charge alone. And I in sooth,
is there aught I need beyond that, with care search out?
Herein is there authority at all with me?
Thou may'st again consign me to some mortal frame;
Or'neath Thy jewelled foot may'st place me, Brow-eyed One!
(32)

IX. My soul is fixed on Thee.

Thou in Whose brow a central eye doth gleam! Thy feet-
the twain- I saw; mine eyes rejoic'd; now, night and day,
Without a thought, on them alone I ponder still!
How I may quit this earthly frame, how I may come
To enter 'neath Thy feet in bliss, I ponder not!

Save Thee, O King, should I Thy servant ponder aught?
Thy service here hath fulness of delight for me! (36)

X. The hope deferred.

Thy beauty only I, a slavish dog, desire,
and cry aloud. O Master! Thou didst show to me
Thy sacred Form in lustre shrin'd, and didst accept
my service. Thou my Glory!- Mine august abode,
In ancient days assur'd, Thou now withhold'st;- and so,
O beauteous Lord!- Thou of the glorious mystic Word!
My King,- sorely indeed hast Thou bruis'd my poor heart! (40)
Hymn XXXIV- uyir unnip pathu

'MY SOUL IS CONSUMED.'

RAPTURE OF LIFE IN CIVAN

I. His praises.

Partner of Umai's loveliness! Destroyer of the 'deeds'
That to this frame cling fast! Thou Guardian of the Bull! Who dwell'st
In Perun-turrai's sacred shrine by well-skilled bards extolled!
When shall I joy, O when exulting sing, henceforth, I too? (4)

II. His condescending love.

And who am I would reach His foot? To me, mere cur, a throne

He gave; enter'd my flesh; mixed with my life; leaves not my
soul.
With crown of honey-dripping-locks, blest Perun-turrai's Lord
On me a gracious boon bestow'd, that heavenly ones know
not! (8)

III. Sacred enthusiasm.

I know myself no more; nor day's nor night's recurrence; He
Who mind and speech transcends with mystic madness
madden'd me;
He owns the angry mighty Bull;- blest Perun-turrai's Lord;
The Brahman used to me wiles I know not,- O Beam divine!
(12)

IV. None like to Him.

And are there other sin-destroyers, say! in this wide world?
Ent'ring me too, He made me His, melting my very bones!
He bound me fast, O joy! Lord, Who in Perun-turrai dwells,
He fills my mind, in eye enshrin'd, midmost in every word!
(16)

V. Cling to Him with reverent love.

Ye who are freed from clinging ties, cling ye where man
should cling!
If ye desire the blissful goal to reach, swift hasten on!
Learn ye the glory of the King, Who crowned with braided
lock

In Perun-turrai dwells; join ye with those who cherish there
His foot! (20)

VI. I am His, body and soul.

Foulness that heaves like billows of the sea He all destroy'd;
My soul and body ener'd,- tills, and quits no more. He Who
In Perun-turrai dwells, with crown of spreading braided locks,
Wreath'd with the moon's bright beams, our Lord Supreme.
This is His wile! (24)

VII. The goal reached.

Glory I ask not; nor desire I wealth; not earth or heaven I
crave;
I seek no birth or death; those that desire not Civan
nevermore
I touch. I've reach'd the foot of sacred Perun-turrai's King,
And crown'd myself! I go not forth! I know no going hence
again! (28)

VIII. Honey or nectar?

Shall I name Thee 'honey from the branch'? 'nectar from the
sounding sea'?
Our Aran! precious Balm! my King! No powers have I to sing
Thy praise,
Who dwell'st in Perun-turrai's shrine, by loamy rice-fields
girt,
Thou Spotless One, Whose sacred Form the holy ash adorns!
(32)

IX. Withdrawal of comfort.

Thee I know I need: and all I need I yet know not;
Ah me! our Aran, precious Balm, Ambrosia, Thou Whose
FOrm is like
The crimson flower, Who dwell'st in sacred Perun-turrai's
shrine,
And still remain'st, the very self within my soul! (36)

X. Prayer permitted still.

While dwellers in the heavenly world do holy deeds, in vain
Bearing a frame of flesh compact, I stand like forest tree:
Thou dwell'st in Perun-turrai's shrine, where honey-dripping
cassia blooms;
Though I'm a sinner, yet I may implore, 'give grace to me!'
(40)
Hymn XXXV- achchap pathu

THE DECAD OF DREAD
or
'ABSORPTION IN DIVINE KNOWLEDGE.'

I. Heretics.

Not the sleek snake in anthill coil'd I dread;
nor feigned truth of men of lies,-
As I, in sooth, feel fear at night of those
who have not learnt the Lofty-One
To know; who near the Foot of the Brow-Ey'd,-

our Lord, crown'd with the braided-lock,-
Yet think there's other God. When these unlearn'd we see,-
AH ME! WE FEEL NO DREAD LIKE THIS! (4)

II. False teachers.

I shudder not, though evil yearnings rise;
nor fear, though sea of deeds o'erwhelm!
Beside His sacred Form, our Lord of lords,-
in which the Two no change discerned,
When name of other gods,- what'er they be,-
by lips profane is but pronounc'd:
If I see those, who loathe not such discourse,-
AH ME! WE FEEL NO DREAD LIKE THIS! (8)

III. The unloving.

I dread not mighty jav'lin, dripping gore;
nor glance of maids with jewell'd arms!
But those that will not sweetly taste His grace,-
Whose glance can melt the inmost soul,-
Who dances in the hallow'd court,- my Gem
unstain'd and pure,- nor praise His Name:-
Such men of loveless hearts when we behold,-
AH ME! WE FEEL NO DREAD LIKE THIS! (12)

IV. The unfeeling.

I dread not chatter vain of parrot-tongues;
nor fear their guileful wanton smile!
If, drawing nigh the Vethian's feet, Whose Form

the sacred ashes white displays,
Men's souls nor melt, nor weep they worshipping,
their eyes with gushing teardrops fill'd:
If these, of tender feeling void, we see,-
AH ME! WE FEEL NO DREAD LIKE THIS! (16)

V. The undevout.

I fear not, though diseases all should come;
nor dread I birth with death conjoin'd!
The crescent moon as ornament He wears,
yet men praise not His roseate Feet,
(Which Mal, though the firm ground He clave, saw not,)
nor join His worshippers devout!
If those that wear not ashes white we see,-
AH ME! WE FEEL NO DREAD LIKE THIS! (20)

VI. Not real worshippers.

I dread not angry flash of gleaming fires;
nor fear, though mountains on me roll !
His shoulders ashes wear, Lord of the Bull,
Sire, passing utterance of speech,-
Yet men praise not His lotus Feet, nor bow,
nor crown them with the full-blown flower!
If those hard hearts, that yield not to His power we see,-
AH ME! WE FEEL NO DREAD LIKE THIS! (24)

VII. Devoid of enthusiasm.

Not guilt unseemly that swift vengeance brings;

nor stroke of instant death I dread!
He dances in the beauteous court, and waves
'mid smoking clouds His fiery axe;
The cassia-wreath, all bright with jewell'd buds,
He wears, of beings First! Yet men
Praise not His Foot! If these, unmov'd by grace we see,-
AH ME! WE FEEL NO DREAD LIKE THIS! (28)

VIII. No high aspirations.

I fear not elephant to pillar chain'd;
nor tiger fiery-eyed I dread!
The Sire, whose crest sweet fragrance sheds,- His Feet
that heav'nly ones may not approach,-
Men praise not, nor with triumph haste
within His shrine to sweetly live !
If we behold these men of wisdom reft,-
AH ME! WE FEEL NO DREAD LIKE THIS! (32)

IX. False shame.

I fear not thunderbolt from out the cloud;
nor changing confidence of kings!
Our Lord of lords the very poison made
Ambrosia, by His gracious act;
He makes us His in way of righteousness;
yet men smear not the sacred ash!
If those who from His side shrink thus we see,-
AH ME! WE FEEL NO DREAD LIKE THIS! (36)

X. Men that worship not.

I dread not arrow that unswerving flies;
nor wrath of death's dread King, I fear !
Him Whose adornment is the mighty moon
men praise not, nor with hymns adore;
They ponder not eith souls subdued, while tears
from brighty beaming eyes pour forth.
These thankless men,- not men !- if we behold,-
AH ME! WE FEEL NO DREAD LIKE THIS! (40)
Hymn XXXVI- tiru pandi pathikam

THE SACRED PANDI

[THE GROWTH OF RAPTURE]

The Lyric of the Sacred Pandi.- Note IV should be studied as
introductory to this very dramatic poem, which is in every
way a remarkable composition; yet I should hardly venture to
affirm that Manikka-Vacagar was its author. In order to
understand it, it is necessary to call to mind the strange
legend of Civan's appearance at Madura as a horseman, or as
He is here called a warrior. The first stanza is supposed to be
uttered by the poet as he contemplates the God entering
Madura on that occasion, surrounded by the other gods, all
on splendid chargers. Civan Himself is mounted upon leader
of a band of foreign merchants, the graces of the
accomplished knight, and the majesty of a king. He has come,
according to His promise, to save His servant from suffering,
and to vindicate His fidelity. The poet in his soul adores his
Deliverer and his God.

In the remaining stanzas he addresses the assembled multitude, and expounds the mystery. 'Fear not as though it were the Avatar of some ruthless conqueror! This horseman is Civan,'- the founder, according to legend, of the dynasty of Pandiyan kings. 'He is the abiding King of Madura, and now He comes in grace to the mortal king of Madura, Arimarttanan.' The whole typifies the sacred war that He wages as the Pathi against the enemies and tormentors of His people's souls. The third stanza skilfully, though by an anachronism, allegorizes the flood that Civan brought upon the city, when at His command the Vaigai overflowed its banks. In the fifth stanza he spiritualizes the idea that Civan appears here as a merchant, a seller of horses. The sixth, referring to His previous appearance at Perun-turrai, hints at His character as a Guru, a giver of spiritual light; and the whole ends with an urgent call to the people to throw aside all foolish delusions, and to march boldly forward under His banner, and accept Him as their King. The way in which the whole legend is allegorized points, it may be thought, to a later period, when the Caiva Siddhanta system had been more developed; and when, under the influence of the Santana Teachers, the whole system was being harmonized. There is here a disposition to make little of the myth, and to bring into prominence its spiritual teaching. This was the second stage of the Caiva development. This however is mere conjecture, and there seems to be scarcely any means for its absloute verification.

The metre is to my ear the most rhythmical of all the species of Tamil poetry. The student should learn to recite and enjoy the verses, if he would fully understand them!

I. The God appears, and is recognised by the Sage.

The Bridegroom of the mountain Maid,- the Pandiyan's
Ambrosia rare,-
The One,- Who is from all diverse,- I worship at His flow'ry
Feet!
Made manifest in grace, He on a charger rides, and thrills my
soul
In Warrior-guise ! no other form beside my inmost soul doth
know ! (4)

II. 'Behold His condescension.'

They gather'd round, bewilder'd all, as in a waking dream;- I
spoke:
'Like sun that veils its beams He comes, His hand divine holds
warrior's spear.
He on a charger rides ! Ye see our race with ruin threatened
sore !
'Tis thus for Madura's king he stays the flowing tide of future
birth !' (8)

III. The Flood in Madura.

'Ye who a soul possess that swims and bathes in rapture's
rushing tide !
A Pandi-king, He mounts His steed, to make all earth the
gladness share.
He takes the form of flood of joy unique, and holds His
servants' hearts.

Plunging in flood of heavenly bliss, O cherish ye His sacred
Foot!' (12)

IV. The Holy War.

'Good friends, persist not in this round of BIRTH ! This is the
time ! The King
Of the good southern land shines forth, and ever draws from
out its sheath
His gleaming sword of wisdom pure, His steed of rapture
urges on,
Makes war with warring BIRTH through the wide world, and
foes confounded flee !' (16)

V. 'How are His good gifts to be gained:' a merchant.

'While there is time, give Him your love, and save yourselves
! Hate ye to Him
Who ate the poison, Whom 'tis hard for him who ate the
earth,
And him of faces four, and all the heavenly ones, to draw
anigh;
Who to His servants stores of grace dispenses, our good
Pandi-lord !' (20)

VI. 'This is His day of grace:' a teacher.

'That gathering darkness may disperse, illusions cease, and all
be clear,
The Splendour urges on His steed. The Minavan himself
knows not

To utter all His praise. Would ye all joy obtain, seek His blest
Foot !
This is the gift in rarest grace the Pandiyan gives, - RELEASE
for aye ! (24)

VII. "He gives audience:' a conquering king.

'When on illusion's charger He in beauty rides, and gathers
round
His waiting hosts; the enmities whose name is "earthly birth"
shall cease
To those who refuge find He gives grace, glorious, vast,
inscrutable.
Draw near the South-king's mighty Foot, Whose conquering
banner proudly waves!' (28)

VIII. 'Receive His gracious gift.'

'In deathless rapture's flood our souls He plunges, shows His
changeless grace;
Drives far away our DEEDS, dissolves the bonds of old
impurity;
And makes us His! Come draw ye near the Pandi-ruler's
mighty Foot.
Press forward, take the gracious boon of Him Who made the
circling world !' (32)

IX. The magic power of His appearing.

'That men may cross the mingling sea of evil DEEDS and
future BIRTH,

The Pandi-king supreme, Who melts the soul of those that love and praise,
Upon His charger came. When this the slender flower-like maidens knew,
Like trees they stood,- their senses rapt, themselves forgot, and all beside !' (36)

X. 'In faith and love cling to Him.'

'As once He conquered death, so now the five sense-kings He conquered too;
And then, in beauteous state, Himself,- and the great Goddess with Him,- sat !
Strong Warrior, on the Bull he came to Minavan, and slew his foes !
O ye of weak and wavering faith ! Draw near, hold fast His roseate Feet !' (40)
Hymn XXXVII- piditha pathu

THE DECAD OF THE 'TENACIOUS GRASP.'

This is one of the most characteristic of the Sage's lyrics, and would seem to belong to a later period than that when the 'cry of the forsaken' (VI) was composed. It is in singular contrast to that lyric. He had meanwhile visited many shrines, and had passed through much struggle; but when he reached what is here called Tiru-toni-puram (the sacred Boat-town), of which the modern name is Shialli, he found a magnificient temple there,that seemed to him like a reproduction on earth of the silver mountain Kailasam, on

which the God dwells in splendour with Parvathi. This shrine
has always been remarkable, but is especially honoured now
as the reputed birthplace of Tiru-nana-sambandhar; who, in
popular estimation, is perhaps the greatest of the Caiva
saints. In his legend we have elsewhere given some notices of
this his home. It has twelve names connected with wild
legends; but is called here 'the sacred Boat-town,' because
when at the end of each aeon the deluge of universal
destruction overwhelms the universe, this shrine floats
securely on the waters,- the everlasting ark ! Here it seems
that the Sage renewed his vows to his guru, from whom he
had somewhat departed in thought and practice. He seems
to regard himself now as a sivanmuthan and declares that he
will henceforth hold fast his allegiance under all
circumstances, in life and through death.

I. Thou art our own !

O King of those above ! - O ceaseless Plenitude
of mystic bliss ! - To me defiled Thou cam'st
Fruit newly ripe, and mad'st me Thine own dwelling-place.
Balm, yielding bliss all earthly bliss beyond !
True meaning's Certitude ! The Foot in glory bright !
My Wealth of bliss ! O Civa-Peruman !
OUR VERY OWN - I'VE SEIZED THEE,- HOLD THEE FAST !
HENCEFORTH,
AH, WHITHER GRACE IMPARTING WOULD'ST THOU RISE? (4)

II. My only Help in this life.

Ever the bull Thou holdest,- King of heaven's glad host !

To me a man of sin Possession true !
Thy slave is foul decay that quits not, merest earth;
within a very nest of worms I lie !
Thou mad'st me Thine, and safe hast kept, lest I should fail
at last; O God, O mighty Sea of grace!
FOR EVERMORE - I'VE SEIZED THEE,- HOLD THEE FAST !
HENCEFORTH,
AH, WHITHER GRACE IMPARTING WOULD'ST THOU RISE? (8)

III. Reality amidst illusions.

O Mother! O my Sire ! My Gem beyond compare !
Ambrosia, ever-precious yield of love !
I, vile one, dwell in short-lived house of worms,
where false illusions ever growing press.
On me Thou hast bestow'd the true and perfect rest;
my Wealth of bliss ! O Civa-Peruman !
UPON THIS EARTH- I'VE SEIZED THEE,- HOLD THEE FAST ! HENCEFORTH,
AH, WHITHER GRACE IMPARTING WOULD'ST THOU RISE?
(12)

IV. Light in the darkness.

Splendour of grace ! Well ripen'd luscious Fruit unique !
King of ascetics stern of all prevailing power !
Science of meanings deep ! Delight transcending praise !
Of mystic sacred musings' Fulness blest !
Thou enterest Thy servant's thought, and all is clear !
My Wealth of bliss ! O Civa-Peruman !

IN EACH DARK HOUR- I'VE SEIZED THEE,- HOLD THEE FAST !
HENCEFORTH,

AH, WHITHER GRACE IMPARTING WOULD'ST THOU RISE?
(16)

V. The One Helper in life's struggles.

Thou only One, to Whom can none compare ! Thou Light
shining within the very soul of me, Thy slave !
On me who knew not the true goal,- of merit void,
O Love unique,- Thou hast choice grace bestowed !
O radiant Form Whose splendour bright no tongue can tell !
My Wealth of bliss ! O Civa-Peruman !
IN WEARINESS - I'VE SEIZED THEE,- HOLD THEE FAST !
HENCEFORTH,

AH, WHITHER GRACE IMPARTING WOULD'ST THOU RISE?
(20)

VI. In death, as in life.

O Pinnagan, our great Possession, Thou hast held
as sacred shrine my empty worthless mind;
Hast given me rapturous joy that knows no bound; hast cut
the root of 'birth,' and made me all Thine own !
O mystic Form, by me in open vision seen !
My Wealth of bliss ! O Civa-Peruman !
IN HOUR OF DEATH - I'VE SEIZED THEE,- HOLD THEE FAST !
HENCEFORTH,

AH, WHITHER GRACE IMPARTING WOULD'ST THOU RISE?
(24)

VII. The revelation of the way to worship.

Thou Who didst teach the way to grasp that Ancient One,
Who cuts the root of every servile 'bond' !
O Being,- Who didst show to me Thy flowery feet;
my worship didst accept; ent'ring my soul;-
Resplendent Lamp ! Thou mystic Form of splendour bright !
My Wealth of bliss ! O Civa-Peruman !
RULER SUPREME - I'VE SEIZED THEE,- HOLD THEE FAST !
HENCEFORTH,
AH, WHITHER GRACE IMPARTING WOULD'ST THOU RISE?
(28)

VIII. The Deity everywhere present .

O Father ! worlds on worlds Thy presence fills !
Thou Primal Deity ! O wondrous One
Who knows no end ! Thy saints devoutly cling to Thee !
My Wealth of bliss ! O Civa-Peruman !
Wild Vagrant, living Germ in being's every form,-
diverse Thyself from every living thing !
ILLUSIONIST - I'VE SEIZED THEE,- HOLD THEE FAST !
HENCEFORTH,
AH, WHITHER GRACE IMPARTING WOULD'ST THOU RISE?
(32)

IX. The rapture of devotion.

The mother's thoughtful care her infant feeds: Thou deign'st
with greater love to visit sinful me, -
Melting my flesh, flooding my soul with inward light,

unfailing rapture's honied sweetness Thou
Bestowest,- through my every part infusing joy !
My Wealth of bliss ! - O Civa-Peruman !
CLOSE FOLLOWING THEE - I'VE SEIZED THEE,- HOLD THEE
FAST ! HENCEFORTH,
AH, WHITHER GRACE IMPARTING WOULD'ST THOU RISE?
(36)

X. The delight of His indwelling.

O Ruler, spotless Gem, Who mad'st me Thine, thrilling
my frame through every pore; in friendly shape
Didst enter it,- as 'twere a vast and golden shrine,-
making this body vile of sweetness full !
Affliction, birth and death, bewilderment,- all links
of life,- Thou hast cut off, O beauteous Gleam !
MY SOUL'S DELIGHT - I'VE SEIZED THEE,- HOLD THEE FAST !
HENCEFORTH,
AH, WHITHER GRACE IMPARTING WOULD'ST THOU RISE?
(40)
Hymn XXXVIII- tiruvesaravu

SACRED SADNESS.

['ABSTRACTION FROM OBJECTIVE THOUGHT.']

I.

My iron mind full oftern didst Thou draw, and melt my frame;
Thy feet to me didst show, as though the sweet cane's
pleasantness;

Thou of the braided lock, where waters wander wave on
wave!
The jackals all Thou mad'st great horses; thus didst show Thy
grace. (4)

II.

Thou Partner of the maid whose words are music! To thine
own
Ambrosia precious, sating every soul ! Master, Thy slave
Rule Thou ! Cut off these earthly 'births.' When Thou didst
pity me
I saw Thy foot in vision clear, and, ah, my soul was freed ! (8)

III.

No hiding place had I; in hell of births and deaths I sank;
No loving hand was stretched to aid; Master, Thou bad'st me
come,
Who didst the poison eat from out the swelling sea ! To me,
How Thou didst show Thy flowery foot, our Deity supreme !
(12)

IV.

Dancer with serpent-girded foot ! Thou of the braided lock !
Lord of the saints crowned with Thy flowery foot ! me dost
Thou save,
From praising meaner gods that others praise. O wondorous
grace !

I ponder how Thou to my soul didst show Thy saving power.
(16)

V.

No lore of wisdom had I, melted not in rapturous tears;-
Yet other gods knew not ! ANd by Thy word, our mighty Lord
!
My soul exulted when I gained Thy foot. To me, Thy slave,
As though one gave to cur a golden seat, Thy grace was
shown. (20)

VI.

Sore troubled by the glancing eyes of damsels, soft of foot,
A poisonous anguish pierc'd my trembling frame; yet by
Thy grace I 'scaped, my Lord, my Owner ! Me Thou bad'st
Fear not,'
And mad'st Thine own,- Ambrosia of the sacred temple court
! (24)

VII.

For me Thou caused'st 'birth' to cease, great Lord of bliss,
Who dwell'st unknown
By even the heavenly ones in Perun-turrai's southern shrine !
Entering in love, melting my heart within, Thou madest me
Thine !
Great Lord, such was the way that Thou didst look on me !
(28)

VIII.

O Ancient One ! First One, that grows not old ! The Endless
Chaunted word ! True Essence ! Burgeoned forth as that
WHICH IS,
AND IS NOT. Entering here, me who in error rolled, Thy grace
Restored, and made Thine own. Such was Thy way, O mighty
One ! (32)

IX. Special manifestation in Idai-maruthur.

Sprang up Thy foot, as sweetly fragrant flower within my
mind, melting my soul !
In every street I wept, and praised Thee, mighty Lord of bliss !
Mercy supreme that as wide ocean rolls, I tasted, plunged
therein !
Father, in Idai-maruthur Thou show'dst Thy grace to me ! (36)

X. No desert in me; all in His grace !

Have I indeed performed ascetic deeds, Ci-va-ya-na-ma
gained to chaunt !
Civan, the mighty Lord, as honey and as rare ambrosia sweet,
Himself He came, entered my soul,- to me His slave gave
grace;
So that I hated, loathed this life of soul in flesh enmeshed,
that day. (40)
Hymn XXXIX- tirup pulambal

THE SACRED LAMENT.

['THE MATURIY OF RAPTURE.']

I. I praise none but Thee.

O Thou Whose way Ayan, from flow'ry lotus sprung, knows
not, nor Mal !
Partner of her whose swelling bosom wears the Gongu
flower ! Whose form
White ash displays ! Owner of blest Arur, begrit with lofty
wall !
Saving Thy flower-like feet, nought else will I Thy servant ever
praise ! (4)

II. To Thee alone I look for help.

Thou of the braided tuft ! Fire-wielder ! Thou Whose weapon
is the dart
Three-leav'd and gleaming ! Light superne ! Lord of the flock !
The soft, white bull
Is thine ! O Lord of Perun-turrai girt by spreading groves ! Thy
slave
Am I. Owner, I know in truth no other present help than
Thee. (8)

III.

Nor friends, nor kin I seek; no city I desire; no name I crave;
No learned ones I seek; and henceforth lessons to be conned
suffice.
Thou dancer, in Kuttalam dwelling blissful, Thy resounding
feet

I'll sek, that as the cow yearns for its calf, my longing soul
may melt. (12)
Hymn XL.- kulaap pathu

THE DECAD OF 'GLORIOUS TILLAI.'

['UNINTERMITTED ENJOYMENT']

I. He enters on a life of absolute renunciation.

The potsherd and the skull I deemed my kin; my soul
dissolved;
Wealth to be sought was Civan's foot alone, I clearly saw;
With soul and body to the earth in worship bent, a slave,
I'VE REACH'D HIM WHERE HE DANCES, LORD OF TILLAI'S
HOME OF JOY! (4)

II. Here shall I be set free.

Through fond desire of those of slender form and gentle
words,
How many deeds soever guilt increasing, I have done,
Nor 'death' nor 'birth' I dread ! He caus'd me to embrace His
feet;
A slave, I'VE REACHED HIM WHO BEARS RULE IN TILLAI'S
HOME OF JOY ! (8)

III. He brought back my wandering mind.

Melting my inmost frame, He killed the germ of twofold
deeds;-

Pluckt out my rooted griefs;- made purely one the manifold;-
So that all former things might perish quite, He entered in !
I'VE REACHED HIM WHO IN LOVE BEARS RULE IN TILLAI'S
HOME OF JOY ! (12)

IV. Civan made known only to disciplined minds.

Who severs not Himself from those whose minds are severed
still
From vain assembles void of sign, and way, and temper
meet,-
The 'goal of bliss,'- Ambrosia's mighty flow,- to chastened
thought
Revealed,- I'VE REACHED HIM WHO BEARS RULE IN TILLAI'S
HOME OF JOY ! (16)

V. The consummation gained in Tillai

This same embodiment bound up with name and quality
To consummate, He cuts off sin that clings ! His servants all
As they draw near, the honey taste of Civan's mercy, and
Are filled, where I've REACHED HIM WHO RULES IN TILLAI'S
HOME OF JOY ! (20)

VI. My being in His hand.

Bud on the bough, then rounded flower, next fruit unripe,
then fruit
Matured,- my frame thus formed He made His own, nor
hence departs;-
That trusting thought may ever cling to Him, as it clings now,

I'VE REACHED HIM WHO BEARS RULE IN TILLAI'S GOLDEN
HOME OF JOY ! (24)

VII. The mighty foot.

The demon's arm for strength renowned, by the same sacred
foot
That pressed upon my head, was crushed, and glorious
rested there;
Thus by His grace I'm freed galling bonds of life, and here
I'VE REACHED HIM WHO BEARS RULE IN TILLAI'S HOME OF
THRILLING JOY ! (28)

VIII.

The sacred foot that walked within the wilds after the wild
Black boar that digs deep down, He planted on my head;
And so surpassing power of the five fierce ones' mighty play
Doth cease, when I'VE REACHED HIM WHO RULES IN TILLAI'S
HOME OF JOY ! (32)

IX.

I lay as one who tills a barren field and reaps no crop;-
'Twas then the gain of penance done of old accrued; and thus
Before the Caivan's roseate lotus foot I bent my worthless
head
His own,- I'VE REACHED HIM WHO BEARS RULE IN TILLAI'S
HOME OF JOY ! (36)

X.

Her form He shares who by His side grows as a tender
bough;-
To Him I with right mind my sacred ministries perform;-
This here, abolishes whate'er results this state can yield;
I'VE REACHED HIM WHO BEARS RULE IN TILLAI'S HOME OF
HEAVENLY JOY ! (40)
Hymn XLI.- arputha pathu

THE MIRACLE-DECAD

[THE UNUTTERABLE EXPERIENCE]

The following decad was composed at Tiru-perun-turrai, and
is probably one of the first sung by our bard. It is in some
respects quite unique among his compositions, and certainly
has not the flowing case and rapture of some of his
subsequent verses; but perhaps it reveals more of himself
than any other. It was put forth, as would seem, immediately
after his conversion; and is a thankful acknowledgment of the
grace that has delivered him (as he now thinks) completely,
and for ever, from the bonds of sensual passion.
The three things which a Caiva saint has to get free from are
sensual passion, wrath, and the infatuation that regards the
phenomenal as the real. Our Sage seems never to have been
troubled with wrathful tendencies; and, in fact, must have
been a very gentle and sweet-tempered man; but it must be
remembered that at the time of his conversion he was yet in
his early youth, the Prime Minister and favourite of the great
Pandiyan king, the virtual ruler of that ancient realm,

boasting a pure and lofty lineage, of prepossessing appearance and manner, instinct with the glow of a poet's enthusiasm; and, in fact, possessing all that the phenomenal world has to give. Remembering, too, the tone and manners of his time and people, it is not to be wondered at that this poem makes acknowledgement of a previous utter absorption in worldly enjoyments, and a habit of mental infatuation,- apparently absolute. From the first and third of the trio of evils, he had very little chance, humanly speaking, of ever becoming free. Yet the history tells us that he had previously sought for light, had consulted teachers of many systems, and had waited in darkness and in bonds for the coming of the Master Whose service should be 'perfect freedom' from sensual thraldom. This poem is his thanks giving for (what he believes to be) his final deliverance. It will be noted that he dwells with persistent monotony on one theme: he is 'free'; the time has not yet come for the analysis of his fellings; or for considering his future career. There is here an almost entire absence of mythology,- the one idea of God that he has before him is the loving Guru Whose feet have crowned the suppliant's head; even Uma, the mother, is not mentioned or alluded to; he utters no invitation to others to join him in praise; his is a gladness with which no stranger can intermediate.

The other poems, sung in the same place soon after, show him recovering from the overwhelming effect of his first glad surprise, and in them he finds it possible to dwell upon other topics.

The Tiruvacagam is a veritable Pilgrim's Progress, and surely reveals the experience of a devout and godly soul. It is possible that in this and in other of the poems, lines may

have been altered and even verses added; for there is a
noticeable discrepancy here and there; but internal evidence
justifies us in concluding that mainly we have here the
unrestrained utterances of a Caiva mystic of the eighth
century.

I. The Truth.

By lust bewilder'd;- in this earthly sphere
caught in the circling sea of joyous life;-
By whirling tide of woman's charms engulf'd;-
lest I should sink with mind perturb'd,
He gave His sacred grace, that falseness all
my soul might flee, and showed His golden feet !
The TRUTH Himself,- He stood in presence there:
THIS MATCHLESS MIRACLE I TELL NOT, I ! (4)

II. The King.

I gave no fitting gift with lavish hand
of full-blown flowers; nor bowed with rev'rence meet.
He grace conferr'd, lest I should tread the paths
of grief, with mind bewildered by soft dames
With fragrant bosoms fair. He came to save,
and showed to me His golden jewell'd feet;
As KING in presence manifest He stood:
THIS MATCHLESS MIRACLE I TELL NOT, I ! (8)

III. The Ineffable Essence.

Busied in earth I acted many a lie;

I spake of 'I' and 'mine,'- illusions old;
Nor shunned what caused me pain; while sins increased
I wandered raving. Me, that BEING RARE,-
By the great mystic Vedas sought in vain,-
held fast in presence there; to lowly me
Essential sweetness was the food He gave:
THIS MIRACLE OF GRACE I KNOW NOT, I ! (12)

IV. The Helper.

To 'birth' and 'death' that cling to man, I gave no thought;
and uttering merest lies went on my way.
By eyes of maids with flowing jet-black locks
disturbed, with passion filled, I helpless lay.
He came ! the anklets on His roseate feet,-
I heard their tinkling sound; nor parts the bliss!
In grace my precious HELPER made me His:
THIS MIRACLE OF LOVE I KNOW NOT, I ! (16)

V. Freedom.

I wealth and kindered and all other bliss
enjoy'd; by tender maidens' charms was stirr'd;
I wandered free in joyous intercourse;
such goodly qualities it seemed were there.
He set me free; to stay the coure of 'deeds'
my foes, He showed His foot-flowers' tender grace,
My spirit stirred, entered within, and made me His:
THIS MATCHLESS MIRACLE I KNOW NOT, I ! (20)

VI. The 'Sea of excellence.'

I gave no thought to 'birth' and 'death,' that yield
their place successive; but with maidens joined
I sank engulfed as by a mighty flood:
their rosy lips my death ! I madly roamed.
The SEA OF EXCELLENCE, Whom neither quality
nor name of excellence defines,-
He came, and tenderly embracing made me His:
THIS MIRACLE OF GRACE I KNOW NOT, I ! (24)

VII. The Father.

Though born a man, unfailing gifts
I laid not at the golden feet; nor did I cull
The cluster'd flowers, by rule and wont prescrib'd;
nor chaunted the 'Five Letters' due. O'ercome
By the full-bosom'd damsels' jet-black eyes
I prostrate lay. SHowing His flow'ry feet,
To me the FATHER came, and made me His :
THIS MIRACLE OF GRACE I KNOW NOT, I ! (28)

VIII. He Whom words express not.

He caused the 'twofold deeds' to cease, that cause
this swing of soul with body joined. He, Whom
'Tis hard to learn by uttered sound to know,
gave me to know Himself: thus made me light !
He cut asunder bonds that clung; fulfilled
with His own mercy's gift sublime my soul's
Desire; and joined me to His servants' feet:
THIS MIRACLE OF GRACE I KNOW NOT, I ! (32)

IX. The Imperishable.

In tangled wilderness of 'birth' supine
I lay ; like wretched cur diseased I roamed;
Did as I lusted; dwelt with creatures vile,
with them complying, satisfied in soul !
He showed me there His flowery fragrant feet,
by Hari and by Ayan unattained;
Th' IMPERISHABLE made ev'n me His own:
THIS MIRACLE OF GRACE I KNOW NOT, I ! (36)

X. The Lord Supreme.

I gave no thought to thronging 'births' and 'deaths,'
but dwelt on tricks, and wiles, and glancing eyes
Of maids with wealth of braided tresses fair;
and thus I lay. The King, our LORD SUPREME,
His jewell'd feet, that traverse all the worlds,
to me made manifest like clustering blooms;
He wisdom gave, and made me all His own:
THIS MIRACLE OF GRACE I KNOW NOT, I ! (40)
Hymn XLII.- chennip pathu

THE HEAD-DECAD

[THE CERTAINTY OF BLISS]

I. Civan a light.

The God of gods; the Warrior true; south Perun-turrai's
Chieftain dear;
The First; the Blissful One, Whose forn the Three could not
attain to know;
The Flower full-blown of LIGHT is He, to all save to His loving
ones, unknown !
UPON HIS MIGHTY ROSEATE FOOT'S PURE FLOWER OUR
HEADS SHALL GLEAMING REST ! (4)

II. Civan the beautiful Sundaran

The eightfold FORM, the Beautiful, the sweet ambrosial Tide
of bliss;
Most Worthy, Prince, of Civa-world; south Perun-turrai's
Warrior-king;
The Beautiful, Who made the Queen with flowing locks part
of Himself;
UPON HI ROSEATE FOOT'S FULL-ORBED FLOWER OUR HEADS
SHALL BLOOMING REST ! (8)

III. Loving and gracious.

Ye maids, the Lord whose eye looked on me sweetly, claiming
service due;
The Warrior-lord, in Perun-turrai girt with cocoa-groves Who
dwells;
Who takes the maidens' armlets bright, and claims our soul
and service true.
UPON HIS ROSEATE FOT'S EXPANDING FLOWER OUR HEADS
SHALL GLEAMING REST ! (12)

IV. Gracious manifestations.

With pious men around, Parabaran' on earth appeared, a
Seer.
Mid saints made perfect, Civa-Lord dances in Tillai's city old.
Mystic ! He comes, enters our homes, makes us His own, our
service claims.
UPON THE MIGHTY ROSEATE FOOT'S FLOWER GIVEN OUR
HEADS SHALL BLOOMING REST ! (16)

V. His disciple.

He gave the boon that I should not vain joys of life as true
regard.
Partner of Umai's grace, He came to sacred Perun-turrai's
shrine.
And, while ambrosia flowing filled our frames, showed us His
foot, and said 'Behold' !
UPON THAT MIGHTY ROSEATE FOOT'S AUSPICIOUS FLOWER
OUR HEADS SHALL REST ! (20)

VI. He gives an assured hope.

Our mind He entered, made us His, destroyed 'ill deeds,' and
piety
That saves bestowed, Unto His jewelled foot when wreath of
flowers we bring,
He'll give our souls release; grant to dwell safe beyond this
threefold world.
UPON THAT FATHER'S ROSEATE FEET, THOSE FULL-BLOWN
FLOWERS, OUR HEADS SHALL REST ! (24)

VII. Fellowship with His saints.

That I might swim this sea called 'birth,' great grace in love
He gave;
Caused me released to join the gracious band of saints, and
made me of their goodly kin.
To save me thus the Lord His truth displayed, in greatness of
His grace !
UPON HIS ROSEATE FEET, WHO SHOWED SUCH MIGHT, OUR
HEADS SHALL BEAMING REST ! (28)

VIII. Unfailing Refuge.

The falsehood of these bodies vile, worm-filled, Thou dost
abolish quite,
'Bright Splendour, Ruler, Lord, our Father,' evermore they
cry, and lift
Adoring hands; their eyes' pure flower with tears o'erflows;
to these Thy saints
THY ROSEATE FEET FAIL NOT; UPON THOSE FLOWERS OUR
HEADS SHALL FLOWER CROWN'D REST ! (32)

IX. Lord of Earth and Heaven.

Me vainly wandering here Thou bad'st to come, didst slay the
'hate of deeds,'
Celestial Lord ! This world Thou dost transcend, Lord of the
realms beyond,
Pleasures of grace shall spring perennial to Thy loving
servants true.

UPON THY ROSEATE FEET'S PURE GOLDEN FLOWER OUR
HEADS SHALL BEAMING REST ! (36)

X. All join in His praise.

The Free,- the Primal Splendour,- Father Triple-eyed-all
being's Germ !
The Perfect,- Lord of Civa-world,- sing, chaunt His name, O
men devout !
Hither draw nigh your bonds to loose ! O bow ye down and
worship here !
UPON THE ROSEATE FOOT, THAT FILLS THE SOUL, OUR
HEADS SHALL GLEAMING REST ! (40)
Hymn XLIII.- tiru varthai

THE SACRED WORD

[GRATEFUL LOVE]

I. The gracious incarnation.

The Lady's Spouse; of mystic word Proclaimer skill'd;
Light seen mid blooming flowers; the faultless Grace
supreme;
Who to His servants grants the boon of justic bright;
the King of virtuous excellence Who reigns benign,
In Perun-turrai girt with fragrant flowery groves;-
Himself hath come, and on this earth, a gracious Form,
Descending hath revealed the Primal Deity.
THAT GRACE WHO KNOW WITH OUR SUPERNAL LORD ARE
ONE ! (4)

II. His condescension.

Mal, Ayan, and the King of heavenly hosts approached
and lowly bowed before Him,- Ican gave them grace !-
Descending to this world, He showed the perfect way
unto the simple dame that dwelt in Idavai,-
Where mansions fair arise with goodly splendour bright,
of sparkling gems, and saints hold converse sweet,-
Grace of abounding excellence He gave.
HIS POWER WHO KNOW WITH OUR SUPERNAL LORD ARE
ONE ! (8)

III.

The crown'd Eternal-One,- King of th' immortal host,-
the rapturous Dancer, as the six sects homage pay,
Ascends the boat, accepts and crowns their service due;
while heaven and earth adore and praise their King.
He grants infirmity should die !- In Perun-turrai's shrine
He dwells in mighty grace ! - In love to her, His bride,
He brought a jewelled net, to catch the mystic fish !
HIS WAYS WHO KNOW WITH OUR SUPERNAL LORD ARE ONE
! (12)

IV.

A woodman's form He bore, on mount Mahendiram
when sore distressed the suppliants came
And sought Him, Civan, mighty Lord, was nigh to save !
That we His servants pondering HIm, should safety win,

The Teacher on a prancing charer mounted came,-
of Perun-turrai's shrine th'Eternal Deity,-
That day His friends from every side He made His own !
THEY WHO HIS NATURE KNOW OUR SUPERNAL LORD ARE
ONE ! (16)

V.

He came. The gods in reverence bowed their heads, and
praised.
A sea of mighty mercy,- He in grace brake off
His servants' bonds, and set us free. Our Deity,-
th' Eternal-One of Perun-turrai's shrine,- that day
Himself passed o'er the sea, whose surging billows rose;
His grace He gave within the lofty walls
Of Lanka's home to the soft-fingered captive maid !
HIS WORTH WHO KNOW WITH OUR SUPERNAL LORD ARE
ONE ! (20)

VI.

Lord of the bow that wrapt the cities three in flames;-
a huntsman's guise he took with guard of dogs around;-
Before Him gathered gods obeying His behests;-
our mighty Lord, in forest wilds where He abode
Took pity on the hunted boar ! Ican, that day,-
our Father, Perun-turrai's King, the Eternal Deity,-
A pig became, wonder unique, and milk bestowed !
HIS DEEDS WHO KNOW WITH OUR SUPERNAL LORD ARE ONE
! (24)

VII.

In their fair garden home 'mid lotus flowers and hum
of bees, the maids with beauteous brows assemble round,
Chaunting bow down, strew full-blown flowers, and praise
our Ican,- radiant Beam of rosy growing light,-
Who ever bides in Perun-turrai's flowery grove,-
our Holy-One. To earth He came,- appeared,- destroyed
Earth-born diversities,- gave grace. His MIGHT OF LOVE
WHO'VE POWER TO KNOW WITH OUR SUPERNAL LORD ARE
ONE ! (28)

VIII.

His breast wears garlands of the opening cassia flower;-
Here, He slew the tiger strong of claw;-
The partner He of Umai, lovely queen;-
of Perun-turrai girt with rich groves King;-
Ican, in great and spotless glory bright;-
He folds the beauteous ones in soft embrace;-
He to the vast sea's king in fiery form appear'd;-
HIS FORM WHO KNOW SHALL UNION GAIN WITH OUR
SUPERNAL LORD ! (32)

IX.

Our mighty Lord with pure white ashes decked;-
Who came Bright Ruler of Mahendiram;-
Ican, Whose planted foot the gods adore;-
the southern Ruler, Perun-turrai's King;-
Who loving pity showed to me that day,

showed me His jewelled foot to melt my soul,
My sorrows soothed, in grace made me His own !
HIS DEEDS WHO KNOW WITH OUR SUPERNAL LORED ARE
ONE ! (36)

X.

The Beauteous-eyed;- the Immortals' Lord and ours;-
Ambrosia to His servants;- Prince Who came
To earth to loose our mighty bonds, that we
a bliss unique in earth and heaven might gain;-
With strong control he sways th' ASSEMBLY wise;-
skilled Leader;- Perun-turrai's King;- that day
To Madura with damsels thronged He came:
HIS WAYS WHO KNOW SHALL UNION GAIN WITH OUR
SUPERNAL LORD ! (40)
Hymn XLIV.- ennap pathikam

DEVOUT MUSINGS.

[JOYOUS EMOTION.]

This poem expresses his intense longing to rejoin at once the
Master and His disciples.

I. Longings for endless joy.

Would birth in earthly forms might cease, devoted love so
might I gain !

O Civa-Peruman, Whose form is beauteous like red lotus-
flower;
Thou art my rare Ambrosia; midst the assembly of Thy saints
Thy sacred grace unique show Thou; be gracious, take me too
and save !
(4)

II. He pleads the promise.

I'm not my own, Thy slave am I; sever'd from Thee no
moment can
I live; a cur, I nothing know,- O Cankaran! In pitying grace
Thou Mighty said'st to me, 'Behold,' and showed'st Thy
jewell'd feet. Our Lord,
And was the promise false that said, 'I sever nevermore from
Thee?' (8)

III. Love that 'maketh not ashamed.'

Melting my frame, granting Thy grace, showing to me Thy
flow'ry feet,
Erewhile Thou madest me Thine own, O Sage, O First of sages
all !
My Bliss, Thou didst dissolve my soul, and dost my life
consume.
Grant me Thy love, King of my soul; that so Thy grace from
shame may shield ! (12)

IV. He laments his deadness of soul.

Of piety I'm void, nor bow at vision of Thy golden feet;

My heart is dead, my lips are seal'd;- yet cause this 'birth' to cease, our Lord !
Pearl-like Thou art, gem-like Thou art ! First One, I utter my complaint:
So oft I've follow'd Thee, henceforth apart from Thee I bear not life ! (16)

V. Spiritual declension.

I see Thy gracious feet no more, which seeing erst mine eyes were glad;
I've ceased to cherish Thee; I've ceased to utter childlike praise; and thus
Tanu, my mighty Lord, I'm lost; the state, that melting thinks on Thee,
By meannesses I've ceas'd to know; 'twere shame to me to see Thee come ! (20)

VI. Supplication.

Thee, Lord supreme, with milk-white ash adorn'd, meeting with grace superne
Thy servants true,
Who dost appear, and show the hav'n of grace,- Thee, glorious Light, I, void
of righteousness,
Extol as my Ambrosia, praising Thee,- praise, glorify, invoke with weepings loud !
Master, thus working in me mightily, in grace O speak, in pity speak ! (24)
Hymn XLV.- yathirai pathu

THE PILGRIM-SONG.

[RAPTURE.]

This is our Sage's wonderful 'psalm of the up-going,' He
commemorates his first visit to Tillai, and thence mystically
sets forth the soul's pilgrimage through the world of sense to
union with Civan on the silver mountain.

I. The setting-forth on the journey.

Our King with head flow'r-wreath'd, BHUYANGAN-LORD,
by mercy's swelling flood that all dissolves,
Commingled ever, like perception's self,
within our souls,- 'O come,' hath said in love,
And made us lowly ones His own ! Come ye
with one accord; behold, the time hath come;
Pass we,- falsehood for ever left behind,-
to enter 'neath the Master's jewelled feet ! (4)

II. The pilgrims's preparation of soul.

Enter no more the juggling senses' net !
BHUYANGAN'S flow'ry feet, the mighty Lord,
Ponder intensely,- other things desire ye not :
dismiss them, let them go, and pass ye on !
With joyous smile He, entering this world,
made us-who were like curs impure- His own,
As it befits to draw anigh the Lord,

let each with no weak faltering step move on ! (8)

III. Earthly ties must be loosed.

Each to himself be his own kith and kin !
each to himself be his own law and way !
For who are 'WE'? what 'OURS'? and what are 'BONDS'?
illusions all,- let these departing flee !
And, with the ancient servants of the King,
taking His sign alone for guiding sign,
Shake falshood off; go on your happy way,
unto BHUYANGAN'S golden foot, - our King ! (12)

IV. Sober, hopeful assurance.

All ye His servants who've become,
put far away each idle sportive thought;
Seek refuge at the Foot where safety dwells;
hold fast unto the end the sacred sighn;
Put off from you this body stained with sin;
in Civan's world He'll surely give us place !
BHUYANGAN'S self, Whose Form the ashes wears,
will grant you entrance 'neath His flow'ry feet ! (16)

V. Faint not, press on !

Free ye your souls from pains of wrath and lust;
henceforth the time shall not be long drawn out !
Beneath our Master's feet with glad acclaim
that we in one may go, in one combine !
Even we in Civan's town shall refuge find,

whose flo'r-wreath'd gates to us shall not be clos'd !
There enter'd we in ecstasy shall sing
the glories only of BHUYANGAN-KING ! (20)

VI. Persevere ! The glorious consummation awaits you.

Praise ye ! Adore ! Bring beauteous flowers !
BHUYANGAN'S foot plant ye within your souls !
Despise adversities of every form !
Henceforth no hindrance bars your happy way
To Civan's town, that fill'd with glory shines
To Civan's foot go we to worship there !
Before the saints that there abide we'll move,
and stand in soul-dissolving rapture there ! (24)

VII. Loiter not, scatter not !

Let those that bide abide,- abide not we
in world that not abides. Straight pass we on
Unto the foot of our BHUYANGAN-KING,
Whose sacred form is milk with golden hue !
All ye that loitering stand delay not now !
Gather in one to march, where'er ye stand !
Unto the Mighty One access henceforth
is hard to gain, if ye should loiter now ! (28)

VIII. The gate opens !

Ye, with the Lord, in rapture infinite
conjoin'd for ever, who have gained to dwell !
In strong illusion henceforth sink not ye,

in sooth; nor utter senseless words profane !
The sacred door where dwells the priceless Gem,
is opening even now. To Civan's town
Come, move we on, to reach the sacred foot
of BHUYANGAN, to Mal divine unknown ! (32)

IX. Anticipate the joys of fruition.

Ah, think how ye may reach the goal ! Your thoughts
correct, and duly chasten'd, ponder this !
Ye, who are sinking now in love's excess,-
enjoying, never sated, the ambrosial grace
Of BHUYANGAN, the Spouse of Her, whose eyes.
are like the gleaming spear that warrior wields,-
Joy ye to go to Civan's jewell'd foot,
nor wallowing lie ye here in falsehood's mire ! (36)

X. They enter in !

Will ye not come this day, and be His own,
and prostrate fall, and worship, and adore?
Those lost in wilderment, who would esteem?
Ye who bewilder'd and confounded stand,
If ye would perfect clearness gain, this do !
Ye who would gain in this wide realm the grace
Of sacred BHUYANGAN, of Civa-world
the King ! Ah, haste ye, hate ye, haste ye on ! (40)
Hymn XLVI.- tirupadai ezhuchi

THE SACRED MARCH

[THE HOLY WAR.]

I.

Strike the sounding drum of the Guru, Wielder of wisdom's
sword;
Spread the white canopy over the Guru, Who mounts the
charger of heaven;
Enter and take to you armour of ashes, fragrant, divine;
Possess we the heavenly fortress, where hosts of illusion
come not ! (4)

II,

Servants of His,- march on in the van; ye Devout ones,- move
on the flanks;
Ye Sages of power illustrious,- come fill up the swelling ranks;
Ye Mystics of strength unfailing,- advance and close up the
rear:
We shall rule the heavenly land, no hosts of evil for ever to
fear ! (8)
Hymn XLVII.- tiruvenba

THE SACRED VENBA

[THE STATE OF 'THOSE WHO HAVE ATTAINED.']

This purports to have been composed immediately after his
return to Perun-turrai, when he was hoping for speedy
consummation, but felt impatient.

I. How shall I endure this state of imperfection?

What shall I do while twofold deeds' fierce flame burns still
out,-
Nor doth the body melt,- nor falsehood fall to dust ?
In mind no union gained with the 'Red Firs's honey'
The Lord of Perun-turrai fair ! (4)
II. How employ the weary time of waiting?

Shall I cry out, or wail, or dance, or sing, or watch?
O Infinite, what shall I do? The Sire Who fills
With rapturous amaze,- great Perun-turrai's Lord
Let all with me bending adore ! (8)

III. The wonder of his conversion.

No sense of fault had I ! Nor of refreshment knew.
In safety's path, by worship at His roseate feet.
He stood on earth, His dart shot forth, and to my thought
Linked Himself;- Perun-turrai's Lord ! (12)

IV. He came in grace.

He stood before me, rooting out my 'twofold deeds,'-
The mighty Ruler Who at last shall cut off 'birth';
Lord of the south; in Perun-turrai great in grace,
Who dwells; Balm of all human woes ! (16)

V. Praise superfluous.

To them that know what word can praise the King? - Him,
Who
All worlds brought forth, Whom Vedic god and Mal knew not;
The mighty Lord, Whose seat is Perun-turrai's shrine;-
In me to-day, and evermore ! (20)

VI. The bliss of His advent.

He filled with frenzy; set me free from 'births'; my soul
With speechless fervours thrilled,- blest Perun-turrai's Lord,-
The Sire in grace exceeding made me His; the balm
For all my pain; the deathless BLISS ! (24)

VII. Leading and light.

He showed the realm where 'births' return no more; He came
In grace that no requital knows, Ambrosia sating not !
This is the light diffus'd within my thought by Him,
The Lord of Perun-turrai's shrine ! (28)

VIII. Condescending love.

Glorious, exalted over all, the Infinite,-
To me mere slave, lowest of all, Thou hast assigned
A place in bliss supreme, that none beside have gained or
known !
Great Lord, what can I do for Thee? (32)

IX. Unparalleled gift.

The three, the thirty-three, all other gods beside

See Thee not, Civan, mighty Lord ! Riding the steed
Hither descending didst Thou come. When at Thy foot
I lowly bow, bliss thrills my frame ! (36)

X. Be not afraid to ask of Him.

Soul, ponder His twain feet Who here made me His own !
Beg for HIs grace ! Behold, He will give all,- the King
Who grace bestows,- Whose seat is Perun-turrai's shrine,-
Dwelling ambrosial in my soul ! (40)

XI. Light and love from His indwelling.

He hath increased delight, hath darkness banished,
For aye cut off afflictions' clinging bond, and light
Of love hath given,- the Lord of Perun-turrai great,
Well pleased to make my heart His home ! (44)
Hymn XLVIII.- pandaayanan marai

THE ANCIENT MYSTIC WORD.

[THE REALITY OF DIVINE GRACE.]

I. No requital of electing grace.

The ancient fourfold mystic word draws not anigh His seat;-
Nor Mal nor Ayan Him have seen; yet me, the most abject,
By grace He made His servant ! To Gokari's King, my heart,
Say, is there any just return ? (4)

II. The great manifestation in Perun-turrai.

Praise Perun-turrai ! There the King, who on the charger
came,
Abides, and gives a mighty flood of honied sweetness forth,
By which my soul's threefold impurity is swept away;-
So roots of 'birth's' wild forest die ! (8)

III. He assumes many characters to save men.

In wilds a Hunstsman; in sea He casts a net;
On land He rides the charger: thus our 'deeds' destroys.
The fair foot-flower of Perun-turrai's Lord praise Thou,
My heart, that error thus may die ! (12)

IV. The centre of Worship.

Householders devout; saints who mighty 'deeds' destroy;-
Those whom 'tis meet the world should bow before, and
praise;-
Immortals too in worship circling move, and laud ! O friends,
In Perun-turrai blest adore ! (16)

V. Come, see the King.

To Perun-turrai drawing near; that woes disperse,
Ponder the King of lofty Gokari; and see
Him Who with Her whose words are music sweet abides
In Utt'ra-koca-mangai's shrine ! (20)

VI. Ever praise the God of Perun-turrai.

The eyes that see Him there are all a rapture of delight;-
The saints that cherish Him are freed from mortal birth;-
The Mighty One, in Perun-turrai dwells for aye;-
My heart, give Him unstinted praise ! (24)

VII. 'Perun-turrai' is the saving word.

This is the purport sole of all men say; all speech
Surpassing, gem-like word, as flawless jewels' sheen !
Utt'ring but 'PERUN-TURRAI,' I'm from 'births' released;
That healing foot fixt in my mind ! (28)
Hymn XLIX.- tirupadai yatchi

THE MARSHALLING OF THE SACRED HOST.

[THE CESSATION OF LIFE'S EXPERIENCES.]

It was no easy taks to work out a version of this lyric, the
rhythmic beauty of which is very remarkable. I have striven,
at the risk of sundry irregularities in metre, to imitate the
flow of the original; but the numberless allusions in a poem,
which sums up the whole Caivite idea of the blessedness of
Civan's final manifestation to the emancipated soul, will give
the reader trouble, if he is at all to enter into its spirit. The
metre itself is very unusual, resembling somewhat that of the
Attys of Catullus, and is much admired by those who use the
poem in their temple service. My rendering is, I believe,
strictly and almost literally exact; but it differs in some
respects from the Tamil paraphrases. The intense mystic
fervour of the song must take itself felt !

I. His appearing.

Eyes the twain His jewell'd Feet beholding shall be glad;-
SHALL IT NOT BE?
Joy amid joys of damsels beautiful shall cease to lure;- SHALL
IT NOT BE?
The round of birth in earthly worlds shall in oblivion pass; -
SHALL IT NOT BE?
Twin flow'ry Feet that Mal knew not adoring shall we bow; -
SHALL IT NOT BE?
To sing with gladsome melody, and dance our endless task; -
SHALL IT NOT BE?
The warriors of the fair Pandi-land's Lord we shall sing; -
SHALL IT NOT BE?
The mystic change for which the heav'ns are glad will come; -
SHALL IT NOT BE?
If He who cast the net-the Woodman,- come, in grace made
manifest to me? (8)

II.

One with one, and five with five,- the life shall last; -SHALL IT
NOT BE?
Thy servants' servants' servants made, we shall be free; -
SHALL IT NOT BE?
The Mother thinks on her young, and rising hastes; so shall
He come; -SHALL IT NOT BE?
The casual qualities that no beginning own shall fill the
thought; -SHALL IT NOT BE?

At 'this is good,' and 'this is ill,' no more shall trembling shake; -SHALL IT NOT BE?
We too to join Thy saints above shall onward pass; -SHALL IT NOT BE?
Th' Ambrosia supreme that fills my loving thought we then shall gain; -SHALL IT NOT BE?
If the bull's Lord, my Master, Whose I am, within my soul shall entering come? (16)

III.

Bonds, changes, qualities, all loos'd and cast aside shall fall away; -SHALL IT NOT BE?
Within my mind, erewhile with fancies fill'd Ambrosia supreme shall flow; -SHALL IT NOT BE?
The Endless, Indivisible shall in us dwell; -SHALL IT NOT BE?
The heav'nly Light, from endless days supreme shall then appear; -SHALL IT NOT BE?
The pains from silly ones with crimson lips shall be dispell'd; -SHALL IT NOT BE?
The sparkling eyes His sacred form shall then embrace; -SHALL IT NOT BE?
Sorrow of grief-ful birth, that from illusions springs, shall all depart; -SHALL IT NOT BE?
If I can, my own loving Lord, in presence meet me here? (24)

IV.

The bliss to rest within His lov'd embrace shall we enjoy; -SHALL IT NOT BE?

In mercy's vast and boundless sea sweetly this day shall we
disport; -SHALL IT NOT BE?
The mystic music of the beauteous gems, within my soul shall
thrilling sound; -SHALL IT NOT BE?
The sacred ashes that the Lord for aye adorn shall we
approach; -SHALL IT NOT BE?
'Mid steadfast loving ones foremost in service there shall I
abide; -SHALL IT NOT BE?
The flow'ry Feet, to even the mystic scrolls unknown, shall we
adore; -SHALL IT NOT BE?
The sweet red water-lily Flower my head shall crown; -SHALL
IT NOT BE?
If Peruman, the gracious, -Ican, He Who owns, arise to visit
me ? (32)

V.

Fond fancies all, that valued earth's illusions vain, shall cease;
-SHALL IT NOT BE?
Before the flow'ry Foot to heavenly ones unknown we'll bow;
-SHALL IT NOT BE?
The perturbations all from blindness sprung shall cease; -
SHALL IT NOT BE?
The mind of loving saints this day shall greatly joy; -SHALL IT
NOT BE?
Entanglement of 'sex diverse,' and self shall now be loos'd; -
SHALL IT NOT BE?
States manifold, their very names unknown, we'll'scape; -
SHALL IT NOT BE?
Innumerous mystic powers my soul shall then possess; -
SHALL IT NOT BE?

If Peruman, the gracious Ican, He who owns, arise to visit me? (40)

VI.

The ashes white upon His sacred golden form all beauteous shine; -SHALL IT NOT BE?
A rain of flowers adoring hands of mighty saints shall shower; -SHALL IT NOT BE?
The heart's intent of damsels bright with slender form shall then appear; -SHALL IT NOT BE?
The sounds from smitten lyre that rise shall multiply delights; -SHALL IT NOT BE?
His servants' feet upon my head shall flourish then; -SHALL IT NOT BE?
Himself to set His servants free shall forthwith come; -SHALL IT NOT BE?
Sweet instruments of music duleet strains shall everywhere rehearse; -SHALL IT NOT BE?
If Ican, Whose of old I am, my Sire, in grace arise to visit me (48)

VII.

The pure gems' wordless music then shall rapture yield; -SHALL IT NOT BE?
The light that hides within my soul sudden shall rise and burn; -SHALL IT NOT BE?
That manifold phenomena may cease the Deity shall come; -SHALL IT NOT BE?

303

Experiences divine unknown before shall unfolding rise; -
SHALL IT NOT BE?
Distraction caused by those whose lovely brows are bows
shall cease this day; -SHALL IT NOT BE?
The Essence excellent that even heavenly ones know not
shall be with us; -SHALL IT NOT BE?
The eightfold qualities that know no bound shall we attain; -
SHALL IT NOT BE?
If He, Whose crest the crescent moon adorns, to make us His
in grace arise? (56)

VIII.

From shell that music breathes the sounds shall then burst
forth; -SHALL IT NOT BE?
The qualities that quit not earthborn race shall fret no more;
-SHALL IT NOT BE?
Delusion that declares this good, or that, shall all die down; -
SHALL IT NOT BE?
Our whole desire shall ask to serve His servants 'neath His
feet; -SHALL IT NOT BE?
The thought of damsels bright of eye shall then rejoice; -
SHALL IT NOT BE?
The bliss of Civan shared by glorious saints we then shall
know; -SHALL IT NOT BE?
The heavenly all-pervasive Light Ambrosial shall we gain; -
SHALL IT NOT BE?
If He, the endless Vedic Lord, to make me His in grace arise
(64)
Hymn L.- Aananda malai

THE GARLAND OF RAPTURE.

[DESIRE OF THE EXPERIENCE OF CIVAN.]

I. How may I join my friends beyond?

Th' Immortals all have gained Thy flower-like feet,
bright as the lightning's glance;- have crossed
The world's wide sea, and bearing golden flowers
they praise ! Reveal in love, I pray,-
Thou Refuge of the stony worthless heart,
how one like me,- distressed,- cast off,-
Sunk in the sea of fond desire,- at length,
how many I come to Thee? (4)

II. Have pity on my lonely grief!

Thou gav'st the station blest I knew not of;
but I knew not Thy grace,- was lost !
Master, no failure is in Thee at ail;
Who comes to aid Thy slave? I cry !
Not joined with Thine own ancient saints,-
who serve and praise Thee many a day,
My Leader loved, here left behind I stay;-
Thou see'st my lonely pain ! (8)

III. I am His - when shall I join Him?

Of virtue void, of penitential grace
devoid, undisciplined, untaught,-
As leathern puppet danced about, giddy,

305

I whirling fell, lay prostrate there !
He showed me wondrous things; He showed the way
to pass to worlds not reached before;
The raft He show'd : when shall I come, a wretch.
to Him Who made me His ? (12)

IV. Am I rightfully abandoned?

I perish, as to perish is my doom;
the blame, Imperishable One,
Thou tak;st; and, if to suffering doomed, I bear
my destined woes, what is the gain?
O Guru-Gem, Who dost defend and rule,-
that I sink not in cruel hell;
Is't good, our Leader lov'd, that Thou withdraw,
and stand not in the midst? (16)

V. Is there no pity?

Thou Who dost cherish men like mother dear,-
uncherish'd, left, a weakling here,-
And must I perish, I a cur ! In love
henceforth Thy goodness show to me !
I've called Thee hast no grace for me,
but now Thou hast no grace for me,-
Vile me, whom Thou 'mid saints didst make Thine own !
I'm he ! Should'st Thou not save ? (20)

VI. I claim Thy consolation.

O King, should'st Thou not show Thy grace?

I, wretched, lie at ruin's door.
And, if Thou bid me not to come to Thee,
who is there here to calm my fears?
Are they who're doomed to die, my fellows all?
'This is unmeet,' will not men say?
O God, Dancer in Tillai's hall, I tremble,
henceforth comfort me ! (24)

VII. I sink powerless before Thee.

Thou mad'st the jackal be a charger fleet !
Didst work enchantments manifold !
The mighty SOuth King's Madura Thou fill'dst
with madness, Perun-turrai's Lord !
O Being hard to reach ! O Avanaci's Sire !
The Pandi kingdom's rushing flood !
O Splendour, infinite, unknown, in sooth
I know not aught to do ! (28)
Hymn LI.- achchop pathikam

THE WONDER OF SALVATION.

[ENJOYMENT INEFFABLE.]

This hymn was composed after he had settled down in Tillai,
his active life finished, and was waiting for the great release.
He surveys, as he was so fond of doing, the whole course
along which his Master had guided him; acknowledges how
often he had fallen through an undisciplined and unpurified
mind; and records with thankfulness that grace him the

victory at last. No rapture is like his! Each verse addresses his Master variously as (1) Father, (2) the Mystic Dancer, (3) the Guru, (4) the High and Lofty One, (5) the Master, (6) the Blissful, (7) again as the Guru, (8) the Author of all things, and (9) the Mother (being one with Umai).

I. The Father's converting grace.

To me, who toiled and moiled 'mid fools, that knew not WAY of final peace,
He taught the WAY of pious love;- and that 'old deeds' might cease and flee,
Purging the foulness of my will, made me pure bliss, took for His own;-
'Twas thus the FATHER gave me grace: O RAPTURE ! WHO SO BLEST AS I ? (4)

II. The mystic Dancer converts the heretic.

A WAY that was no rightful WAY I followed, deeming it the WAY,-
That I might seek no meaner WAY, but only seek HIS sacred grace
To gain, - He, Whom no signs describe, His mystic DANCE has given to know !
'Twas thus the DANCER gave me grace: O RAPTURE ! WHO SO BLEST AS I ? (8)

III. The Teacher leads and guards in the way of truth.

Me trusting every lie as truth, - plunged in desire of women's charms,-

He guarded that I perished not with soul perturb'd,- the Lord Superne,

On whose left side the Lady dwells ! He brought me nigh His jewell'd feet,-

'Twas thus my GURU gave me grace: O RAPTURE ! WHO SO BLEST AS I ? (12)

IV. The Lofty One purifies by discipleship.

To me, - born in this clay, and doom'd, o'erworn, to perish, and to fall, -

Love inconceivable He gave;- made me His own;- caused me to wear

His own perfumed ashes white;- that I the way of purity

Should reach, the LOFTY gave me grce: O RAPTURE ! WHO SO BLEST AS I ? (16)

V. The Master relieved my soul of its fear.

Afflicted sore by glancing eyes of silly damsels, soft of foot,-

I stood, my mind by sorrow pierced; and then Thy grace I gain'd,- was sav'd,-

Ev'n I, O MASTER mine ! Thou bad'st Thy servant come; 'Fear not, 'Thou said'st !

'Twas thus that grace to me was given: O RAPTURE ! WHO SO BLEST AS I ? (20)

VI. The Last-One saved me from sensual servitude.

Birth of this frame that burns and falls I took for true,- did many deeds;

In converse joy'd with maidens wreathed in flowers, with lustrous armlets deck'd.

My bonds He cut, made me His own, cleansed foulness so no trace was left !

'Twas thus the LAST-ONE gave me grace: O RAPTURE ! WHO SO BLEST AS I ? (24)

VII. The Guru's esoteric teaching.

Prostrate it was my fate to fall in 'wilderment of fair ones' charms.

In gentle love He led me forth, loosing the prison bars of 'bond';

Showed me the way to 'scape; and taught the meaning of the mystic OM

'Twas thus the GURU gave me grace: O RAPTURE ! WHO SO BLEST AS I ? (28)

VIII. The First saved me by gift of personal devotion.

My troubled soul was whirled around in circling tide of death and birth;

I fell, enamoured with the charms of those with jewels rare adorned;

The Lord, whose Form the Lady shares, in mercy drew me to His feet.

'Twas thus the FIRST-ONE gave me grace: O RAPTURE ! WHO SO BLEST AS I ? (32)

IX. Saves me with a Mother's love.

With those that knew not right or good,- men ignorant,- I
wandered too.
The First, the Primal Lord Himself threefold pollution caus'd
to cease;
Even me He took as something worth,- like dog in sumptuous
litter borne !
'Twas thus the MOTHER gave me grace: O RAPTURE ! WHO
SO BLEST AS I ? (36)

END OF TIRUVACAGAM.

Printed in Poland
by Amazon Fulfillment
Poland Sp. z o.o., Wrocław

51293930R00177